Pollution Law
Handbook

Recent Titles from Quorum Books

Evaluating Employee Training Programs: A Research-Based Guide for Human Resources Managers
Elizabeth M. Hawthorne

Current Budgeting Practices in U.S. Industry: The State of the Art
Srinivasan Umapathy

Developing Negotiation Skills in Sales Personnel: A Guide to Price Realization for Sales Managers and Sales Trainers
David A. Stumm

Training in the Automated Office: A Decision-Maker's Guide to Systems Planning and Implementation
Randy J. Goldfield

The Strategist CEO: How Visionary Executives Build Organizations
Michel Robert

America's Future in Toxic Waste Management: Lessons from Europe
Bruce W. Piasecki and Gary A. Davis

Telecommunications Management for the Data Processing Executive: A Decision-Maker's Guide to Systems Planning and Implementation
Milburn D. Smith III

The Political Economy of International Debt: What, Who, How Much, and Why?
Michel Henri Bouchet

Multinational Risk Assessment and Management: Strategies for Investment and Marketing Decisions
Wenlee Ting

Staffing the Contemporary Organization: A Guide to Planning, Recruiting, and Selecting for Human Resource Professionals
Donald L. Caruth, Robert M. Noe III, and R. Wayne Mondy

The Court and Free-Lance Reporter Profession: Improved Management Strategies
David J. Saari

Pollution Law Handbook _____

A GUIDE TO FEDERAL ENVIRONMENTAL LAWS

Sidney M. Wolf

Q Quorum Books

NEW YORK • WESTPORT, CONNECTICUT • LONDON

Library of Congress Cataloging-in-Publication Data

Wolf, Sidney M.
  Pollution law handbook.

  Includes index.
  1. Pollution—Law and legislation—United States.
I. Title.
KF3775.W58   1988   344.73′04632   87-13094
                         347.3044632
ISBN 0-89930-141-X (lib. bdg. : alk. paper)

British Library Cataloguing in Publication Data is available.

Library of Congress Catalog Card Number: 87-13094
ISBN: 0-89930-141-X

First published in 1988 by Quorum Books

Greenwood Press, Inc.
88 Post Road West, Westport, Connecticut 06881

Printed in the United States of America

The paper used in this book complies with the
Permanent Paper Standard issued by the National
Information Standards Organization (Z39.48-1984).

10 9 8 7 6 5 4 3

To Walt and Mary,
who were friends indeed
when I was most in need.

Contents

Preface

This handbook is a practical reference and overview of the eight major federal statutes concerned with controlling pollution. There are many federal statutes which involve environmental protection, but the eight selected for the handbook provide the principal authority for regulating air, water, and land pollution and toxic substance releases into the environment.

The handbook is not intended to describe every single provision of each statute, for some of these laws are exceptionally lengthy and brimming with minute requirements. The handbook does, however, contain the many crucial details of each law. To attorneys and laypersons alike, many of these statutes when read in their original statutory text seem convoluted, confusing, and complex. They defy ready understanding even after several careful, painstaking readings. Few of the eight statutes were drafted with easy reading, plain language, and good organization in mind—this being the result of the many interests and legislative minds that formulated the laws and of the complex issues addressed by each law.

This work is designed to make the eight statutes more comprehensible both in general and as to their many essential details. The descriptions of the laws' provisions are presented in a coherent manner which is lacking in the often scattered organization of the statutory texts, and this is done by breaking down each law into the important areas it covers. These statutory descriptions are organized in a format that enables the reader to find the requirements and subjects that constitute each statute. Many of the concepts and provisions of the statutes are complex and defy overly simple description, but the handbook does provide descriptions of the statutory provisions that make them understandable without sacrificing the many needed details of these laws.

Each chapter begins with a highly detailed listing of the contents of that chapter. It is recommended that you refer to it before beginning to read the chapter in order to find the appropriate topic or requirement in the statute for which information is sought or to obtain a general overview of the statute's contents.

The handbook has two principal intended uses. The first is simply to provide a good understanding of a particular statute's provisions without the difficulty commonly associated with finding, reading, and researching the statute itself. The second is to employ the handbook in conjunction with reading the statutory text to provide better comprehension of the statute which might be elusive without such a reference aid. The handbook is not meant, by any means, to be a substitute for close and detailed examination, understanding, and application of the pollution control laws which the book describes. If the reader wants or needs to know the exact language and dictates of the statutes, then the statutory source must be researched and consulted. The statutory text for each law can be found in the *United States Code*, which is the official codification of federal laws. Unofficial codifications, which feature annotations on judicial construction and interpretation of federal statutes, can be found in the *United States Code Annotated* and the *United States Code Service*. The general table of contents provides the citations where each statute can be found in these three federal statutory codes.

Abbreviations

ATSDR	Agency for Toxic Substances and Disease Registry
BADCT	"best available demonstrated control technology"
BART	"best available retrofit technology"
BAT	"best available technology economically achievable"
BCT	"best conventional control technology"
BMP	"best management practices"
BOD	biological oxygen demand
BPJ	"best professional judgment"
BPT	"best practicable technology currently available"
CERCLA	Comprehensive Environmental Response, Compensation, and Liability Act

CERCLIS	Comprehensive Environmental Response, Compensation, and Liability Information System
DOL	Department of Labor
EP	extraction procedure
EPA	Environmental Protection Agency
FDF	"fundamentally different factor"
FIFRA	Federal Insecticide, Fungicide, and Rodenticide Act
FWPCA	Federal Water Pollution Control Act
LAER	"lowest achievable emission rate"
MSDS	"material safety data sheets"
NAS	National Academy of Sciences
NCP	National Contingency Plan
NIOSH	National Institute for Occupational Safety and Health
NPAR	"nonbinding preliminary allocation of responsibility"
NPDES	National Pollutant Discharge Elimination System
NPL	National Priorities List
NRC	Nuclear Regulatory Commission
OMB	Office of Management and Budget
PCBs	polychlorinated biphenyls
POTWs	publicly owned wastewater treatment works
PSD	"preventing significant deterioration"
RACT	"reasonably available control technology"
RCRA	Resource Conservation and Recovery Act
RI/FS	Remedial Investigation/Feasibility Study
SDWA	Safe Drinking Water Act
SIC	Standard Industrial Classification
SIPs	State Implementation Plans
TSCA	Toxic Substances Control Act

1 Federal Clean Water Act (33 U.S.C. §§ 1251 et. seq.)

GENERALLY

DEFINITIONS

GENERALLY

The Federal Water Pollution Control Act (FWPCA) was originally enacted in 1972 and amended with major provisions by legislation in 1977, 1981, and 1987. It is commonly referred to as the Clean Water Act, the title of the 1977 amendments. The latest amendments constitute the Water Quality Act of 1987.

The principal objective of the FWPCA is to restore and maintain the chemical, physical, and biological integrity of the nation's waters. Three major national goals are expressed to achieve this objective:

1. Eliminating the discharge of pollutants into navigable waters by 1985
2. As an interim goal, achieving by July 1, 1983, wherever attainable, water quality that is swimmable and fishable and allows for recreational uses, and
3. prohibiting the discharge of toxic pollutants in toxic amounts.

The FWPCA also establishes a national policy that federal financial assistance be provided to construct publicly owned wastewater treatment works (POTWs). The Environmental Protection Agency (EPA) is given the principal responsibility for administering the FWPCA.

Moreover, Congress adopted the policy that the states retain strong and primary responsibility for the management and enforcement of water pollution control, with EPA keeping ultimate authority.

The FWPCA utilizes technology-based effluent limitations and standards, receiving water quality standards, and a discharge permit program—to implement these standards—as the basic means of achieving the act's goals.

The two basic types of standards applied to direct dischargers into navigable waters are effluent limitations and receiving water quality standards. Effluent limitations directly restrict the amount of a pollutant which a source can discharge into the water. Receiving water quality standards establish the chemical and biological quality that will be required for a body of water and refer to the maximum concentration of a pollutant that is allowed. Water quality standards are generally aimed at allowing or sustaining a particular kind or category of use for the water. Once the use is determined, then specific effluent limitations can be established for dischargers that will allow water quality to reach and sustain the use that is chosen or designated. The various uses which these receiving water quality-based effluent standards can be employed to attain or protect include recreation, propagation of fish, plant, and wildlife, and use as a public water supply.

The FWPCA requires all dischargers in any industry category to comply with minimum levels of pollutant discharges, called effluent limitations or standards. The major kind of national effluent limitations are based on technology, that is, they are set at discharge levels that can be reached through the use of certain statutorily specified concepts of pollution control technology. There are two prevailing types of technology-based standards which the FWPCA makes relevant for industries that discharge directly into the water. These are "best available technology economically achievable" (BAT) and "best conventional control technology" (BCT) standards. The technology standard which is mainly applied to POTW discharges is "secondary treatment."

The FWPCA distinguishes between two classes of industrial pollutant dischargers: (1) persons discharging directly into navigable waters, and (2) persons discharging into POTWs, called indirect dischargers because their wastes ultimately can make it into the water through the treatment works. For indirect dischargers, the FWPCA provides for national pretreatment standards. Pretreatment standards cover pollutants that are determined not to be susceptible to treatment by the POTW or that would interfere with its operations. The pretreatment standards, which are set by EPA, require the industry to treat its wastes to an acceptable effluent level before discharging into the sewer system.

The FWPCA authorizes the states to establish water quality criteria and receiving water quality standards, subject to EPA approval. The receiving water quality standards refer to the maximum concentration of pollutants allowed in a body of water. When the EPA-established national effluent limitations are too low to attain or sustain the state-designated receiving water quality standard for a body of water, the state can impose more stringent effluent limitations. EPA itself can also establish receiving water quality standards and then impose effluent limitations to attain and sustain these levels of receiving water quality, without being required to utilize the technology-based effluent limitations that may be less stringent.

The heart of the FWPCA is a permit system known as the National Pollutant Discharge Elimination System (NPDES). The FWPCA prohibits discharges into navigable waters unless authorized by an NPDES permit. Through the terms and conditions written into the NPDES permit, both effluent limitations and receiving water quality standards are primarily implemented and enforced. The NPDES permit must be consistent with effluent limitations and water quality standards, whichever is stricter, and other requirements of the FWPCA. Whenever EPA technology-based effluent limitations are insufficient to meet state or federal receiving water quality standards, then they must be made stricter and must be included in NPDES permits to the extent necessary to meet the water quality standards. A discharger into a POTW may be required to comply with pretreatment regulations but is not required to obtain an NPDES permit. The POTW is, however. EPA is required to conduct an NPDES permit program, but states may assume EPA authority for the program, in whole or in part, in lieu of EPA, provided EPA determines the state meets federal requirements for an EPA-approved program.

The FWPCA also establishes a permit system for the discharge of dredged and fill materials, which is administered by the Corps of Engineers.

In furtherance of the national policy stated in the FWPCA that federal financial assistance be provided to construct POTWs, federal grants are authorized for the construction of these facilities. However, the legislation also seeks to phase out federal grants as the primary means of building POTWs and gradually to shift the burden of payment to state and local governments. Under the 1987 amendments the construction grants would end in fiscal 1990. Beginning in fiscal 1989, a new federal grants program would take effect which provides seed grants to capitalize state-run revolving funds. Local governments could borrow from the revolving funds to build POTWs and related projects but would have to pay back the loans. The federal grants to start the state loan funds, called capitalization grants, replace the direct construction grants but would end in 1994. Thereafter the state loan funds would be self-sustaining from repayments of loans, including interest.

The Water Quality Act of 1987, which amended the Clean Water Act, established several new programs either to study water quality problems or to provide funds for efforts to protect selected major bodies of water. The new programs included the establishment within EPA of a Great Lakes National Program Office, continuation of the Chesapeake Bay Program to coordinate federal and state efforts to improve water quality in the Bay, grants to affected states for cooperation in implementing a Chesapeake Bay management plan, creation of a Clean Lake Program requiring states to survey and submit reports to EPA on lake quality, grants to states to develop and implement state Nonpoint Source Management programs, and a National Estuary Program which authorizes EPA or the states to initiate management conferences for affected governmental bodies to develop comprehensive plans to manage the protection of nominated estuaries.

The FWPCA has been given teeth as is reflected in an assortment of administrative and judicial remedies for violations of requirements established pursuant to the act, such as NPDES permits, federal effluent limitations, and federal pretreatment requirements.

DEFINITIONS

Discharge is a key term in the FWPCA and means the addition of pollutants to navigable waters from a point source* or from a vessel.

*A point source is any discernible, confined, and discrete conveyance, including but not limited to any pipe, ditch, channel, tunnel, conduit, well, discrete fissure, container, rolling stock, concentrated animal feeding operation, vessel or other floating craft, or a landfill leachate collection system, from which pollutants are or may be discharged, but does not include return flows from irrigated agriculture.

Pollution means the manmade or man-induced alteration of the chemical, physical, biological, or radiological integrity of the water.

Pollutant includes dredged soil, solid waste, incinerator residue, sewage, garbage, sewage sludge, munitions, chemical wastes, biological materials, radioactive materials, heat, wrecked or discarded equipment, rock, sand, cellar dirt and industrial, municipal, and agricultural waste discharged into the water. If a discharge does not contain a pollutant as defined by the FWPCA, then the discharge is not subject to regulation under the act and an NPDES permit is not required for it. The FWPCA expressly excludes from the term *pollutant*, sewage from vessels, as this kind of discharge is governed by provisions in the act governing marine sanitation devices. The FWPCA also excludes from the term *pollutant*, water, gas, or other material when injected into a well to facilitate production of oil or gas, or water derived from oil and gas production and disposed in a well in a manner the state approves as not harmful to surface water or groundwater.

The term *toxic pollutant* means any pollutant or combination of pollutants, including disease-causing agents, which will cause death, disease, behavioral abnormalities, cancer, genetic mutations, physiological malfunctions (including reproductive malfunctions), or physical deformities, in organisms or their offspring.

WASTE TREATMENT WORKS' GRANTS AND PLANNING

Generally

For the purpose of achieving the goals of the FWPCA, the act requires, and financially supports with federal grants-in-aid, waste treatment facilities and state pollution control programs.

Title II Grants for Construction of Treatment Works (Expiring in 1990)

Under Title II of the FWPCA, EPA is authorized to dispense billions in direct grants to states, municipalities, and multijurisdictional governments to construct publicly owned treatment works (POTWs). Most of the money has been given to construct municipal treatment works. EPA administers the Title II grants and disperses them to projects within the states according to a statutory allotment formula for distribution of the funds to each state. The states, in turn, set priorities for spending the money on treatment works and other water pollution control activities within their borders. The Title II construction program expires in fiscal 1990.

After October 1984, eligibility for the Title II grants was generally limited to projects for secondary treatment and more stringent processes and facilities. EPA is allowed to make grants for POTW projects of less stringency than secondary treatment, but the grants cannot exceed 20 percent of the total amount allotted to the state for construction grants.

After October 1984, Title II grants to the states distributed by EPA were opened up for projects to control combined stormwater and sanitary sewer overflows if this kind of discharge was made a major priority for funding by the state. Also after October 1984, the federal share of funding the cost of constructing treatment works was reduced from a maximum of 75 percent of total costs to 55 percent. If a particular treatment works received a grant before October 1984 and the state makes a commitment to provide further grant funds prior to October 1, 1990, the POTW will remain eligible for the 75 percent federal share for the continuation and completion of the project. In the case of any project for which an application for a construction grant was made before October 1984 and which at that date was subject to a judicial injunction prohibiting its construction, the project is also eligible for the 75 percent maximum federal share for construction costs. Federal construction grants are paid on a staged basis which keeps pace with construction.

EPA-funded POTW projects are required to adopt a system of charges in which users of the treatment system must pay a proportionate share of the costs of operation, maintenance, and replacement of the system. The FWPCA allows a POTW to utilize lower charges for low-income residential users, and still not violate the proportionate charge requirement, if EPA determines that the reduced charges for low-income customers were adopted after public notice and hearing. EPA must establish guidelines for payment of waste treatment costs and charges by users of waste treatment services, including user classifications, criteria for the adequacy of charges, and model rate and user charges. EPA may exempt from the user charge requirement any industrial user that discharges 25,000 gallons or less of sanitary wastes into the treatment works system, if the wastes do not adversely affect the facility or contaminate sludge.

A federal construction grant cannot be made for a sewage collection system except under the following two circumstances: (1) it is for the replacement or major rehabilitation of the existing collection system and is necessary to the total integrity and performance of the waste treatment works, or (2) the grant is for a new collection system in an existing community with current or planned capacity which is adequate to treat the collected waste.

It is up to each state to establish a priority list for spending federal funds on eligible treatment works, and the priorities must be according to categories of treatment works. The FWPCA specifies several categories of projects that must be included on a state priority list, and the state may include additional categories. While the determination of priorities to be given to different categories of waste treatment projects is up to each state, there is an exception where EPA determines, after public hearing, that a specific project fails to comply with applicable provisions of the FWPCA. In these cases, EPA may require the state to rearrange its priorities. If the state places any sewer improvement project on its priority list, 25 percent of the funds allocated to the state must be obligated to a sewer improvement category. No federal funds can be spent for the control of discharges from separate storm sewer systems.

EPA may make Title II construction grants for treatment works using innovative and alternative treatment processes that meet EPA guidelines. EPA is prohibited from making grants to a municipality unless the grant applicant, among other things, demonstrates that innovative and alternative treatment has been fully studied and evaluated, including reclamation and reuse of water, recycling techniques, land treatment, confined disposal of pollutants, and more efficient use of energy and resources. States are required to set aside from 4 percent to 7.5 percent of their allotment to fund innovative or alternative treatment technologies. EPA is to set aside a minimum of 4 percent of the construction grants available to the states for rural states with innovative treatment works in small towns with fewer than 3,500 people.

In any case in which a dispute arises with respect to awarding a contract for construction of treatment works by a recipient of funds and a party to the dispute files an appeal with EPA for resolution of the dispute, EPA must make a final decision on the appeal within 60 days after it is filed.

Waste Treatment Planning

The FWPCA encourages and financially assists comprehensive planning related to water pollution control activities and waste treatment facility activities. Many of these planning programs and requirements are related to waste treatment facilities built by Title II construction grants. With the eventual elimination of this kind of grant, many of the planning demands associated with it will become less relevant or totally irrelevant.

Several major water pollution control and waste treatment facility planning programs are established by the FWPCA. It authorizes the establishment of waste management plans and practices to achieve the goals of the legislation. These plans and practices are to apply the best practicable treatment technology to waste treatment works receiving Title II construction grants. Statewide water quality planning is authorized, as are the development and implementation of areawide waste treatment management plans, river basin plans, and state water quality implementation plans.

One of the most important planning requirements has been the obligation of states to establish areawide waste management jurisdictions in areas of urban-industrial concentrations with substantial water quality problems. The areawide waste jurisdictions are to develop waste management plans to implement and govern waste treatment facility construction and operation activities that have been funded by Title II grants. These agencies and plans have come to be known as 208 agencies and plans because it is in this section of the 1972 legislation that the provisions for this activity were located. States are also allowed to join together in interstate areawide waste management planning endeavors.

The 208 planning agency created for a designated areawide waste management area must prepare plans that include the identification of treatment works that are necessary to meet municipal waste treatment needs for a 20-year period and that are likely to be candidates for Title II grants. The 208 plans are to be revised yearly and should include developmental priorities and time schedules for initiating and completing treatment projects.

After a 208 waste management agency has been designated for an area and after its plans have been approved by EPA, Title II construction grants can only be made to projects conforming to the plans. No Title II construction grants may be made unless EPA determines either that a 208 plan is being implemented for the area and the proposed treatment works is included in such a plan or that reasonable progress toward construction is being made. The treatment works must also comply with state plans developed under the Clean Water Act.

The 208 areawide planning agency is responsible for establishing a regulatory program to implement the waste treatment management requirements of the FWPCA. This regulatory program is to control the siting, modification, and construction of any facility within its jurisdiction which may result in waste discharges. The 208 agency must see that the discharge of industrial wastes into treatment works meets the FWPCA's applicable pretreatment requirements. The 208 agency also has regulatory responsibilities for nonpoint sources of pollution. No NPDES permit can be issued for a point source that does not conform with the 208 areawide waste management plan.

Title VI Capitalization Grants (Successor to Title II Grants) and State Water Pollution Control Revolving Funds

The Water Quality Act of 1987 added a new Title VI to the FWPCA which establishes a grant program to provide seed funding for starting state-administered Water Pollution Control Revolving Funds, also authorized by the new Title VI. The grants, called capitalization grants because they capitalize the loan funds, are meant to provide a transition from largely federal financing to build POTWs, in the form of Title II construction grants, to state and local financing of POTWs through money from the state revolving funds. The states are to use the revolving funds to provide loans for the construction of POTWs and other pollution control activities. The state funds are revolving because they are to be replenished and maintained in perpetuity through repayments, with interest, of the loans. The $8.6 billion authorized for Title VI capitalization grants will be provided for fiscal years 1989 through 1994, replacing the Title II construction grants, which are to expire after fiscal year 1990. After 1994 the capitalization grants will be terminated, and POTWs will have to be financed by loans from the self-sustained state revolving funds and other state and local financial sources.

In order to receive a capitalization grant, a state must enter into an agreement with EPA and become obligated to conform to the requirements of the act for obtaining such a grant. Among other things, the state must commit itself to do the following: (1) deposit into the state's revolving fund at least a 20 percent match (EPA may require a higher match) of federal capitalization grants made to the state; (2) make binding loan commitments for the construction of treatment works and other eligible water pollution activities within one year of receiving a federal capitalization grant; (3) abide by the restriction that capitalization grants cannot be used for any other purpose, if at all, until first being used to satisfy the need to maintain progress toward compliance with the enforceable goals and requirements of the FWPCA, including the secondary treatment compliance date of July 1, 1988, for POTWs; and (4) require any treatment project that is constructed in whole or in part prior to fiscal year 1995 with funds made directly available by capitalization grants to meet several of the requirements imposed on projects that receive Title II construction grants. As to the last requirement with which the state must agree, that the capitalization grants to POTWs conform with certain portions of the FWPCA previously applied to Title II grant-funded projects, these provisions require the following: (1) application of the best practicable waste treatment technology; (2) limitation of assistance to projects for secondary treatment or more stringent treatment; (3) consideration of alternative waste treatment techniques in project designs; (4) agreement not to subject related sewer collection systems to excessive filtration; (5) consideration of innovative and alternative treatment technologies; (6) consideration of potential recreation and open space opportunities in the planning of the proposed facility; and (7) compliance with the Davis-Bacon Act labor wage provisions in the construction of POTWs.

In order to be eligible for capitalization grants, a state must establish a loan fund call a State Water Pollution Control Revolving Fund. As mentioned before, the federal capitalization grants provide seed funding for the state loan funds, and the states are to match the federal contribution with at least 20 percent of their own funds. The revolving fund is to be maintained by repayment to the fund of loans made to municipalities for eligible water pollution projects. With the repayments, which include interest on the loans, the state fund is designed to continue in perpetuity to finance water pollution projects in the future and to relieve the federal government of this responsibility.

The use of financial assistance from a state revolving fund is restricted to three purposes: (1) construction of POTWs; (2) implementation of the Nonpoint Source Control Program in a state; and (3) development and implementation of a conservation and management plan in the state for the National Estuarine Program. Wastewater treatment projects (but not other eligible kinds of projects) that receive assistance from the revolving fund must be on the state priority list. Assistance to these treatment projects may be provided regardless of the rank of the project on the priority list. Financial assistance from the revolving fund must be based on an annual intended use plan prepared by the state. The state must provide an opportunity for public comment and review in formulating the intended use plan.

Money from a revolving fund may be used to make loans but is not to be used to provide direct grants. Loan funds may not be used for direct loans to support the nonfederal share of a POTW receiving a construction grant under Title II, with the limited exception of the case where the loan is truly necessary to allow construction of the POTW to proceed. The loan fund may be used to buy or refinance loans for POTWs whose loans were received after March 7, 1985. A state may only make a loan from the revolving fund if the recipient establishes a dedicated source of revenue for repayment of the loan. In addition to being used for loans, the revolving fund may be used for loan guarantees or for the purchase of insurance to improve credit access or reduce interest rates for local financing of treatment works. The revolving fund may also be used as security for state bonds issued to finance local POTW projects, if bond proceeds are deposited in the fund. Finally, the find may be used to guarantee financing for similar revolving funds established by municipal or intermunicipal agencies to fund treatment and pollution control projects.

Construction grant funds from Title II can be transferred to a state revolving fund established under Title VI. The transfers cannot exceed 50 percent of the construction grant funds available in fiscal year 1987 and 75 percent in fiscal 1988. The transferred Title II construction grant funds are treated as capitalization grants and are deducted from the allocation of capitalization grants which the state is entitled to receive later.

DISCHARGES OF POLLUTANTS AND FWPCA STANDARDS

Generally—Effluent Limitations and Receiving Water Standards

The discharge of any pollutant is unlawful, except when in compliance with the FWPCA provisions authorizing technology-based effluent limitations, water quality effluent standards, toxic effluent standards, pretreatment standards, new source performance standards, aquaculture permits, NPDES permits, and dredge and fill permits. It is important to note that any effluent limitations which EPA establishes are specifically applied to point sources, not nonpoint sources. The FWPCA makes it unlawful to discharge any radiological, chemical, or biological warfare agent or high-level radioactive waste into navigable water.

The FWPCA provides for the establishment by EPA of national effluent limitations for controlling discharges by industries and municipal sewage treatment works. The states and EPA are also authorized to establish receiving water quality standards.

EPA is required to establish various statutorily specified technology-based effluent limitations that prescribe minimum standards of performance for a municipal or industrial discharge which restrict the amount of a pollutant released by such a source without regard to the quality of the receiving body of water. The general purpose of the technology-based standards is to set minimum control requirements that must be met by dischargers.

It is important to realize that the technology-based effluent limitations to be established by EPA are national in scope. There must be national uniformity for these standards by class or category of industries—or more simply put, for industrial groups. The national standards apply regardless of the quality of the receiving waters. These discharge standards are often confusedly called technology-based standards, but they are in fact performance standards because they require a specific level or limit on a pollutant's discharge rather than designating that a particular kind of technology be used by the discharger. The technology-based standards are so named because the effluent limitation applied to an industrial group across the nation must be determined in accordance with the degree of restriction on the pollutant's discharge which is attainable by applying considerations of technological and economic feasibility specified by the act. These considerations differ for different kinds of categories or sources of pollutants and are embodied in different technology-based standards like secondary treatment, BAT, BCT, and BPT, which are discussed below. An effluent limitation means any restriction, including schedules of compliance, established by the state or EPA on quantities, rates, and concentrations of chemical, physical, biological, and other constituents that are discharged from point sources into waters. The effluent limitations authorized by the FWPCA are directed at point sources.

Where EPA's technology-based effluent limitations are inadequate to achieve a particular use for the receiving water desired by a state, then the state can establish more stringent effluent limitations that may be necessary to attain or sustain its desired water use. EPA can establish its own effluent limitations related to water quality for the purpose of reducing or eliminating a pollutant's concentration in the receiving water, regardless of or in addition to technology-based effluent limitations. The receiving water quality standards that can be established either by EPA or a state identify the intended uses of a body of water and specify the biological and chemical character necessary to attain or sustain these uses. These water quality standards refer to the maximum concentration of pollutants allowed in a body of water. The use of water quality standards is encouraged where necessary to protect public health and welfare. Receiving water quality standards, whether established by a state or EPA, are implemented by effluent limitations imposed by regulatory authorities upon dischargers at levels necessary to reach and maintain receiving water quality standards.

POTW Dischargers, Secondary Treatment Standard, and Sewage Sludge

Generally

By July 1, 1977, POTWs were required to meet effluent limitations for pollutants based on secondary treatment, as defined by EPA. Secondary treatment generally is a level of treatment that involves microbological digestion of organic materials in the wastewater. In addition to effluent limitations for a POTW based on secondary treatment, more stringent effluent limitations than secondary treatment may be imposed if necessary to meet state receiving water quality standards or any EPA or state treatment standard or schedule of compliance.

EPA is required to issue environmentally protective regulations for the disposal of sewage sludge by a POTW into navigable waters. These sewage sludge disposal guidelines, at the very least, must (1) identify sludge uses, including disposal; (2) specify factors to be taken into account in determining the measures and practices applicable to sewage sludge use or disposal, including costs; and (3) identify concentrations of pollutants that interfere with sludge use or disposal. The FWPCA states that the manner of disposing of sewage sludge is a local determination except that it is unlawful for a POTW to dispose of sludge in any way other than in accordance with the guidelines.

EPA must identify toxic pollutants that may be present in sewage sludge in concentrations that can harm public health and the environment. EPA must promulgate regulations on acceptable management practices and numerical limitations for toxics in sludge. EPA must update its toxic sludge regulations at least every two years.

EPA is prohibited from issuing any permit, including an NPDES permit, authorizing the dumping of sewage sludge into the ocean after December 31, 1981. For the purposes of the ocean discharge prohibition sewage sludge is considered to be any POTW waste which, when dumped in in the ocean, may result in the unreasonable degradation or endangerment of human health, welfare, amenities, or the marine environment, ecological systems, or economic potential.

Extension of Secondary Treatment Deadline

The FWPCA allows an extension of the 1977 statutory deadline for secondary treatment or any other more stringent limitations for a POTW up to July 1, 1988, when necessary construction cannot be completed in time to meet the deadline, or when the federal government has failed to make funding available in time to achieve secondary treatment by the 1977 deadline. This postponement of the secondary treatment requirement is available only to POTWs in existence as of July 1, 1977, or approved pursuant to waste treatment grant provisions prior to June 30, 1974, for which construction has to be completed within four years of approval. POTWs in existence or approved after these dates cannot obtain a secondary treatment compliance postponement. Application to EPA for the extensions must be filed no later than August 4, 1987. If a POTW is granted an extension of the secondary treatment deadline, its NPDES permit must contain a schedule of compliance requiring compliance on the earliest date it can be achieved, but in no event later than July 1, 1988. The compliance extension may include other terms and conditions relating to general requirements for waste treatment plants, toxic discharges, and other requirements of the FWPCA.

Relaxation of Secondary Treatment for Marine Waters

In addition to the general postponement allowed for compliance with the statutory deadline for secondary treatment, EPA is also allowed to give a more specific variance that can relax the secondary treatment requirement for POTWs that discharge into marine waters. Simply put, EPA's secondary treatment requirements may be relaxed for POTWs that discharge into marine waters. EPA, with the concurrence of the state, can issue an NPDES permit that relaxes the secondary pretreatment requirements for a POTW for the discharge of any pollutant into marine waters if the POTW can demonstrate to EPA compliance with nine conditions: (1) there must be an existing water quality standard for the pollutant for which the modification from secondary treatment is requested; (2) the discharge of pollutants under a modified requirement will not interfere, alone or in combination with other pollutants, with the attainment or maintenance of water quality standards to assure protection of public water supplies, recreational uses, and fish and wildlife resources; (3) the POTW has established a pollution monitoring system that involves scientific investigations necessary to study the effects of the discharge; (4) the modified requirements will not require additional compensating pollution control requirements on other point and nonpoint sources; (5) pretreatment requirements for discharges into the

POTW will be enforced; (6) in communities with over 50,000 people, the POTW requires pretreatment of toxic pollutants and has a pretreatment program in effect; (7) to the extent practicable, the POTW will establish a schedule for eliminating the discharge of toxic pollutants from nonindustrial sources into the POTW; (8) there will be no new or substantially increased discharge of the pollutant for which the modification is requested above the volume specified in the NPDES permits; and (9) at least primary treatment is being provided for the marine discharge.

In order for an NPDES permit to be issued to a POTW seeking the marine discharge variance, there must be an assurance that water providing dilution does not contain significant amounts of previously discharged effluent from the treatment works. The modification may not be issued for estuarine waters if, at the time of the application, the waters do not support a balanced indigenous fish and wildlife population or allow recreational activities, or exhibit water quality below the receiving water quality standards adopted to protect public water supplies, wildlife, or recreational facilities. The prohibition applies regardless of any causal relationship between such characteristics and the applicant's discharge.

The marine discharge modification is available only for a POTW built on or before July 1, 1977. A POTW in existence as of July 1, 1977, must apply for the marine discharge exemption no later than December 31, 1982. However, a POTW which prior to December 31, 1982, had an existing contract to discharge its sewage into another POTW that had received or applied for a marine discharge modification prior to this date, in its own right may apply for a modification before March 6, 1987. The FWPCA prohibits an NPDES permit for a POTW from being modified to allow the discharge of sewage sludge into marine water.

Industrial Dischargers—Technology-Based Effluent Limitations

Generally

In general, EPA is authorized to establish national effluent limitations for categories and classes of point sources other than POTWs. The FWPCA requires that the effluent limitations set by EPA be uniform for categories or classes of the point source to which they are applied, regardless of the quality of the receiving waters. EPA is authorized to prohibit discharges of any radiological, chemical, or biological warfare agent or high-level radioactive waste into navigable waters.

The FWPCA devised a technology-based system of federal effluent limitations for industrial discharges directly into the water. That is, the effluent limitations are set at levels that could be reached through the application of these statutorily specified concepts of pollution control technology. Four major types of national technology-based effluent standards can be applied to direct industrial dischargers: "best practicable technology currently available" (BPT), "best available technology economically achievable" (BAT), "best conventional control technology" (BCT), and "best available demonstrated control technology" (BADCT).

The original 1972 Federal Water Pollution Control Act provided EPA with only BPT and BAT standards to use for setting effluent limitations. The BPT standards were to be the first phase of regulation when established by the 1972 act, requiring BPT effluent limitations for EPA picked water pollutants to be achieved by July 1, 1977. In the second phase of regulation, the BPT standards were to be replaced with the BAT standards, which were considered stricter, and these standards were to be achieved by polluters by July 1, 1983. In other words, the regulation would shift from BPT to BAT standards for industrial dischargers.

The 1977 amendments made a midcourse correction in the FWPCA by eliminating the July 1, 1983, BAT deadline and instead designated three categories of pollutants—conventional, toxic, and nonconventional—and the kind of technology-based effluent standard and compliance deadline to be applied became a matter to which of the three categories did a pollutant belong. The 1977 amendments established a new type of standard—BCT standards—and they were to be used for conventional pollutants. BAT standards were to be restricted to use for toxic and nonconventional pollutants. In general, these BCT and BAT standards are to be met by dischargers within three years after being promulgated, but compliance cannot be delayed beyond March 31, 1989, for statutorily designated toxic and conventional pollutants. The BPT limits are still applicable in a few NPDES permits, but ultimately they will be replaced by the BCT standards for conventional pollutants and BAT standards for toxic and nonconventional pollutants. The BADCT standard is essentially the same as the BAT standard and applies to effluent limitations set for new sources, which are discussed in a subsequent section. In sum, with the BPT standards eventually being phased out, the prevailing technology-based standards for industrial dischargers are BAT and BCT standards.

Conventional Pollutants

The FWPCA requires dischargers of conventional pollutants identified by the 1977 amendments to comply with effluent limitations established by EPA based on the use of BCT within three years after the limitations are promulgated, but in no case later than March 1, 1989. Conventional pollutants under the FWPCA subject to the deadline for BCT compliance are biological oxygen demand (BOD), suspended solids, fecal coliform, and pH. EPA may designate other conventional pollutants. The heat component of any discharge is not a conventional pollutant under the legislation and thus cannot be made subject to the BCT standards.

EPA is to define BCT in accordance with factors specified in the act. EPA is to identify the degree of effluent reduction attainable through the application of BCT, including specifying measures and practices, for categories and classes of industrial sources. It is important to note that in setting BCT standards for conventional pollutants EPA designates the category or categories of point sources to which the effluent standards will apply. That is, the effluent limitations are set on an industry group basis and not on a facility-by-facility basis. The BPT, BADCT, and BAT standards for other pollutants are likewise directed at industry groups and not individual facilities.

Toxic Pollutants

One of the main purposes of the FWPCA is to establish a national policy of prohibiting the discharge of toxic pollutants in toxic amounts. The FWPCA defines toxic pollutant to mean any pollutant that will cause death, disease, behavioral abnormalities, cancer, genetic mutations, physiological malfunctions (including malfunctions in reproduction), or physical deformities in organisms.

The FWPCA requires EPA to set effluent limitations or prohibitions for toxic pollutants which are based on the use of the "best available technology economically achievable," or BAT, for the industrial group to which point sources belong. As noted before, all EPA technology-based standards are to apply to industry groups and cannot be applied on a facility-by-facility basis.

The BAT standards or prohibitions for toxic pollutants established by EPA are, at the very least, to be set for 65 statutorily specified toxic pollutants. The 1977 amendments required the effluent limitations to be established for these 65 toxic pollutants no later than July 1, 1980. When the 1987 amendments were enacted, EPA had not yet promulgated effluent limitations for two categories of toxic pollutants in the list of 65: (1) pesticides and (2) organic chemicals and plastics, and synthetic fibers. The 1987 legislation required EPA to establish pretreatment and BAT effluent discharge limitations for these two categories of toxic pollutants no later than December 31, 1986. For the 65 designated toxic pollutants, industrial dischargers must comply with EPA's BAT effluent limitations within three years after they had been promulgated, but no later than March 31, 1989.

EPA is to identify the degree of effluent reduction that is achievable through the application of BAT technology on industrial categories. The availability of discharge control technology and considerations of technological and economic feasibility determine whether BAT can be set for toxic pollutants. The BAT standard must result in reasonable further progress toward eliminating the discharge of the toxic pollutants if EPA finds that this elimination is technologically and economically achievable for the industry group to which the limitation is to apply.

EPA may revise the list of toxic pollutants subject to BAT effluent limitations or prohibitions, and may add or remove toxic pollutants from time to time. In revising the list, the factors which EPA must take into account include toxicity, persistence, degradability, presence and importance of affected organisms in the water, and extent to which effective control is or may be achieved by other regulatory means. EPA's determination on including or excluding toxic substances on the list is regarded as final, and is judicially reviewable only if arbitrary and capricious, in which case EPA is to promulgate a revised limitation. For other toxic pollutants added to the list, the BAT effluent limitations are to be achieved no later than three years after the effluent limitations have been established by EPA.

EPA may set effluent standards, including prohibitions, for toxic pollutants besides BAT-based effluent limitations. EPA may only impose a toxic pollutant effluent standard or prohibition that is more and not less stringent than would be achieved by a BAT effluent limitation. The stricter effluent standard or prohibition for toxic pollutants, unlike a BAT effluent limitation, need not be based on the availability of pollution control technology to reach the standard. The stricter toxic pollutant effluent standard or prohibition must be set at a level which EPA determines provides an "ample margin of safety." The toxic effluent standards set by EPA are to be reviewed by the agency at least every three years. The factors which EPA must take into account in establishing a stricter toxic pollutant effluent standard or prohibition include the toxicity of the pollutant, its persistence and degradability, the presence and importance of affected organisms in the water, the nature and extent of the toxic pollutant on these organisms, and the extent to which effective control is or may be achieved by other regulatory measures. When establishing a stricter toxic effluent standard or prohibition, EPA is to designate the category or categories of industrial sources to which it applies. EPA may include the disposal of dredged materials in the category sources to which it applies, but only in consultation with the Department of the Army.

In establishing a toxic pollutant effluent standard or prohibition stricter than a BAT limitation, EPA is to allow a 60-day review period and, upon request, hold a full public hearing, including allowing the opportunity for cross-examination and making a verbatim record available to the public. The standard or prohibition must be promulgated within 270 days after publication in its proposed form. The toxic pollutant effluent standard or prohibition is to take effect no more than one year after promulgation. EPA may postpone compliance by an industrial category if the stricter standard or prohibition cannot be feasibly achieved within the one-year deadline, in which case the standard or prohibition is to take effect on the earliest date compliance is technologically feasible, but in no event more than three years after promulgation. EPA's promulgation of a stricter toxic pollutant effluent standard or prohibition is final and is judicially reviewable only if not based on substantial evidence, in which case EPA is to revise the standard.

EPA is authorized to issue regulations to supplement effluent limitations for industrial categories for the purpose of controlling the runoff of toxic and hazardous materials. For specific pollutants which EPA must regulate as toxic pollutants, it may also issue regulations to control plant site runoff, spills or leaks, sludge or waste disposal, and drainage from raw material storage, which is associated with the manufacturing processes of the regulated industrial category and which may contribute significantly to water pollution. The regulations are to rely on the use of "best management practices" (BMP) to control the nonpoint toxic and hazardous pollutant discharges. The BMP standards are to be made part of any NPDES permit issued to a point source with which the nonpoint source pollution is associated.

Nonconventional Pollutants

Any industrial pollutant not specifically identified by EPA as conventional or toxic falls into a third category, commonly called nonconventional pollutants. EPA is to set effluent limitations for nonconventional pollutants which are based on the use of BAT and are to be established on an industry category-by-category basis. The deadline for complying with the BAT standards for nonconventional pollutants is no later than three years after they are promulgated, but in no case later than March 31, 1989, for nonconventional pollutants, for which EPA has set BAT standards as of February 4, 1987.

The availability of discharge control technology and considerations of technological and economic feasibility determine whether BAT effluent limitations can be set for nonconventional pollutants. The BAT standard must result in reasonable further progress toward eliminating the discharge of the nonconventional pollutants if EPA finds this elimination is technologically and economically achievable for the industry group to which the limitation is to apply.

Variances: Modification and Extension of Effluent Limitations

The kind of pollutant discharged—whether conventional, toxic, or nonconventional—determines if a postponement or relaxation of effluent limitations can be obtained by an industrial discharger for a technology-based effluent limitation.

The FWDCA authorizes four major variances from technology-based effluent limitations on industrial dischargers: (1) an economic variance from BAT effluent limitations for nonconventional pollutants; (2) a water quality-related variance from BAT effluent limitations for five nonconventional pollutants; (3) an innovative technology postponement of up to two years after the BAT compliance date for nonconventional pollutants and BCT compliance date for pollutants; and (4) fundamentally different factor (FDF) variance which allows relaxation for an individual facility of BAT and BCT effluent limitations when the facility is fundamentally different with regard to noncost factors from other facilities in the industry group to which it belongs and the effluent limitation applies.

For industrial dischargers, the FWPCA allows an economic variance from BAT effluent limitations for nonconventional pollutants based on the individual facility's capability to afford the BAT limitation. If granted, the variance will be incorporated in the discharger's NPDES permit. This economic variance is not available for toxic pollutants, which are also subject to BAT standards. In order to obtain an economic BAT variance, the discharger of the nonconventional pollutant must demonstrate to EPA that the modified limitation will (1) represent the maximum use of technology within the economic capability of the discharger and (2) result in reasonable further progress toward eliminating the discharge of the nonconventional pollutant.

EPA, with the concurrence of the state, may grant a water quality variance for a particular facility for any of five nonconventional pollutants. The five eligible nonconventional pollutants are ammonia, chlorine, color, iron, and total phenols. EPA may list additional nonconventional pollutants to be eligible for the variance. If granted, the variance is incorporated in the discharger's NPDES permit. The water quality variance is not available for conventional pollutants, toxic pollutants, or heat discharges. In order for a discharger to obtain this type of relaxed BAT standard for nonconventional pollutants, it must show that (1) at a minimum there will be compliance with a BPT standard; (2) the granting of the modification will not result in additional requirements for other dischargers; (3) the modification will not interfere with the attainment or maintenance of water quality standards that assure the protection of public water supply, recreational activities, and fish and wildlife resources; and (4) there will not be an unacceptable risk posed to human health or the environment because of bioaccumulation, persistence in the environment, chronic toxicity (including cancer, genetic damage, or birth defects), or synergistic properties. If these conditions are met, then EPA, with concurrence of the state, must relax the BAT effluent limitation. An industrial discharger who applies for a water quality-related variance from a BAT standard may also apply during the same time period for the previously described economic variance from the BAT standard for the same pollutant.

In response to a petition, EPA may list other nonconventional pollutants, in addition to the five specified in the act, for which the BAT effluent standard can be modified. To be allowed for a particular industrial group, this listing must occur before the deadline for submitting applications for a modification, which is 270 days after the promulgation of an effluent limitation for the particular nonconventional pollutant. A petitioner may file an application for a modification simultaneously with a petition for listing the nonconventional pollutant. Before listing a nonconventional pollutant as eligible for a modification, EPA must first determine whether the pollutant meets the criteria for being listed as a toxic pollutant. If EPA determines that the pollutant meets these criteria, it must be listed as a toxic pollutant, and it is thus not eligible for a nonconventional pollutant modification. If EPA determines that the pollutant is not a toxic pollutant and that adequate information is available to make a decision regarding modification requests then EPA must list the pollutant as eligible for modification requests. The burden of proof for a listing petition is on the applicant.

An extension to postpone the statutory compliance date which the FWPCA imposes on BAT effluent standards for nonconventional pollutants and BCT effluent standards for conventional pollutants is authorized for up to two years when certain types of innovative effluent reduction technology are proposed for use by the discharger. EPA, or a state after consultation with EPA, may extend the BAT and BCT deadlines in an NPDES permit if the discharger proposes to meet the effluent limitation requirements. The discharger must agree to use innovative production processes or control techniques that will reduce effluent levels to a significantly greater degree than required by the limitation and that will move toward zero pollution or significant cost reduction in pollution control. Moreover, the proposed innovative system must have potential for industrywide application.

EPA is authorized to modify an effluent limitation for an individual facility within an industry group to which the limitation applies if the facility is found to be fundamentally different from other facilities within the industry group on the basis of statutorily specified factors. This fundamentally different factor (FDF) variance is reserved for individual facilities and is not meant to generally relax or retreat from effluent limitations imposed on an industry group. The FDF variance is given on the basis of noncost factors. The cost of compliance cannot be used to justify an FDF variance.

A facility must satisfy four criteria to the satisfaction of EPA before an FDF variance allowing alternative requirements to be used can be granted. First, a facility must be fundamentally different from the factors EPA considered in establishing the effluent limitation. These factors include the age of the equipment and facilities, the process employed, the engineering aspects of the types of control techniques, process changes, and other factors deemed appropriate by EPA. Cost is specifically excluded, independent of the other factors, as a basis for establishing a fundamental difference with regard to an individual facility and relaxing an effluent limitation. The second criterion requires that the application for an FDF variance be based on either of two kinds of information: (1) solely on information and supporting data that have been submitted to EPA during the rulemaking process and that specifically raise the factors which are fundamentally different for the facility; or (2) the aforementioned information, plus information and data which the applicant did not have a reasonable opportunity to submit during the rulemaking for the effluent limitation. The third criterion is that the alternative requirement being requested can be no less stringent than justified by the facility's fundamental difference from the rest of the industry group with respect to the factors specified in the act. The fourth criterion requires that if FDF relief is granted, the alternative requirement will not result in a nonwater quality environmental impact that is more harmful than the impact considered by EPA in establishing the effluent limitation.

An application for an FDF modification must be made within 180 days after the establishment or revision of the effluent limitation for which the variance is sought. An application does not cancel out the facility's obligation to comply with the effluent limitation which is the subject of the FDF modification request. EPA has 180 days to make a decision on an FDF modification application. If the application is denied, the facility must comply with the original compliance date for the effluent limitation. EPA must impose a system of fees for receiving and processing an FDF application.

New Source Performance Standards

When enacted in 1972, the FWPCA required the promulgation by EPA of effluent limitations for certain designated major new sources of pollution. The new source provisions of the law were meant to advance water pollution control by forcing technology. Unlike sources existing when the 1972 legislation was enacted, these new sources were to bypass the BPT stage of effluent limitations and instead comply with effluent limitations based on the more advanced "best available demonstrated control technology" (BADCT). The BADCT standard is tougher than the BPT standard and, in practice, is similar to the BAT standard which the FWPCA imposes on existing sources discharging nonconventional and toxic pollutants. A BADCT new source effluent limitation may include, where practicable, an absolute prohibition on effluent discharges. A new source means any source whose construction was begun after the publication of proposed regulations for the BPT standards which EPA was required to promulgate by the 1972 legislation. The new sources to which the national BADCT standards of performance apply include, at the very least, 27 specific new sources listed in the 1972 provisions of the FWPCA. EPA was also given the authority to add new sources to these 27. It must be stressed that the new source performance standards do not apply to all newly built facilities, but only to those belonging to an industrial group which is on the EPA list of industry groups. If a facility is a member of an industry group not on the list, then it must comply with whatever BPT, BAT, or BCT effluent limitation that is applicable to the pollutant discharged by a facility in an industry group for which EPA has promulgated one of these kinds of effluent limitations.

In establishing or revising new source performance standards based on BADCT, EPA must take into account the cost of achieving effluent reduction and any nonwater quality environmental impacts or energy requirements. The new source performance standards are to be revised from time to time as technology and alternative technologies change. EPA's new source performance standards are applicable to any new source owned or operated by the federal government, not just private facilities.

Each state is allowed to develop a system under its own law for applying and enforcing new source performance standards in the state. The state can administer the new source performance standards if EPA finds that the enforcement of these standards will be required at least to the same extent by state law as by federal law for EPA. The state's new source performance standards are not applicable to federal facilities.

New sources are protected from being subject to quickly changing standards. Any facility that is constructed to meet a new source performance standard in effect at the time it is built may not be subject to any more stringent standards for ten years from the date of the completion of the construction or during the period of tax depreciation or amortization provided by the Internal Revenue Code, whichever period ends first.

Federal Water Quality Related to Effluent Limitations

EPA can establish federal effluent limitations that are tied to protecting desired uses of water, in addition to its establishing the various national technology-based standards for POTWs and industrial dischargers. EPA can set effluent limitations related to water quality for a point source or group of point sources to the extent necessary to sustain various uses of water, such as for public water supply, the propagation and protection of fishlife and wildlife, agricultural and industrial needs, and recreational uses. EPA can impose the effluent standard related to water quality even if the source is meeting an applicable EPA-established, technology-based national effluent limitation.

Before establishing the federal water quality-based standard, EPA must issue notice, and within 90 days of the notice it must hold a public hearing. The purpose of the hearing is to determine the social and economic costs of achieving the water quality-based effluent standards and whether they can be attained with existing or alternative control technologies. If an industry point source at the hearing demonstrates that there is no reasonable relationship between the costs and benefits, then EPA must adjust the limitation for this particular industry source.

EPA, with the concurrence of the affected state, can modify federal water quality-related (but, not technology-based) effluent limitations for nontoxic pollutants if the applicant demonstrates at the time the effluent limitation is proposed that there is no reasonable relationship between the economic and social costs and benefits to be obtained from achieving the proposed limitation. EPA, with the concurrence of the affected state, may also modify federal water quality-related (but not technology-based) effluent limitations for toxic pollutants for a single period not to exceed five years. The condition is that the applicant demonstrate at the time the toxic effluent limitation is proposed that the modified requirement represents the maximum degree of control within the economic capability of the owner of the particular source, and will result in reasonable further progress (beyond BAT) toward attaining the water quality sought by the effluent limitation.

Pretreatment

EPA must establish pretreatment standards for the discharge of pollutants by industries into POTWs. These dischargers to the POTW are often called indirect dischargers. The pretreatment standards are applied to pollutants that are not susceptible to treatment by the treatment works or that would interfere with the operation of the POTW. The pretreatment standards are meant to prevent the discharge of any pollutant that interferes with, passes through, or is otherwise incompatible with the POTW. The function of pretreatment standards is to have the indirect discharger pretreat its wastes to an acceptable level before they are discharged into the sewers leading to the POTW.

EPA must establish a compliance date for the pretreatment standards it issues, which is no later than three years after the standards are promulgated. EPA is to revise the pretreatment standards when appropriate to reflect changes in pollution control technology for pretreatment. State and local governments are allowed to impose pretreatment standards that do not conflict with those established by EPA.

A two-year extension for compliance with a pretreatment standard is available to any existing, but not new, indirect discharger who intends to comply with the standard by using an innovative pretreatment system. The extension is not available unless the applicant can demonstrate that the innovative system has the potential for industrywide application, and the EPA or state-approved pretreatment program concurs with the proposed extension. The innovative pretreatment modification cannot be used if it causes or contributes to a violation of the POTW's NPDES permit or sewage sludge requirements.

The pretreatment standards are directly enforceable by EPA against dischargers into the POTW. EPA may notify a discharger into a POTW of a violation. If the POTW does not institute an enforcement action within 30 days, EPA may bring a civil enforcement action against the indirect discharger, including a restraining order, in federal district court. EPA has the authority to ban or restrict new sewer hook-ups to keep the POTW from taking effluent contributions that can cause it to violate its NPDES permit.

The effluent reductions dictated by a pretreatment standard for toxic pollutants may be revised to allow increased discharges into the POTW to reflect the removal of the toxic pollutants achieved by the POTW. This has come to be known as a removal credit. The POTW can seek EPA's permission to relax the pretreatment standard for a toxic pollutant from indirect dischargers if it can be determined that the POTW does not violate any toxic effluent limitation with which the industry would have to comply had it been a direct discharger, and if the discharge into the POTW does not interfere with sludge use or disposal in accordance with the act.

A new source introducing pollutants into a POTW must comply with EPA regulations for new sources and pretreatment. When EPA promulgates new source performance standards, it must simultaneously promulgate pretreatment standards for the new source.

EPA is authorized to modify a pretreatment standard for an individual facility within an industry group to which the limitation applies if the facility is found to be fundamentally different from other facilities within the industry group on the basis of statutorily specified factors. This fundamentally different factor (FDF) variance is reserved for individual facilities and is not meant to generally relax or retreat from effluent limitations for an industry group. The FDF variance from pretreatment standards is given on the basis of noncost factors. The cost of compliance cannot be used to justify an FDF variance.

A facility must satisfy four criteria to the satisfaction of EPA before an FDF variance allowing alternative pretreatment requirements to be used can be granted. First, a facility must be fundamentally different with the factors EPA considered in establishing the effluent limitation. These factors include the age of the equipment and facilities, the process employed, the engineering aspects of the types of control techniques, process changes, and other factors deemed appropriate by EPA. Cost is specifically excluded, independent of the other factors, as a basis for establishing a fundamental difference with regard to an individual facility and relaxing a pretreatment standard. The second criterion requires that the application for an FDF variance be based on either of two kinds of information: (1) solely on information and supporting data that have been submitted to EPA during the rulemaking process and that specifically raises the factors which are fundamentally different for the facility; or (2) the aforementioned information, plus information and data which the applicant did not have a reasonable opportunity to submit during the rulemaking for the pretreatment standard. The third criterion which the applicant for an FDF modification must demonstrate is that the alternative requirement being requested can be no less stringent than justified by the facility's fundamental difference from the rest of the industry group with respect to the factors specified in the act. The fourth criterion requires that, if FDF relief is granted, the alternative requirement will not result in a nonwater quality environmental impact more harmful than the impact considered by EPA in establishing the pretreatment standard.

An application for an FDF modification must be made within 180 days after the establishment or revision of the pretreatment standard for which the variance is sought. An application does not cancel the facility's obligation to comply with the pretreatment standard which is the subject of the FDF modification request. EPA has 180 days to make a decision on an FDF modification application. If the application is denied, the facility must comply with the original compliance date for the pretreatment standard. EPA must adopt a system of fees for receiving and processing an FDF application.

Thermal (Heat) Discharges

The FWPCA includes heat in its definition of a pollutant. Though effluent limitations can be set for thermal discharges, the heat component of any discharge is specifically excluded as a conventional pollutant and thus is not subject to any BCT standard for conventional pollutants. Any standard established for a point source must require that cooling water intake structures reflect the best technology available for minimizing adverse environmental impact.

Heat discharge limitations cannot be more stringent than required to assure the protection and propagation of the balanced, indigenous population of shellfish, fish, and wildlife in and on the body of water to which the heat discharge limitation applies. If the discharge source can demonstrate that the heat discharge standard would be more stringent than necessary to assure protection and propagation of aquatic life, EPA or the state can grant a modified standard allowing an alternative heat discharge limitation. The FWPCA protects the discharger receiving this heat discharge variance from being subjected to more stringent limitations in the future if the variance was granted after October 18, 1972, and otherwise does not violate effluent limitations or adversely affect aquatic life. The period for which a discharger allowed the heat discharge variance will be protected from other more stringent requirements is for up to ten years or during the Internal Revenue Code's tax depreciation or amortization period, whichever period is shorter.

STATE WATER QUALITY PROTECTIONS

State Receiving Water Quality Standards

The FWPCA allows states to adopt receiving water quality standards consisting of the designated uses of the water body. These state water quality standards are subject to EPA approval. A state submits to EPA the receiving water quality standards and implementation plans for their enforcement, along with the state's own effluent limitations needed to maintain or attain the water quality uses established by these standards. If EPA fails to approve the state standards, it must adopt federal standards for the state. When federal effluent limitations are too low to attain or sustain the state's water quality standards, EPA must set more stringent effluent limitations. Subject to approval by EPA, the state is required to identify and establish the maximum pollution loads or concentrations for those waters within its boundaries for which federal effluent limitations and heat discharge limitations have been set but which are not strict enough to satisfy state water quality standards.

State water quality standards are intended to protect public health or welfare, enhance water quality, and otherwise carry out the purposes of the FWPCA. The water quality standards consist of a designation of the use of the receiving body of water which is involved and the water quality criteria to be employed which will sustain such uses. The minimum requirements for these standards may be to protect various uses of water, including public water supply, propagation and protection of fishlife and wildlife, recreational purposes, and agricultural, industrial, and other uses.

At least every three years, the state must hold public hearings to review and make necessary modifications to its water quality standards consisting of designated uses of the water. EPA is to review new or revised standards. EPA may approve them as submitted, or require the state to make the changes necessary to comply with the FWPCA. Should the state fail to make the necessary changes, EPA may do so for the state, following notice and a hearing.

State Standards More Stringent Than Federal Standards

The FWPCA preserves the right of states and their political jurisdictions to impose more stringent water quality requirements than those issued by EPA, but they may not be less stringent.

State Toxic Load Reduction Programs—Individual Control Strategies and Effluent Limitations for Toxic Hot Spots

The FWPCA requires states to develop individual control strategies for toxic hot spots in waterways expected to remain polluted with toxic materials even after the strictest treatment requirements have been met. Every state is required to undertake a progressive program of reducing toxic pollution loads or concentrations in their waters where BAT effluent limitations are not sufficient to meet state water quality standards or water quality objectives of the act for protecting public health, public water supplies, aquatic life, and recreational values. By February 4, 1989, the states must submit to

EPA a list of their water bodies that do not meet state water quality standards because of toxic pollutants, despite the implementation of the BAT effluent limitations, new source performance standards, and pretreatment standards. These segments of water listed by the state might be termed "toxic hot spots." For each segment of waters on this list, the state must determine the specific point sources discharging toxic pollutants that are believed to be preventing or impairing the water quality and the amount of each toxic pollutant discharged by each source.

The state submission to EPA of toxic hot spots should include an individual control strategy for each which it determines will produce a reduction in the discharge of toxic pollutants from point sources. The control strategy submitted to EPA must include effluent limitations and receiving water quality standards for toxic pollutants that are sufficient, along with existing controls, to achieve the applicable water quality standard as soon as possible, but no later than three years after the date of the establishment of the strategy. The individual control strategies for toxic hot spots are implemented through the terms and conditions imposed by a state in NPDES permits.

Not later than 120 days after the submittal is due, EPA must approve or disapprove the control strategies submitted by a state. If a state fails to submit control strategies or EPA does not approve the control strategies submitted by a state, then not later than one year after the submittal is due, EPA, in cooperation with the state, must develop an appropriate control strategy. Persons may petition EPA to consider a navigable water for listing as a toxic hot spot which would make it subject to an individual control strategy for toxic pollutants.

State Water Quality Planning and Inventories

States are required to engage in water pollution control planning. Each state must submit for review to EPA a proposed continuing planning process for pollution control. EPA cannot approve a state taking over responsibility for administration of the NPDES permit program unless the state has an approved continuing planning process. To be approved by EPA, the state's continuing planning process must include the following eight elements: (1) effluent limitations and compliance schedules at least as stringent as federal law; (2) all the elements of any applicable areawide management plan and basin plan; (3) total maximum daily load or concentration for pollutants in receiving waters; (4) procedures for revision; (5) adequate authority for intergovernmental cooperation; (6) adequate provisions for implementation; (7) control of the disposal of residual wastes from wastewater treatment plants; and (8) an inventory and priority ranking for the construction of wastewater treatment works to meet federal effluent limitations.

States are required to prepare and submit at least every two years to EPA a water quality inventory, and EPA is required to transmit these state water quality inventories, together with an analysis, to Congress. Each state is also required to prepare and submit to EPA for approval an identification and classification of all publicly owned fresh water lakes in the state.

MANAGEMENT OF NONPOINT SOURCES OF POLLUTION

The Water Quality Act of 1987 amended the Clean Water Act to add new provisions establishing a national policy whereby the states would develop and implement programs for the control of nonpoint sources of water pollution. This legislation authorized $400 million in federal grants over four years to the states and combinations of adjacent states to implement nonpoint source pollution management programs.

Each state must submit to EPA a report that identifies state waters which, without additional action to control nonpoint sources of pollution, cannot reasonably be expected to attain or maintain water quality standards or the goals and requirements of the act. The state report must also set out the categories, subcategories, or, where appropriate, particular nonpoint sources that add significant pollution to the identified waters. The report should include the management practices used for the nonpoint sources which are determined to add the significant pollution causing the waters not to comply with water quality standards.

The states or combination of states must also prepare and submit to EPA management programs for implementation. These programs are to identify the best management practices (BMP) and measures which the state will undertake to control the nonpoint source pollution that can or does cause waters not to meet water quality standards. When identifying BMP for various nonpoint source categories and subcategories to reduce nonpoint source pollution, the state can focus on specific categories or subcategories or watersheds where nonpoint pollution is a significant problem and can set priorities for control efforts among them. To achieve implementation of BMP, the state management program can utilize, among other measures, nonregulatory or regulatory programs for enforcement, technical assistance, financial assistance, education, training, technology transfer, and demonstration projects. The state management program is to include a schedule containing annual implementation milestones and providing for use of BMP at the earliest possible date. The state management programs should be developed and implemented, to the maximum extent practicable, with the involvement of local and other entities with expertise and experience in control of nonpoint sources of pollution. To the maximum extent practicable, the states must develop and implement management programs on a watershed-by-watershed basis.

The states must submit their nonpoint pollution source reports and management programs to EPA by August 4, 1988. EPA has six months to approve or disapprove the submissions, or they are deemed approved. EPA may disapprove a program or a portion of it upon determination, among other considerations, that it is not likely to satisfy the goals and requirements of the act, or that the practices and measures of the proposed program are not adequate to reduce nonpoint source pollution and to improve water quality. The state has three months to revise a disapproved program, and EPA has three months to approve or disapprove the revised program. If a state fails to submit a program, or if it is not approved, a local public agency or organization with expertise in and adequate authority to control nonpoint sources may, with approval of the state, develop and implement a program for its area.

In cases where waters in a state with an approved program are not meeting applicable water quality standards or the goals and requirements of the act because of upstream pollution from another state, the state may petition EPA to convene and EPA must convene, or EPA may initiate without a state petition, an interstate management conference to develop an agreement on control measures for the upstream pollution. The interstate management agreement cannot supersede or abrogate water rights established by interstate water compacts, Supreme Court decrees, or state water laws. The agreements also cannot apply to any pollution subject to the Colorado River Basin Salinity Control Act. Citizen suits cannot be used to compel an interstate management agreement.

Federal grants to implement a state nonpoint source management program cannot exceed 60 percent of the implementation costs. No grant can be made unless EPA determines that the state has made satisfactory progress in the preceding year in meeting its implementation schedule.

PERMITS

Introduction

The FWPCA has established two permit systems to control discharges into bodies of water. One is a permit system known as the National Pollutant Discharge Elimination System (NPDES). The FWPCA prohibits discharges by municipal and industrial dischargers into navigable waters unless authorized by an NPDES permit. The second permit system is for the discharge of dredged and fill materials into navigable waters. The NPDES permits are sometimes referred to as 402 permits and the dredge and fill permits as 404 permits, after the sections of the FWPCA containing the provisions governing these permits.

EPA administers the NPDES permit program, and the Corps of Engineers administers the dredge and fill permit program. Both the NPDES and dredge and fill permit programs may be delegated to states that apply for the responsibility and must demonstrate they have adequate programs to carry out the respective permit programs.

The FWPCA also requires EPA or states to certify compliance with the act and state water pollution control laws for facilities that require any other type of federal permit or license.

National Pollutant Discharge Elimination System (NPDES) Permit

Generally

No discharge of effluents is permitted except as authorized by an NPDES permit. The permit system is the basic mechanism for enforcing federal and state effluent limitations, water quality standards, and other requirements governing pollutant discharges. Virtually all point sources, including POTWs, are required to obtain a permit.

Compliance with an NPDES permit is deemed compliance with the FWPCA effluent limitations and water quality standards because these limitations and standards are the conditions on which the permit is based. Compliance with an NPDES permit is not necessarily regarded as compliance with toxic substance standards, and the discharger must meet newly established toxic substance standards before a permit has been revised to include them. EPA is required to prescribe permit conditions that insure compliance with the FWPCA, including conditions on data and information gathering, reporting, and other requirements it deems appropriate.

All permits are to be issued for fixed terms, but not to exceed five years. A copy of each permit application and each permit issued is to be made available to the public for inspection and copying. An NPDES permit may be revoked or modified for cause, including, but not limited to, the following reasons: (1) violation of any permit condition; (2) obtaining of a permit by misrepresentation or failure to disclose all relevant facts, and (3) change in any condition that requires either a temporary or permanent reduction or elimination of a permitted discharge.

Permits issued for the discharge of pollutants from vessels are subject to Coast Guard regulations for the transportation, handling, and storage of pollutants. Dischargers of sewage from vessels are exempt from the NPDES permit requirement. Permits are required for the disposal of sewage sludge resulting from the operation of POTWs. EPA is authorized to issue regulations governing the disposal of sewage sludge. NPDES permits cannot be required for agricultural irrigation return flows or for stormwater runoff from oil, gas, and mining operations.

States can acquire EPA approval to take on the responsibility of administering the NPDES permit program, in place of EPA, for all or part of the program.

In cases where a POTW is unable to meet the requirements of its NPDES permit because of operational or design failure, neither EPA nor a state-approved program can impose a permit requirement that indirect dischargers of conventional pollutants pretreat them to allow the POTW to comply with the permit. This restriction does not affect federal authority to implement pretreatment requirements or take enforcement action, state and local authority to conduct pretreatment programs, state authority to establish effluent limitations, nor does it relieve the POTW from meeting the requirements of the FWPCA. Finally, the restriction against conventional pollutant pretreatment in the cause of POTW failure does not preclude the POTW from pursuing other feasible options available to meet its responsibility to comply with the NPDES permit.

State Permit Programs

States can acquire EPA approval to grant NPDES permits in lieu of EPA. The FWPCA directs EPA to promulgate guidelines establishing the minimum procedural and other elements for an approvable state permit program.

In general, a state seeking EPA approval to run the NPDES program totally in place of EPA must meet EPA's minimum guidelines for an adequate program for the program elements of monitoring, reporting, enforcement, funding, and personnel. The FWPCA provides detailed requirements for the delegation of the NPDES permit program in which the state must show that, among other things, it has the authority: (1) to issue permits which (a) comply with the FWPCA effluent limitations, water quality-related effluent limitations, new source performance standards, toxic effluent limitations and pretreatment standards, and ocean discharge criteria, (b) are for fixed terms no more than five years, (c) terminate or modify existing permits for cause, including violations of any permit condition, for misrepresentation or failure to make full disclosure of facts in the permit application, or for any change in any condition that requires either a temporary or permanent reduction or elimination of the permitted discharge, and (d) control the disposal of pollutants into wells; (2) to issue permits that enforce the inspection, monitoring, entry, and recordkeeping requirements of the FWPCA and engage in these activities to the same extent allowed the federal government; (3) to insure that the public, and other states affected, receive notice of permit applications and provide a public hearing before issuing permits; (4) to insure that EPA receives notice of permit applications; (5) to insure that other states affected by the issuance of a permit may submit written recommendations to the permitting state, and EPA, and that the affected state be informed of the recommendations that are not accepted and the reasons for not accepting them; (6) to insure that no permit be issued if the Corps of Engineers determines that operations in navigable waters would be substantially impaired; (7) to abate violations of a permit or the permit program, and employ civil and criminal penalties and other methods of enforcement; (8) to require that the permitting state receive (a) notice of the introduction to any POTW of toxic pollutants, pollutants from new sources, and other discharges that would be otherwise subject to effluent limitations if they had been discharged directly into the water—for the purpose of insuring that any permit for a POTW includes the condition requiring the identification of pollutants from significant sources which are subject to pretreatment standards, (b) notice of any substantial change in the volume or character of pollutants introduced into the treatment works by sources using them at the time of the permit issuance, and (c) notice of information of the quality and quantity of effluents introduced to each POTW and their anticipated impact on the quality and quantity of POTW discharges; (9) to ensure that individual users of the POTW comply with the payment of charges according to the proportionate payment system, toxic and pretreatment effluent standards, and the inspection and recordkeeping requirements of the FWPCA. Furthermore, EPA cannot approve of the delegation of a state permit program if the state does not have an approved continuous planning process.

EPA has ninety days to determine whether to approve a total state program submitted to it. If EPA approves the state program, it may no longer issue NPDES permits in the state. EPA is to disapprove the total state program if it determines that the program does not meet the minimum statutory requirements and guidelines for the program elements. If the EPA finds that the state program does not comply with the FWPCA, it must notify the state of necessary modifications and revisions necessary to meet statutory requirements and EPA approval.

EPA may withdraw its approval of a state NPDES program after notice and hearing, and after a state's failure to take corrective action.

The act allows partial EPA delegation of the NPDES permit program to a state. The partial program is only temporary, for it is meant to give the state time to phase in a fully delegated program. At a minimum, partial delegation would allow a state either to administer permits for a major category(ies) of discharges into the state's waters or to assume responsibility for a major component of the permit program. With respect to a partial permit program covering administration over a major category of discharges, EPA may confer approval if it finds that the state program covers in a complete fashion all the discharges under the jurisdiction of a state agency or that the partial program represents a significant and identifiable part of the state's NPDES program. Under the partial assumption option, EPA may approve a partial or phased program, but can do so only if the partial program represents a significant and identifiable part of the state's NPDES program, such as all major industrial dischargers or all major POTWs. To obtain approval under this option, the state must also submit a plan approved by EPA to assume administration by phases of the remainder of the state's NPDES permit program.

A state may return or EPA may withdraw approval for a partially delegated

NPDES permit program, but the authority for state return and EPA withdrawal is subject to conditions. In the case of an approved partial permit program covering administration of a major category of a state's point source discharges, the entire permit program related to the category and being administered by one of the state's agencies must be returned or be withdrawn. In the case of an approved partial and phased program covering administration of a major component of the NPDES program, return or withdrawal can be approved only if the entire phased component is returned or withdrawn. The capacity to return or withdraw a partial NPDES program does not authorize a state to return parts of a program approved prior to February 4, 1987.

Measures provided by the FWPCA enable EPA to control state NPDES permit programs. A state with a permit program must transmit a copy of each permit application to EPA and give notice to EPA of every action related to the permit application.

A state NPDES permit may not be issued if EPA objects in writing within ninety days of receiving notice because issuance of the permit may affect water quality in another state or the proposed permit violates the guidelines and requirements of the act. EPA's written objection is to contain a statement of the reasons for the objection and the effluent limitations and any conditions that the permit would include if it had been issued by EPA originally. If EPA objects to the issuance of a permit, the state may request a public hearing on EPA's objection, and if the state does not resubmit the permit that has been corrected to meet the objection within thirty days after the completion of the hearing, or, if no hearing is requested within ninety days after the date of the objection, EPA itself may determine whether to issue the permit.

EPA may waive its right to object to individual permit applications. At the time EPA approves delegation of a state NPDES permit program, it may waive the right to review permit applications to the state for any category of point sources within the state. EPA may also promulgate regulations establishing categories of point sources that are exempt from its review in any state with an approved permit program.

Anti-Backsliding and NPDES Permits

The term *backsliding* has come to refer to the practice whereby effluent limitations or other treatment and control restrictions imposed in an NPDES permit are relaxed when the permit is renewed, reissued, or modified by EPA or a state regulatory authority. As has been explained previously, the NPDES permit is the chief instrument used by regulatory agencies to implement the water pollution control measures adopted pursuant to or required by the FWPCA.

The FWPCA generally prohibits backsliding, except in certain narrowly defined circumstances. Despite the exceptions to backsliding described below for BPJ ("best professional judgment") and water quality-based permits, in no event may either kind of permit be renewed, reissued, or modified to contain a less stringent effluent limitation than is required by existing effluent guidelines, and in no event may a water quality-based permit be changed to contain a less stringent effluent limitation if the relaxed standard would result in a violation of an applicable state water quality standard. Whatever backsliding that is allowed is restricted to BPJ and water quality-based permits. To the extent that permits do not relate to BPJ or water quality-based standards, they cannot be revised under the exceptions to the backsliding prohibition when the permit is renewed, reissued, or modified.

Before explaining the exceptions to the backsliding prohibition, the concept of "best professional judgment" (BPJ) should be explained since a major exception is allowed for BPJ permits. BPJ usually refers to EPA's or a state's best engineering judgment in determining the appropriate effluent limitations for an NPDES permit in certain instances. One of the most common situations concerns issuing a permit before effluent limitations are promulgated for a particular industrial category being permitted. Thus the regulator has the flexibility and duty to exercise its best professional judgment in determining appropriate effluent limitations during this interim which will achieve water quality standards. Exercise of this best professional judgment by permit writers may also be required after effluent limitations are issued, or when a facility requests a variance of the discharge limitations, or when more stringent discharge limitations are being considered than the technology-based ones.

The FWPCA generally prohibits backsliding for BPJ permits. However, the prohibition against backsliding for BPJ permits is subject to the following exceptions: (1) there have been material and substantial alterations or additions to the permitted facility which justify the less stringent effluent limitation in the BPJ permit; (2) information is available which was unavailable at the time the BPJ permit was issued and which would have justified less stringent effluent limitations at the time; (3) EPA determines that technical mistakes or mistaken interpretations of law were made in issuing the BPJ permit; (4) a less stringent effluent limitation is necessary because of events over which the BPJ permit holder has no control and for which there is no reasonably available remedy; (5) the BPJ permit holder has received an effluent limitation variance; or (6) the BPJ permit holder has installed the treatment facilities required to meet the effluent limitations of the previous permit and has properly operated and maintained the facilities but nevertheless has been unable to achieve the previous effluent limitations.

Backsliding is also generally prohibited for water quality-based NPDES permits, subject to the same exceptions previously mentioned as allowed for a BPJ permit but the one of technical mistakes or mistaken interpretations of law.

A limitation is imposed on the exception that allows a BPJ or water quality-based permit to be relaxed because the permit holder has installed and operated required treatment facilities but nevertheless has not been able to achieve the effluent limitations required in its permit. The limitation requires that in no event can the exception be used to adjust a BPJ or water quality-based permit to a level less stringent than the level of pollution control actually being achieved. The level can never be less stringent than required by effluent guidelines in effect at the time of permit renewal, reissuance, or modification.

Neither the new information exception (in the case of BPJ and water quality-based permits), nor the mistake of fact or law exception (in the case of BPJ permits) allows a permit to be adjusted to require less stringent effluent limitations for any revised waste load allocation in a body of water or any alternative grounds for translating water quality standards into an effluent limitation, except in one narrow situation. This situation is one in which the cumulative effect of a revised waste load allocation results in a decrease in the amount of pollutant discharges into waters covered by the allocation; the revised allocations are not the result of a discharger eliminating or greatly reducing its discharges due to complying with the requirements of the act; or for reasons unrelated to water quality. Where an applicable water quality standard has not been attained, the total maximum daily load of pollutants or other waste load allocation may be revised in the NPDES permit only under two circumstances. First, the cumulative effect of the revised effluent limitations based on the total maximum daily loads or waste load allocation must assure attainment of water quality standards. Second, the daily maximum load of pollutants or the waste load allocation may be revised only if the designated use of the receiving waters which is not being attained is changed in accordance with regulations concerned with establishing water quality standards.

Where water quality in the receiving waters exceeds or equals that required by applicable water quality standards or the levels needed to protect the actual or designated uses of the receiving waters, backsliding from water quality-based effluent limitations is prohibited except to the extent that EPA or an approved NPDES state agency acts in accordance with the procedures and the decision standards of the anti-degradation policy governing state-established water quality standards.

NPDES Permits for Stormwater Discharges

As a general rule, prior to October 1, 1992, neither EPA nor a state with an NPDES permit program can require an NPDES permit for discharges composed entirely of stormwater. There are four exceptions to this general prohibition, and they apply to: (1) discharges for which an NPDES permit was issued prior to February 4, 1987; (2) discharges from an industrial activity; (3) municipal separate stormwater discharges in communities over 100,000 persons; and (4) discharges which EPA or a state determines violate a water quality standard or is a significant contributor of water pollutants. The relief from the NPDES permit requirement prior to October 1, 1992, is given only to discharges composed entirely of stormwater. Storm sewers that discharge pollutants introduced by other means, in addition to stormwater, are required to have a permit.

The relief from the NPDES permit requirement for municipal separate storm sewers is temporary, ending on October 1, 1992. After this date, all municipal separate storm sewers are subject to effluent limitations and NPDES permits. The FWPCA establishes a schedule for the development of regulations, issuance of permits, and compliance by point sources concerning industrial and municipal separate sewer system discharges of stormwater. A deadline of February 4, 1989, has been set for EPA to establish regulations governing permits for industrial stormwater discharges and for communities over 250,000 persons with municipal separate storm sewers. These activities must file for a permit by February 4, 1990, and EPA must make an issuance decision for them by February 4, 1991. Industrial stormwater dischargers and municipal separate stormwater systems in communities with over 250,000 people must comply with permits after they are issued as expeditiously as practicable, but in no event later than three years after being issued. A different schedule for developing regulations, issuing permits, and compliance is applied to municipal separate stormwater systems in communities with 100,000 to 250,000 people. EPA regulations must be promulgated by February 4, 1991, permit applications must be filed by February 4, 1992, and EPA must make its permitting decisions by February 4, 1993. The municipal separate stormwater system in these medium-sized communities must comply as expeditiously as possible with their permits, but in no case later than three years after issuance.

NPDES Permits and Ocean Discharges

EPA is required to prepare environmentally protective guidelines governing NPDES permits for ocean discharges. The ocean discharge guidelines are for determining the degradation caused to the ocean and are to be based on seven statutory criteria: (1) the effect of the pollutant's disposal on human health or welfare, including but not limited to aquatic life, wildlife, shorelines, and beaches; (2) (a) the effect of pollutant disposal on marine life, including the transfer, concentration, and dispersal of pollutants through biological, physical, and chemical processes, (b) changes in marine ecosystem diversity, productivity, and stability, and (c) species and community population changes; (3) the effect of pollutant disposal on aesthetic, recreation, and economic values; (4) the persistence and permanence of the pollutants; (5) the effect of disposal at varying rates, particular volumes, and concen-

trations of pollutants; (6) possible locations and methods of disposal or recycling of pollutants, including land-based alternatives; and (7) the effect on
alternative uses of the oceans, such as mineral exploitation and scientific
study.

An NPDES permit cannot be issued if there is insufficient information on
any proposed ocean discharge for EPA to make a reasonable judgment on
any of the guidelines for ocean discharges.

Sewage Sludge and NPDES Permits

An NPDES permit is required for the disposal of sewage sludge into
navigable waters. EPA has the responsibility to issue, and revise from time
to time, guidelines for the disposal and use of sewage sludge. After December
31, 1981, EPA is prohibited from issuing any permit, including any NPDES
permit, for the disposal of sewage sludge into the ocean.

Aquaculture and NPDES Permits

EPA is authorized to permit the discharge of a specific pollutant or pollutants under controlled conditions from aquaculture projects that are approved and supervised under EPA or state NPDES permit programs. EPA
is to issue regulations that establish the procedures and guidelines to carry
out these aquaculture projects.

Dredge and Fill Permits

The FWPCA establishes a permit system for the discharge of dredged
and fill materials. Permits are issued by the Corps of Engineers.

The Corps chooses the sites where dredged and fill materials may be
disposed. EPA and the Corps jointly establish the guidelines that govern
the designation of disposal sites. The guidelines might prohibit a site for
disposal, but the Corps may choose it anyway by taking into account the
beneficial economic impact of the site on navigation and anchorage. EPA
still has ultimate authority to restrict or prohibit disposal at any site if it
finds unacceptably adverse environmental impacts.

General permits are authorized for statewide, regional, and national application for any category of activities which the Corps determines may be
alike and will, individually or cumulatively, have minimal adverse effects on
the environment.

States may be delegated responsibility to administer the Corps' dredge
and fill permit program. The authority of any state to control the discharge
of dredged and fill materials into its waters is not limited or precluded by
the FWPCA. A state thus may impose more stringent dredge and fill re-

quirements than required in a federal permit. The states are authorized to require federal facilities to obtain dredge and fill permits.

A violation of any condition or limitation of a permit from the Corps of Engineers is subject to a judicial civil monetary penalty of up to $25,000 per day.

State or EPA Certification for Federal Permits or Licenses

An applicant for any one of the many federally issued permits or licenses is required to obtain certification that discharges to the water will comply with the FWPCA requirements from the state in which the discharge occurs as a condition for obtaining the federal permit or license. EPA gives the certification where the state does not have authority. State or EPA certification must include any effluent limitations or other limitations and monitoring requirements necessary to assure that the applicant for federal license or permit will comply with the FWPCA and state law. The state certification requirement applies to all federal permits, and not just to EPA-issued NPDES permits. The certification provision gives the state veto power over the EPA discharge permit. A state wishing to impose more stringent requirements than EPA may do so either by denying certification or by causing the NPDES permit not to be issued or by attaching tougher standards as conditions to be included in the federal permit. Failure or refusal by the state or EPA to act on certification within a reasonable time, not to exceed one year, waives the certification requirement. When granted, the certification becomes a condition attached to the federal license or permit.

The state or interstate agency must provide public notice and a hearing before granting certification. EPA must be notified when a federal agency receives a permit application and the required state certification. If EPA determines that the water quality of another state may be affected in other than the state where the discharge originates, EPA is to notify the state affected within 30 days after it received notice of the federal permit or license application. If the other state finds that the discharge will violate its water quality requirements, it may notify EPA and the licensing or permitting agency and object to the issuance of the permit. Based on the recommendation and other evidence, the federal license or permitting agency may deny the permit or license or impose conditions to insure compliance with the affected state's water quality requirements.

Certification continues in effect after being issued, unless the state certifying agency notifies EPA of a change in circumstances that removes the reasonable assurance that there is compliance with effluent limitations and water quality standards. Such changes of circumstances include changes occurring since certification in the construction or operation of the facility, changes in the characteristics of the water into which the discharge is made, changes in the water quality criteria, effluent limitations, or other requirements.

After construction of a federally licensed or permitted facility has been approved, EPA or the state pollution control agency may supervise the operation of the facility to assure that it will not violate effluent standards. After notification of noncompliance by the state, or EPA, the federal licensing agency may, following a public hearing, suspend or revoke the license or permit. A federal permit or license of a facility may be suspended or revoked by the federal agency that issued the permit or license whenever a judicial judgment has been rendered under the FWPCA that the facility violates effluent requirements.

INSPECTIONS, RECORDKEEPING, REPORTS, AND ACCESS TO INFORMATION

The FWPCA authorizes EPA to require each point source to install, use, and maintain monitoring equipment, to sample effluents, to establish and maintain records, and to provide such other information as EPA may require.

EPA may enter any premises where effluent source records are located, in order to copy records, inspect monitoring equipment, and sample any effluents which the owner or operator is required to sample. A state administering the NPDES permit program is allowed to utilize its procedures for inspection, monitoring, and entry if EPA determines they are equivalent to federal authority and requirements.

Any information, records, or reports obtained by regulatory authorities must be available to the public, unless entitled to protection as a trade secret. However, the trade secret information kept from the public may be disclosed to federal government officials administering and enforcing the law. A criminal penalty of a maximum fine of $1,000 or imprisonment of up to one year, or both, can be imposed on any EPA official convicted of knowingly or willfully disclosing confidential information obtained during the inspection and monitoring of a discharger.

EPA SUBPOENA POWER

EPA has the power to issue subpoenas for the attendance and testimony of witnesses and for the production of papers, books, and records, and EPA may administer oaths. Except for effluent data, EPA will protect this information as confidential if it is shown to EPA that making such information public would divulge trade secrets or processes. However, this information can be divulged to federal officials to carry out the purpose of the act. EPA may institute suit in federal district court to subpoena the appearance of witnesses and the production of information in connection with establishing effluent limitations and administering the NPDES permit program. EPA has the power to audit the records of any recipient of financial assistance under the FWPCA. For purposes of the audit, EPA and the U.S. comptroller general may have access to any books, documents, or papers of any grant recipients.

FEDERAL ENFORCEMENT AND CIVIL SUITS

Civil and Administrative Enforcement

When faced with a violation of the FWPCA, EPA has the option of issuing an administrative order requiring compliance, instituting a Class I or Class II administrative proceeding against the violator, or bringing a civil action in federal district court for penalties and injunctive relief. The federal government may also prosecute criminal suits for violations of the act. The violations for which EPA may issue administrative compliance orders, institute Class I and Class II administrative proceedings, or bring a civil suit in federal court include those pertaining to the following: NPDES and dredge and fill permits; federal technology-based effluent limitations; federal water quality-related effluent limitations; federal new source performance standards; federal pretreatment standards; federal regulations relating to inspection, monitoring, and recordkeeping by point sources; federal aquaculture permit requirements; federal sewage sludge requirements; or any condition or limitation implementing an NPDES permit or a dredge and fill permit.

In states with approved NPDES or dredge and fill permit programs, EPA either can institute an enforcement action itself or EPA may proceed to notify the person of the alleged violation and the state of its finding. If the state does not undertake appropriate enforcement action within 30 days of EPA's notification to it, then EPA must issue an administrative order to the accused violator requiring compliance or may bring a civil action in federal district court.

When EPA determines that violations of NPDES permit conditions or limitations by a person are so widespread as to appear to result from the state's failure to enforce the permit conditions or limitations effectively, it must notify the state of this finding. EPA must give public notice of the state's widespread lack of enforcement of permits if it continues more than 30 days after the initial notice to the state. Thereafter, during what is commonly called a period of federally assumed enforcement, EPA may itself enforce permit conditions or limitations through compliance orders or civil suits until EPA has been satisfied that the state will properly undertake enforcement action.

EPA is authorized to bring enforcement actions without first depending on and proceeding through the state. EPA is to issue a compliance order or bring a civil action for a violation of a discharge limitation or of a state or federally issued NPDES or dredge and fill permit.

A compliance order issued by EPA must specify the nature of the violation and the time for compliance. EPA is to take into account the seriousness of the violation and any good faith efforts to comply with the law in establishing the time for compliance. EPA must forward a copy of any compliance order issued to the state agency of the state in which the violation occurred and to other affected states. Service of a compliance order to a corporation must include a copy of the order to an appropriate corporate officer. An order relating to violations of the recordkeeping, monitoring, and sampling requirements of the FWPCA is not to take effect until the person to whom it is issued has an opportunity to confer with EPA.

EPA may institute an action in federal district court for civil penalties against a party who has violated the FWPCA or an EPA compliance order. The federal court can impose a civil penalty of up to $25,000 per day for each violation which EPA proves in a civil action brought by it.

The FWPCA also authorizes EPA civil actions brought in federal district court for a violation of pretreatment requirements. When EPA finds that a source is introducing pollutants to a POTW in violation of the act, it may notify the POTW and the state of the violation, and if the POTW does not institute a civil suit in 30 days, EPA may seek injunctive relief to require the POTW and the source to take necessary action for compliance.

EPA may utilize two kinds of administrative actions and penalties—Class I and Class II—against accused violators of the FWPCA. EPA may choose one or the other, but not both, against a violator. The difference between the two penalties is that the Class I version uses an informal administrative proceeding and a single monetary penalty imposed on a per violation basis only, whereas the Class II version employs a formal administrative process and monetary penalties that are assessed on a per violation per day basis. The Corps of Engineers is given similar authority to assess Class I and Class II administrative penalties for violations of dredge and fill permits.

In the case of a Class I administrative action, EPA may assess a monetary penalty of up to $10,000 for each violation, except that Class I penalties against a violator cannot exceed $25,000 in any one enforcement action conducted by EPA, regardless of the number of violations or number of days of violations. Before issuing an order assessing a Class I penalty, EPA must give notice of the proposed penalty to the alleged violator and give 30 days for that person to request what is an informal hearing. The hearing is not bound by the requirements and conditions of the Federal Administrative Procedures Act.

If EPA uses the Class II penalty, it can impose a monetary penalty of up to $10,000 per day for each violation. The Class II penalty cannot exceed $125,000 for the violations in a single EPA administrative enforcement action of this type. The Class II penalty is governed by the formal hearing and other rigorous procedural demands imposed by the Federal Administrative Procedures Act.

EPA can commence proceedings in federal district court for permanent or temporary injunctions to restrain any violation for which it is authorized to issue a compliance order. Notice of commencement of an EPA suit must be given to the appropriate state.

A state may be joined as a party whenever the federal government brings a judicial action against one of its cities. A state becomes monetarily liable for judgments and expenses of litigation incurred against a city when state law precludes its cities from raising revenues to pay judgments.

EPA may ask the Justice Department to represent the federal government in any civil or criminal action. If the Justice Department does not notify EPA within a reasonable time that it will appear in a civil action on EPA's behalf, then EPA attorneys are authorized to represent the federal government in civil enforcement actions.

Criminal Actions

The FWPCA allows the federal government to proceed criminally against violators of the FWPCA and authorizes criminal penalties for persons convicted of these violations. The criminal penalties apply to dischargers or individuals who knowingly or negligently violate or cause the violation of major provisions of the act.

Punishment by a fine of between $2,500 and $25,000 per day, or imprisonment for up to a year, or both is available against any person convicted of negligently violating the following kinds of provisions of the FWPCA: federal technology-based effluent limitations; federal water quality-related effluent limitations; federal new source performance standards; federal pretreatment standards; federal inspection, monitoring, or recordkeeping requirements; federal aquaculture permit requirements; federal sewage sludge requirements; conditions or limitations implementing the foregoing standards and requirements in an NPDES permit; requirements imposed by an approved state pretreatment program; or any requirement of a dredge and fill permit. The same kind of criminal penalty can be imposed on a convicted violator who negligently introduces into a sewer system or POTW a pollutant or hazardous substance that causes or may reasonably be anticipated to cause personal injury or property damage or that causes the POTW to be in violation of its NPDES permit. Second and subsequent convictions for negligent violations are punishable by a fine of up to $50,000 per day for each violation, or by imprisonment of up to two years, or both.

Negligent violations of the FWPCA are subject to stiffer criminal penalties than knowing violations. The criminal penalty for a person convicted of knowing violations is a fine of $5,000 to $50,000 per day, or imprisonment for up to two years, or both. For subsequent convictions for knowing violations, the maximum monetary and prison penalties are doubled.

An enhanced felony penalty is provided for conviction of a knowing violation of the FWPCA which involves, in addition, knowingly placing another person as a result of the violation in imminent danger of death or serious bodily injury. This enhanced knowing endangerment penalty applies to all the violations mentioned above for knowing and negligent criminal acts, except for violations of state-approved pretreatment program requirements or the introduction of pollutants into a sewer system which causes personal injury, property damage, or POTW noncompliance with its NPDES permit. The criminal penalty for conviction for knowing endangerment is a fine of up to $250,000 for individuals, up to $1 million for organizations, or imprisonment of up to 15 years, or both a fine and a prison term. Furthermore, if a conviction of a person for knowing endangerment is committed after a first conviction, the maximum fine and prison term are doubled.

Any person who knowingly makes any false material statement, representation, or certification in any application, record, report, plan, or other document filed or required to be maintained under the FWPCA, or who knowingly falsifies, tampers with, or renders inaccurate any monitoring device or method required to be maintained under the act is subject upon conviction to criminal penalties that include a fine of up to $10,000 or imprisonment for up to two years, or both. Second and subsequent convictions double the maximum fine and prison term that can be imposed.

Imminent Hazard Enforcement

EPA is authorized to initiate a federal district court action to immediately restrain a pollution source presenting an imminent and substantial hazard to human health or welfare.

CITIZEN SUITS

A citizen may bring a civil suit in federal district court against any person, including the United States or any other government agency, alleged to be in violation of any effluent limitation, new source performance standard, toxic pollutant standard, pretreatment standard, state certification of a federal license or permit, an NPDES permit, or an EPA compliance order. A citizen may also bring a civil suit against EPA for failure to perform any nondiscretionary duty under the FWPCA.

Before a citizen suit may be brought, a 60-day notice must be given to EPA and the state in which the violation occurred. As long as EPA or the state is undertaking appropriate criminal or civil action against the violator, a citizen suit is precluded. When such an EPA or state enforcement action is pending in federal or state court, a citizen may intervene as a matter of right. The 60-day notice requirement for citizen suits does not apply in cases involving violations of new source performance standards and toxic effluent standards. In these instances, notice is to be given to EPA as the agency prescribes in its regulations. EPA and the Justice Department must be notified when a citizen suit is initiated. No consent judgement can be entered in a citizen suit in which the United States is not one of the parties before a 45-day period following the receipt of a copy of the proposed judgment by EPA and the Justice Department.

Litigation costs may be awarded in citizen suits, but only to the prevailing or substantially prevailing party. In actions for a temporary restraining order or temporary injunction, the court may require the filing of a bond or equivalent security.

JUDICIAL REVIEW OF EPA ACTIONS

Judicial review is restricted to federal courts of appeal for suits seeking review of EPA promulgation of new source performance standards, EPA approval of state new source standards, EPA promulgation of toxic pollutant standards, EPA promulgation of pretreatment standards, EPA approval of state NPDES programs, EPA approval or promulgation of effluent limitations, issuance or denial of NPDES permits, and EPA's promulgation of any individual control strategy for a toxic pollutant. The aforementioned EPA actions are not subject to review in any criminal or civil enforcement proceeding. Review of EPA actions can be instituted by any interested person in the federal circuit court encompassing the federal judicial district in which the person resides or transacts business. The suit must be brought within 120 days of the issuance of the applicable standard or decision or it is barred. Litigation costs may be awarded in judicial review suits, but only to the prevailing or substantially prevailing party.

EMPLOYEE SAFEGUARDS

Employees who assist in carrying out the provisions of the act are protected. Employers are prohibited from discharging or discriminating against any employee who institutes or causes to be instituted or testifies or is about to testify in proceedings in connection with the administration or enforcement of the FWPCA.

Employees who are fired or discriminated against for instituting or testifying in proceedings may, within 30 days after the firing or discrimination has occurred, file a complaint with the Department of Labor. The Department of Labor can order rehiring or compensation of such employees.

Any employee who is discharged or laid off, threatened with the same, or otherwise discriminated against because of any effluent limitations or order issued under the act, may ask EPA to conduct a full investigation. EPA must investigate after receiving such a complaint, and at the written request of any party, it must hold public hearings on not less than a five-day notice.

FEDERAL PROCUREMENT PROHIBITION

Federal agencies are prohibited from entering into contracts for the procurement of goods and services with any person who has been convicted of any offense under the FWPCA if the contract is to be performed at the facility where the violation occurred. EPA is to establish a procedure to inform all federal agencies of the procurement prohibition against the convicted party. The president may exempt any contract, loan, or grant from the prohibition if it is determined that it is in the paramount interest of the United States.

MARINE SANITATION DEVICES

The FWPCA establishes regulation of marine sanitation devices. EPA, in consultation with the Department of Transportation, is required to establish standards for marine sanitation devices to prevent the discharge of untreated or inadequately treated sewage into navigable waters from vessels, except vessels not equipped with installed toilet facilities. After being issued, these federal standards preempt regulations or laws for marine sanitation devices of any state or political subdivision. However, a state may impose more stringent standards for vessels used primarily as residences. A state can enforce federal standards.

It is unlawful to make or sell any vessel not equipped with a federally certified marine sanitation device, to remove or render inoperative or modify a certified marine sanitation device, and to operate any vessel without a certified and working marine sanitation device.

Injunctive relief may be obtained in federal district court to restrain violations of the equipment requirements for marine sanitation devices. The sale of vessels without marine sanitation devices, or wrongful removal or modification of them, is subject to a civil penalty not to exceed $5,000. The operation of a vessel without a marine sanitation device or the violation of a marine sanitation device requirement is subject to a civil penalty not to exceed $2,000.

2   Clean Air Act (42 U.S.C. §§ 7401 et. seq.)

OVERVIEW
AIR QUALITY CONTROL REGIONS
AIR QUALITY CRITERIA
NATIONAL AMBIENT AIR QUALITY STANDARDS
STATE IMPLEMENTATION PLANS
   Generally
   Submission and Approval of a SIP
   Attainment Deadlines for SIP of National Ambient Air Quality Standards
   SIP Modification or Postponement
     SIP Revisions
     Primary Nonferrous Smelter Orders
     Temporary Emergency Suspension for Fuel Burning Sources

OVERVIEW

The Clean Air Act was enacted in 1970 and extended and substantially amended in 1977. The purpose of this lengthy and complex piece of legislation is "to protect and enhance the quality of the nation's air resources in order to promote the public health and welfare and the productive capacity of its population."

Two kinds of air pollution standards are provided by the Clean Air Act as its chief means of controlling air pollution. One type is national ambient air quality standards, and the other is point source emission limitations and standards. The national ambient air quality standards determine the concentrations of pollutants allowed in the surrounding air. The ambient air quality standards are implemented by limitations on emissions at the sources to insure that the prescribed concentrations in the ambient air are attained and maintained. Emission standards limit pollution emissions at the source regardless of ambient air concentrations. These source standards include those for new sources, hazardous air pollutants, motor vehicles, fuels, and aircraft.

EPA is required to publish a list of air pollutants which it determines have adverse effects on the public health and welfare. The listing sets in motion the process in which EPA establishes national ambient air quality standards. For each pollutant which EPA places on the list, a criteria document must be compiled and published. These criteria documents consist of the scientific data that have been collected on the health effects of the pollutants and methods for controlling emissions of those pollutants. In setting ambient air quality standards, EPA must rely on the criteria for pollutants which EPA had previously promulgated.

EPA can promulgate two types of national ambient air quality standards for stationary sources—primary and secondary. Primary air quality standards are for the purpose of protecting public health, and secondary standards for protecting public welfare.

EPA, with state participation, establishes air quality control regions throughout the nation, with each state representing at least one region. The national primary and secondary ambient air quality standards are to be achieved in the air quality control regions through State Implementation Plans (SIPs). The SIPs are of central importance because they provide the central regulatory framework to enforce the requirements for nonattainment areas and for preventing significant deterioration (PSD) in attainment or nondegradation areas, often also called PSD areas. Nonattainment areas are those air quality control regions that have failed to achieve the national ambient air quality standards by the deadlines prescribed in the Clean Air Act. Attainment or nondegradation areas are air quality control regions that meet or are cleaner than what is required by national ambient standards. PSD requirements established by EPA are directed at attainment or nondegradation areas and are meant to make sure that the air remains clean and conforms with the ambient air quality standards. Through the SIPS the states set emissions standards for stationary sources to achieve the national ambient air quality standards set by EPA, as well as to achieve any emission standards established by the state itself.

EPA is empowered to set two types of national emission standards for stationary sources in addition to the national ambient air quality standards it establishes. EPA is required to set performance standards for new and newly modified stationary sources. EPA can also set national emission standards for hazardous air pollutants.

The Clean Air Act provides for emissions standards and regulatory measures to control air pollution from motor vehicles and aircraft. EPA must issue regulations prescribing emission standards for new motor vehicles or engines, to regulate emissions from heavy-duty vehicles, to regulate emissions of particulate matter from all motor vehicles by using the best available technology, and to regulate carbon monoxide and hydrocarbons from light vehicles.

The act prohibits the sale or importation of motor vehicles that do not comply with standards established by EPA. EPA is authorized to establish a program for the testing and certification of motor vehicles or engines to determine compliance with emission standards established by EPA.

AIR QUALITY CONTROL REGIONS

The Clean Air Act encourages the development of air pollution control programs at the regional level. The 1970 Clean Air Act required EPA to divide the country into air quality control regions, and included the regions already established prior to the 1970 act. The 1970 act authorized EPA to designate interstate areas or major intrastate areas as air quality control regions that were necessary or appropriate for attaining or maintaining ambient air quality standards.

The Clean Air Act Amendments of 1977 required the states to submit to EPA a list of the air quality control regions that met national ambient air quality standards, those that did not, or those for which there were insufficient data to determine whether or not the national ambient air quality standards were being met. After 1977 the states were to revise the lists from time to time. These lists are used for the purpose of determining the applicability of the requirements of the act relating to preventing significant deterioration in attainment areas and relating to achieving compliance in nonattainment areas.

The governor of each state is allowed to revise the boundaries of air quality control regions for the purpose of improved air quality management, with the approval of EPA.

AIR QUALITY CRITERIA

EPA establishes air quality criteria that are to investigate and determine the effect of a pollutant on public health and welfare. Before EPA can establish national ambient air quality standards, it is required to issue, and revise from time to time, a list of air pollutants which EPA determines can or do adversely affect public health or welfare. No later than 12 months after a pollutant has been included on this list EPA is to issue air quality criteria for the pollutant. The criteria are to include information on any known or anticipated adverse effects on health or welfare.

At the same time EPA issues air pollutant criteria it is also to provide information describing methods for reducing or eliminating the pollutant emissions, along with the costs of these methods.

The 1977 amendments required EPA to prepare criteria for nitrogen oxides that cover short-term exposures. The short-term nitrogen oxide criteria were to include various carcinogenic and potentially carcinogenic derivatives of nitrogen oxides.

NATIONAL AMBIENT AIR QUALITY STANDARDS

The Clean Air Act requires EPA to establish national ambient air quality standards for each pollutant for which it has issued air quality criteria. These national ambient air quality standards are ceilings for individual pollutant concentrations in the ambient air which are not to be exceeded anywhere in the United States.

EPA can issue two kinds of ambient air quality standards—primary and secondary. Primary standards are to be set at a level of air quality required to protect public health. Secondary standards are set at a level of air quality needed to protect the public welfare. The primary air quality standards must be set at a level that allows an adequate margin of safety which is necessary to protect public health. The public welfare sought to be protected by secondary ambient air quality standards encompasses virtually all aspects of the environment and society other than human health and includes effects on soil, water, crops, vegetation, synthetic materials, animals, wildlife, weather, visibility, climate, property damage, transportation hazards, and effects on economic values and on personal comfort and well-being.

At the same time EPA issues an air quality criterion for any pollutant, it must publish proposed national and ambient air quality standards for the pollutant to the extent needed. EPA is to allow a reasonable time for public comments, but no later than 90 days after proposing an ambient air quality standard EPA must issue final ambient air quality regulations.

Primary ambient air quality standards are to be achieved as promptly as possible after being promulgated, but no later than three years after a SIP for implementing the standards has been approved by EPA. Secondary ambient air quality standards are to be attained at some reasonable time after being issued.

At the time the 1977 amendments were enacted, national ambient air quality standards were not being complied with in areas called nonattainment areas. The 1977 amendments extended the deadlines for compliance by requiring all SIPS to be reviewed, and where the standards were being violated the SIPs were to be revised and submitted for EPA approval no later than January 1, 1979. The deadlines for compliance with existing national ambient air quality standards in nonattainment areas were extended to December 31, 1982. However, this primary ambient air quality deadline could be extended to as long as December 31, 1987, for photochemical oxidants or carbon monoxide in areas experiencing severe problems in attaining these standards. In order to have the deadline extended for photochemical oxidants or carbon monoxide, the state must demonstrate that attainment is not possible by the December 31, 1982, deadline, despite the implementation of all reasonably available measures.

Air quality criteria and the ambient air quality standards on which they are based are to be reviewed by EPA at least every five years after December 31, 1980. EPA also has an independent scientific review committee which reviews air quality criteria and ambient air quality standards, with the first review to be completed by December 31, 1980 and subsequent reviews every five years.

EPA was required to establish national primary ambient air quality standards for short-term exposures for nitrogen oxides by August 31, 1978, unless EPA determined that the criteria showed no significant evidence that the standards were required to protect public health.

The 1977 amendments required that EPA determine whether certain previously unregulated pollutants should be regulated by national ambient air quality standards, by hazardous air pollutant standards, or by new source performance standards. EPA had one year after the enactment of the 1977 amendments to determine whether cadmium, arsenic, and polycyclic matter (and two years for radioactive pollutants) cause or contribute to air pollution and endanger public health. If EPA finds that any of these substances endanger human health, it must regulate the pollutant by ambient air quality standards, by hazardous air pollutant emission standards, or by new source performance standards, or some combination of actions, whatever is appropriate.

STATE IMPLEMENTATION PLANS

Generally

A major premise of the Clean Air Act is that the prevention and control of air pollution should be the primary responsibility of state and local governments.

The chief instrument for exercising state authority in carrying out the national ambient air quality standards of the Clean Air Act is through the state implementation plans (SIPs) established by the FWPCA. The major purpose of the state implementation plan is to establish the state regulatory framework and control strategy to attain or maintain the national ambient air quality standards established by EPA. Each state is to carry out its primary responsibility for assuring air quality within its borders by submitting to EPA an implementation plan specifying the manner in which national ambient air quality standards will be achieved and maintained within the state's air quality regions.

Submission and Approval of a SIP

Within nine months after the promulgation of a national ambient air quality standard, each state, after public hearings, must submit to EPA for its approval a plan for the implementation of the ambient standard in every air quality region in the state. EPA has four months to approve or disapprove a state implementation plan in whole or in part. EPA cannot extend the deadline for submission of a SIP, except in the case of a SIP for a national secondary ambient air quality standard, which EPA can postpone for up to 18 months. EPA cannot exceed the deadline for the submission of a SIP implementing a primary ambient air quality standard. A state must hold public hearings after reasonable notice before adopting an implementation plan and submitting it to EPA.

EPA has the authority to approve or disapprove state implementation plans. If a state submits a SIP which EPA finds unsatisfactory, or fails to submit one in whole or in part, EPA must promulgate a SIP for that portion of a state plan that is missing or inadequate. An EPA-approved state implementation plan has the force and effect of federal law and may be enforced by EPA in federal courts.

The Clean Air Act specifies requirements for the contents of a SIP which are the approval criteria EPA must use in determining whether a SIP is acceptable. The contents of a SIP must include, among other things: (1) attainment of the national ambient air quality standards within the time prescribed by the act; (2) emission limitations and timetables for attaining and maintaining ambient standards; (3) monitoring and data collection practices and measures for ambient air quality; (4) a program for emission limitation enforcement and the regulation of the construction, modification, or operation of stationary sources, including a permit program to regulate the construction or expansion of major emitting facilities in nondegradation and nonattainment areas; (5) prohibitions for stationary sources which will prevent attainment or maintenance of ambient air quality standards in another state or interfere with nondegradation measures in another state; (6) adequate assurances of personnel, funding, and authority to carry out an implementation plan, monitoring requirements for stationary source emissions, and periodic reporting on emissions; (7) an inspection and testing program for motor vehicle emissions; (8) revision of the plan in accordance with revisions of ambient air quality standards or for better methods of achieving the standards; (9) prohibitions on the construction or modification of any major stationary source after June 30, 1979, whose emissions will cause or contribute to nonattainment, unless the plan meets the nonattainment requirements of the act; (10) compliance with the nondegradation requirements of the act; and (11) major stationary sources to pay fees to defray the costs of preconstruction permit programs.

The SIP must also contain measures to notify the public of areas that do not meet national primary ambient air quality standards and advise the public of air pollution health hazards.

Attainment Deadlines for SIP of National Ambient Air Quality Standards

A SIP is to provide for attainment of a primary national ambient air quality standard as expeditiously as possible, but no later than three years from the date of EPA approval of the SIP. For secondary standards, the SIP must specify attainment within a reasonable time.

A governor may request EPA to extend the three-year attainment period for up to, but no longer than, two years for a SIP implementing a primary national ambient air quality standard if the request is made at the time the SIP is originally submitted. In order to get the extension, the governor must show the unavailability of technology for specified emission sources to achieve compliance within the three-year attainment period. EPA will require compliance for all other sources for which compliance is technologically feasible. The SIP must also require that the noncomplying sources follow reasonable interim measures of control which EPA has established.

SIP Modification or Postponement

The modification of SIP requirements by a state or EPA is expressly prohibited except as specifically provided in the act. The permissible extensions, variances, suspensions, or other modifications of SIP requirements are SIP promulgations and revisions, sulfur oxide emission exemption orders for primary nonferrous smelters, temporary emergency suspensions, national interest exemptions for federal facilities, and delayed compliance orders.

SIP Revisions

Each state is to revise its SIP, after public hearings, as may be necessary to take into account the revisions of national ambient air quality standards or the availability of improved or more expeditious methods of achieving such standards. A state is required to revise its implementation plan whenever EPA finds that the plan is substantially inadequate to achieve the national ambient air quality standards which it implements or to otherwise comply with any additional requirements of the Clean Air Act.

EPA is to approve revision of any SIP applicable to an air quality region if it determines that the SIP contains the necessary elements of an approvable plan required by law and if the plan has been adopted by the state after reasonable notice and public hearings.

Primary Nonferrous Smelter Orders

The Clean Air Act allows a special exemption for primary nonferrous smelters which postpones compliance with the sulfur oxide emission standards of a SIP. The exemption is meant to enable primary nonferrous smelters to attain or maintain compliance with the national ambient air quality standards for sulfur oxides, and can be granted for no other reason.

Either EPA or a state may issue orders granting the exemption. The exemption is available only to primary nonferrous smelters that were in existence at the time the 1977 amendments were enacted. To be eligible for the exemption, the source must adequately demonstrate to EPA that it will be unable to comply with the SIP's sulfur oxide limitations by the due date because there are no means of emission control technology applicable to the smelter to enable it to achieve compliance with the sulfur oxide limitations which has been adequately demonstrated to be reasonably available, as determined by EPA. In determining the reasonable availability of such means, EPA must take into account energy considerations and the cost of compliance, health, and environmental impacts other than on air quality.

A primary nonferrous smelter may be granted for up to two extensions, not exceeding three years each, but the second postponement cannot extend beyond January 1, 1988. The second extension is to be subject to a compliance schedule that includes increments of progress toward compliance with the postponed sulfur oxide emission limitation as expeditiously as practicable. The smelters are required to use interim measures during the extensions which in EPA's judgment assure the attainment and maintenance of national ambient air quality standards for sulfur oxides. The interim requirements are to include monitoring and reporting and the necessary measures to avoid imminent and substantial endangerment to human health. The interim measures are also to include the use of continuous emission reduction technology. EPA may waive the use of continuous emission control technology upon a showing that it will be so costly as to result in a permanent or prolonged temporary shutdown of the smelter.

Temporary Emergency Suspension for Fuel Burning Sources

The Clean Air Act authorizes a temporary suspension of SIP requirements for up to four months for fuel burning sources when necessitated by an energy or economic emergency. The owner or operator of the fuel burning source must request a suspension from the governor, and the governor must petition the president to determine and declare that a national or regional energy emergency exists. If the president declares an energy emergency, the governor may issue source-by-source temporary suspensions for up to, but no more than, four months but only if he or she finds there is a temporary energy emergency involving high unemployment or the loss of needed energy supplies and the emergency suspension will alleviate the unemployment or energy loss. EPA can disapprove a suspension issued by a governor if it determines that it does not meet the law's requirements. The governor may not issue a suspension for any SIP requirement promulgated by EPA, but the president can.

Temporary Emergency Suspension for a Proposed SIP Revision

The governor of a state may issue a temporary emergency suspension for a source's emissions allowed in a proposed SIP revision which the state has approved and submitted to EPA but which EPA has not acted on during the four-month period it must approve or disapprove the revision. The suspension cannot exceed four months and must only be to prevent unemployment or plant closings at the source. This kind of temporary emergency suspension cannot be granted if the plant would close anyway regardless of the proposed SIP revision.

National Interest Exemption from SIP for Federal Facilities

While federal facilities are generally required to comply with state and local air pollution control requirements, the president may exempt any federal emission source if it is in the paramount national interest.

Delayed Compliance Orders from SIP

A state, or EPA, after a 30-day notice to the state, may issue enforcement orders extending the date of compliance for any stationary source that is not in compliance with the final compliance date required by federal law to be implemented by a SIP for the attainment of a national ambient air quality standard. The order cannot be issued until after public notice and opportunity for a hearing, and it must contain a schedule for compliance.

The delayed compliance order must require compliance as expeditiously as practicable, but not later than July 1, 1979, or three years after the date for final compliance which is specified in the SIP, whichever is later. The delayed compliance order is limited to no more than three years, but may be extended to five years for sources that undertake to use new innovative emission control technology that is likely to be more effective in reducing emissions or the energy costs from emission controls.

The issuance of a delayed compliance order, in the case of a major stationary source, serves as notice for purpose of noncompliance penalties if the affected source does not comply by the delayed compliance data. A source receiving a delayed compliance order must comply with all interim requirements which EPA deems reasonable and practicable, and the interim requirements are to include measures necessary to protect substantial endangerment of health and for compliance, as far as possible, with the SIP. EPA may revoke a delayed compliance order and take enforcement action if it determines that the conditions on which the order was based no longer exist or that the source is in violation of interim requirements or other conditions of the delayed compliance order. EPA is to terminate an order upon a determination on the record, after notice and hearing, that the inability of the source to comply no longer exists. If the source demonstrates that the prompt termination of the order would result in undue hardship, the termination is to become effective at the earliest practicable date on which the undue hardship ends.

As long as the source is in compliance with a delayed compliance order, no enforcement action can be taken. Where a source wishes to comply by replacing the facility, terminating operations, or completely changing production processes, it may receive an extension requiring no interim steps before final compliance if it agrees to post a bond or surety equal to the cost of compliance had the owner decided to comply by installing control equipment.

For major stationary sources, no delayed compliance order issued by a state can take effect until EPA determines it meets the requirements of the law. In the case of sources other than major stationary sources, EPA may revoke any order issued by the state if the order is not in accordance with the law, and then EPA may proceed with whatever enforcement measures it deems appropriate, including issuing a delayed compliance order. A state or any of its political subdivisions may enforce more stringent requirements or a more expeditious compliance timetable than contained in an EPA-issued delayed compliance order.

Tall Stacks and Dispersion Techniques Banned as a Means of Meeting Air Quality Standards in SIPs

EPA is prohibited from banning or restricting any stack height. However, the Clean Air Act does restrict the use of tall stacks and other dispersion techniques as a means of compliance with SIPs. The stack height of any stationary source which exceeds good engineering practice or any dispersion technique cannot be credited toward the amount of emission reduction required by a SIP. In other words, tall stacks cannot be used in meeting ambient air quality standards.

The term *dispersion technique* includes any intermittent or supplemental control of air pollutants varying with atmospheric conditions. Good engineering practice is defined to mean the height necessary to insure that emissions from the stack do not result in excessive air pollution concentrations near the source due to atmospheric conditions or terrain. Good engineering practice for stack height means a stack that is no more than 2 1/2 times the height of the source, unless EPA is shown that a greater height is needed to avoid excessive pollution concentrations.

There is one exception to the prohibition on the use of tall stacks in meeting national ambient air quality standards. For federally owned coal-fired steam electric generating power plants that began operations prior to July 1, 1957, emission limitations established for these sources may take into account the effect of the entire height of stacks for which a construction contract was awarded prior to February 8, 1974.

Indirect Source Review and the SIP

EPA is prohibited from requiring a SIP to contain an indirect source review program as a condition for approval, except for federally funded highways, airports, and other major federally assisted or federally owned or operated indirect sources. An indirect source is any source, such as a road, highway, or parking lot, which attracts mobile sources of pollution. An indirect source review program may be included in a SIP, but it is not required. EPA may approve and enforce an indirect source program if it is adopted and submitted by a state.

SIP Consultation and Delegation to Local Governments

The SIP must provide for consultation with local governments in accordance with regulations prescribed by EPA.

EPA is authorized to delegate enforcement authority to local government in the case of a SIP promulgated by the agency. The delegation is to be initiated by an application of the chief executive officer of the local government, and EPA may grant the delegation if it finds that the local government has adequate regulatory authority under state or local law.

SIPs and Interstate Pollution Abatement

SIPs must contain provisions that prohibit any stationary source within the state from emitting any air pollutant in amounts that will either prevent the attainment or maintenance by any other state of any national ambient air quality standard, interfere with any other state's efforts to prevent significant deterioration of air quality, or impair visibility in another state.

SIPs are required to provide written notice to adjacent states at least 60 days prior to construction for any proposed new or modified stationary source within that state whose emissions may prevent the other state from meeting significant deterioration requirements or from attaining or maintaining national ambient air quality standards. A state or local government may petition EPA for a finding that a major source in another state does or will prevent the affected state from meeting significant deterioration requirements or meeting national ambient air quality standards. EPA has 60 days to respond, and if it makes a finding of interstate pollution, then it is a violation of the host state's SIP for any proposed new or modified source to begin construction or operation. The source in the host state is in violation even if it has a permit that was granted by the state in which it is located.

It is also a violation for an existing source to operate for more than three months after EPA has found that it interferes with another state's ability to meet significant deterioration requirements or national ambient air quality standards. EPA may allow the continued operation of the source causing interstate air pollution beyond the three-month period for up to three years if the source complies with the emission limitations and compliance schedule imposed by the agency to bring about compliance with the out-of-state SIP as expeditiously as practicable. A delayed compliance order would also be available for the source.

SIP Revisions for International Pollution

The Clean Air Act allows EPA to revise a SIP upon the petition of an international agency or the secretary of state if EPA finds that the emissions originating in a state may reasonably be anticipated to endanger the health or welfare of persons of a foreign country.

SIPs and Transportation Controls

SIPs must include transportation controls if necessary to assure attainment or maintenance of national ambient air quality standards. Transportation control measures can include a parking surcharge regulation, management of parking supply, preferential bus/carpool lanes, retrofits on vehicles, gas rationing, and reduction of on-street parking places.

If EPA promulgates a SIP for a state, no parking surcharge regulation may be required by the SIP. A state can adopt a surcharge regulation on its own and present it as part of its SIPs, and EPA is not prevented from approving the parking surcharge. EPA cannot promulgate any standard, plan, or requirement relating to the management of parking supply or preferential bus/carpool lanes, unless the promulgation has been subjected to at least one public hearing for which there has been reasonable public notice. To the extent necessary and practicable, each state must provide for periodic inspection and testing of motor vehicles to enforce compliance with applicable emission standards.

Conflict of Interest and State Boards

The SIPs must require that any board or body with permit issuance or enforcement authority have a majority of members who do not have a significant financial interest in sources subject to regulation.

EMISSION LIMITATIONS

Generally

The term *emission limitation* or *standard* means any requirement set by a state or EPA which limits the quantity, rate, or concentration of emissions of air pollutants on a continuous basis, including any requirement relating to the operation and maintenance of a source to assure continuous emission reduction.

The SIP must include limitations and schedules and timetables for compliance with such limitations, and such other measures regarded as necessary to insure the attainment and maintenance of national ambient air quality standards.

The states bear the principal responsibility for establishing emission limitations to achieve and maintain EPA's national ambient air quality standards. However, EPA has far-reaching and primary responsibility to set motor vehicle and motor vehicle engine emission limitations, as well as aircraft emission limitations; to establish new source performance standards and hazardous emission standards; and to regulate the sale of fuel and fuel additives.

National New Source Performance Standards

EPA is required to establish national standards of performance for new sources in any category of sources designated as contributing to air pollution which endangers public health or welfare. EPA is required to issue, and revise from time to time, a list of categories of stationary sources. EPA is to identify those sources on the list which it determines contribute significantly to air pollution and endanger public health or welfare. EPA must propose national standards of performance for new sources 120 days after an industrial category has been listed by EPA. A new source means any source that is constructed or modified after EPA proposes regulations establishing emission standards applicable to that source.

The standard of performance is to reflect the degree of emission limitation and the percentage reduction achievable through the application of the best technological system of continuous emission reduction which EPA determines has been adequately demonstrated, taking into account the cost of achieving the emission reduction, and nonair quality health and environmental impacts and emergency requirements. In addition to allowable limitations, the new source standard for a fossil fuel burning stationary source must include a requirement for achieving a percentage reduction in emissions compared to emissions that would have resulted had the fuel been treated or cleaned prior to use. In calculating the percentage reduction requirement for fossil fuel burning sources, EPA may credit the source for fuel cleaning or a reduction in the pollution characteristics of the fuel prior to combustion.

It is unlawful for an owner or operator of any new source to operate it in violation of a new source standard. The new source may utilize any means of emission reduction to comply with a new source performance standard, unless EPA has established a design, equipment, work practice, or operational standard, or some combination of these, after determining it was infeasible to prescribe or enforce a standard of performance.

If a state or any political subdivision of a state establishes an emission standard that is more stringent than the federal standard, the new source need not comply with the state standard but must comply with the federal standard.

A state may be delegated the authority to enforce EPA's new source performance standard if EPA approves an implementation procedure for the delegation which the state may develop and submit to the agency. EPA retains authority to enforce the new source standards in any state with a delegated program.

The governor of a state may petition EPA to issue new source performance standards for industries that have not yet been covered by such standards, to revise priorities for standard setting, to issue revised standards when better technology becomes adequately demonstrated, or to issue standards for unregulated hazardous pollutants.

States are required to establish emission limitations for existing sources in any source category for which EPA sets a new source performance standard where the pollutant is not covered by a national ambient air quality standard or national hazardous pollutant standard. The state standards must take into account the remaining useful life of the existing sources. If the state fails to adopt such standards for existing sources, then EPA may do so in its place.

Exempt from new source performance standards are grain elevators with a storage capacity of less than 2.5 million bushels.

EPA cannot generally require any new or modified stationary source to employ a particular technological system of continuous emission reduction to comply with the new source performance standard. Where numerical emission limitations would be infeasible to prescribe or enforce, EPA is authorized to set new source performance standards as design, equipment, work practice, or operational standards, or some combination of these. An emission limitation is considered infeasible to prescribe or enforce whenever a pollutant cannot be emitted through a conveyance or it is impracticable to measure the pollutant's emissions. The alternative design, equipment, work practice, or operational technologies for new sources are to reflect the best systems of continuous emission reduction which EPA determines has been adequately demonstrated, taking into account any nonair quality health and environmental impacts and energy requirements.

EPA is authorized to grant waivers from the new source performance standards to permit a source to use innovative continuous emission reduction systems or other types of innovative control technology. The EPA waivers are to be for no more than seven years after the date on which the first waiver is granted for the source, or four years after commencement of the source's operations, whichever is earlier. Before EPA can grant a technology innovation waiver, it must have the consent of the governor of the state where the source is located and find that (1) the proposed system has not been adequately demonstrated, (2) there is the substantial likelihood that the innovative technology will achieve greater emission reductions than required by new source performance standards or an equivalent reduction at lower economic, energy, or nonair quality environmental costs, and (3) the source has shown that the new technology will not cause or contribute to an unreasonable risk to public health, welfare, or safety from its operation or malfunction. EPA must impose terms and conditions on an innovative technology waiver which assures that emissions from the source will not prevent the attainment or maintenance of any national ambient air quality standards.

If a waiver is terminated because of a failure to operate as planned, EPA is to grant an extension of the requirements for compliance with the new source performance standards to allow a source up to three years to achieve compliance. This extension must establish emission limits and a compliance schedule containing increments of progress that require compliance as expeditiously as practicable and include measures in the interim to minimize emissions.

National Hazardous Pollutant Emission Standards

EPA is authorized to establish emission standards for hazardous air pollutants. A hazardous air pollutant is defined as an air pollutant which causes, or contributes to, air pollution that may reasonably be anticipated to result in an increase in mortality or an increase in serious irreversible or incapacitating reversible illness.

The process for establishing hazardous air pollutant emission standards begins with EPA publishing a list including each hazardous air pollutant for which it intends to establish an emission limitation. Proposed regulations establishing emission standards for these hazardous air pollutants, together with a notice of public hearing to be held within 30 days, are to be published within 180 days after the listing of the pollutant. Not later than 180 days after the publication of these regulations EPA is to prescribe an emission limitation for the hazardous pollutant unless, on the basis of information presented at the hearings, it finds that the pollutant clearly is not hazardous.

The hazardous air pollutant standard is to be set at a level which in EPA's judgment provides an ample margin of safety to protect the public health from such hazardous air pollutants. If EPA finds that it is not feasible to prescribe or enforce an emission standard for a hazardous air pollutant, it may promulgate a design, equipment, work practice, or operational standard which it determines is adequate to protect the public health from the pollutant with an ample margin of safety. The infeasibility of a hazardous air pollutant emission standard is defined to include the infeasibility of means to constrain or capture the pollutant or the impracticality of measurement methods because of technical or economic limitations. EPA may permit the use of alternative means of emission limitations for purposes of compliance, if, after notice and public hearing, EPA is satisfied that these alternatives will achieve emission reductions that are at least equivalent to EPA's design, equipment, or operational standards.

The emission standards for hazardous air pollutants apply to both new and existing sources. A new source means any stationary source that is constructed or modified after EPA proposes regulations establishing emission standards applicable to the source. After the effective date of an emission standard, no one can construct a new source or modify an existing source that emits a hazardous air pollutant unless EPA finds that the source is properly operated will not cause emissions in violation of the standard.

EPA may grant a waiver to an existing source for up to two years extending the time for compliance with the hazardous air pollutant emission standards if EPA finds that the extension is necessary for the installation of controls and that steps will be taken during the interim to assure that public health will be protected from imminent endangerment. The president may exempt any stationary source for up to two years if the technology needed to implement the standards is not available and the operation of the source is required due to national security. This exemption may be extended for one or more additional periods, each of which cannot exceed two years.

A state may be delegated the authority to enforce EPA's hazardous pollutant emission standards if EPA approves an implementation procedure for the delegation which the state may develop and submit to the agency.

Atomic Power Plants

Atomic power plants licensed by the Nuclear Regulatory Commission (NRC) may be exempted from an EPA, state, or local emission standards if the NRC finds that it would endanger public health or safety, subject to an appeal to the president to abrogate the exemption within 90 days after such a finding.

Use of Local or Regional Coal to Prevent Economic Disruption or Unemployment—Additional Emission Limitations

EPA or the president or president's designee may require a major fuel burning stationary source (over 250 million Btu's per hour or its equivalent) not in compliance with a SIP or under a coal conversion order to use locally or regionally available coal to prevent severe local or regional economic disruption or employment that might result from the use of other fuels. The governor of a state may petition the president to exercise this authority.

If such a prohibition is imposed, the major fuel burning source must enter into long-term contracts, which are to be at least ten years in duration, for supplying local or regionally available coal. For good cause, the president or president's designee may grant an exception by permit, rule, or an order.

The major fuel burning source must also enter into a contract to acquire any additional means of emission limitation that may be required after switching to coal as a fuel. The fuel burning source must comply with the schedules, timetables, or other requirements which the governor or EPA establishes to assure compliance.

PREVENTION OF SIGNIFICANT DETERIORATION IN ATTAINMENT AREAS

Generally

The 1977 amendments included new provisions for preventing significant deterioration (PSD) of air quality in areas that are cleaner than required by the national ambient standards. These clean air areas are commonly called attainment or nondegradation areas. The PSD provisions are meant to require clean air areas to remain clean.

The Clean Air Act states five purposes which the PSD provisions should achieve: (1) protect the public health and welfare from adverse effects which in EPA's judgment may be anticipated from air pollution; (2) preserve, protect, and enhance air quality in national parks, national wilderness areas, national monuments, national seashores, and other areas of special national or regional natural, recreational, scenic, or historic value; (3) insure that economic growth will be consistent with the preservation of existing clean air resources; (4) assure that emissions from one state will not interfere with the SIP provisions to prevent significant deterioration for any other state; (5) and assure that any decision to permit increased air pollution subject to the PSD provisions is made only after careful evaluation of all the consequences of such a decision and after adequate procedural opportunities for informed public participation in the decision-making process.

The SIP is to contain emission limitations and other measures to prevent significant deterioration in an air quality region.

Designation and Redesignation of Three Statutory PSD Classifications for Sulfur Oxides and Particulates

Clean air areas can be designated under three classifications where the air quality is cleaner than required by ambient air quality standards for the pollutants sulfur oxides and particulates. The three classes establish how much additional pollution from sulfur oxides and particulates will be allowed from additional growth in an area. For each classification the act specifies the maximum allowable increases or increments in the concentration of ambient air pollution from sulfur oxides and particulates in an area.

Areas subject to PSD provisions for sulfur oxides and particulates may be designated as either Class I, II, or III. Class I areas require the most stringent regulation and allow the least degradation. Class II areas allow moderate increases in sulfur oxide and particulate pollution in the ambient air. Class III areas allow the greatest increases in sulfur oxide or particulate emissions and involve the least amount of regulation of the three classes.

The Class I areas were initially designated to include only certain federal areas in existence as of August 1977, and they included all international parks, all national wilderness areas and national memorial parks larger than 5,000 acres, and all national parks larger than 6,000 acres. These are mandatory Class I federal areas and cannot be redesignated. All other areas of the nation are Class II, unless redesignated as Class I or Class III in the manner allowed by the Clean Air Act.

With certain exceptions, states are free to redesignate the classification of a PSD area, including federal lands, as long as PSD requirements are followed. The exceptions are mandatory federal Class I lands, certain federal areas that cannot be redesignated as Class III, and Indian lands, which may only be redesignated by an appropriate Indian governing body. The federal areas that may not be redesignated as Class III, only Class I or Class II, include national parks or national monuments established after August 1977 which are larger than 10,000 acres and other federal lands over 10,000 acres which are national monuments, national primitive areas, national preserves, national recreation areas, national wild and scenic rivers, national wildlife refuges, and national lakeshores and seashores.

Prior to the redesignation of any area, notice must be given to the public and, if the area includes any federal lands, to the appropriate federal land manager. If a state proposes to redesignate an area to the least restrictive Class III area, it must first get approval of the local governments which represent the majority of residents in the area. The state must demonstrate that the redesignation will not cause PSD violations in any other areas.

EPA may disapprove the redesignation of any area only if it finds, after notice and opportunity for a public hearing, that the redesignation does not meet procedural requirements.

Maximum Allowable Increases in PSD Classes

Sulfur Oxides and Particulates

The statute specifies the maximum increase that will be allowed for ambient air concentrations of sulfur oxides and particulates for each PSD class. These maximum allowable increases are determined with reference to exceeding baseline concentrations for sulfur oxides and particulates specified in the Clean Air Act. The maximum allowable increases above the baseline concentrations are the quantitative measure of determining significant air quality deterioration under the PSD provisions. Specific maximum numerical increments or increases are established for each class for ambient air concentrations of sulfur oxides and particulates against which allowable increases are measured. The baseline concentration for sulfur oxides and particulates is the ambient concentration level that exists at the time for the first application for a permit in an area subject to PSD requirements, based on air quality data available to EPA or the state and on the monitoring data which the permit applicant is required to submit. The statute provides the rules for the accounting of emissions, that is, determining whether particular emissions are to be included in the baseline concentration or are to be counted against allowable increases.

Regardless of the allowable increments for sulfur oxides or particulates for each class, in no case can pollutants exceed ambient standards. Hence, the ambient standards for sulfur oxides and particulates represent the uppermost ceilings beyond which pollution concentrations cannot rise. Every SIP is to provide assurances that the maximum allowable increases over baseline concentrations will not occur.

Hydrocarbons, Carbon Monoxide, Photochemical Oxidants, Nitrogen Oxides, and other Pollutants

The PSD allowable increases initially applied only to sulfur dioxides and particulates and set increments for them. By August 1979 EPA was also to issue PSD regulations for hydrocarbons, carbon monoxide, photochemical oxidants, and nitrogen oxides. Whenever EPA promulgates national ambient air quality standards for any other pollutants, it must issue PSD regulations for these standards not more than two years afterwards. These nondegradation regulations must include specific measures that are at least as effective as allowable numerical pollution increments, and may include such increments, emission density requirements, or other measures. For any pollutants other than sulfur oxides and particulates, no area classification is required if the SIP submitted to EPA contains provisions which as a whole will carry out the nondegradation requirements of the PSD provisions at least as effectively as an area classification plan.

PSD Preconstruction Requirements and Permits for Major Emitting Facilities

Generally

The key mechanism for implementing the PSD requirements in clean air areas is by the preconstruction review and permit procedures established by the act. No major emitting facility may be constructed in one of the classified areas unless a permit has been issued for the proposed facility which contains emission limitations conforming with PSD requirements. Construction subject to a permit also includes modification of a major emitting facility, with modification defined as any physical change or change in the method of operation of a stationary source which increases the amount of any air pollutant emitted by such a source or which results in the emission of any air pollutant not previously emitted. A major emitting facility is defined as any facility falling into one of 28 source categories specified by the statute and emitting 100 tons yearly of any air pollutant, plus any other source not listed by the statute which actually emits or has the potential to emit 250 tons yearly or more of an air pollutant.

Before a PSD permit application may be filed, a detailed air quality analysis must be conducted for each regulated pollutant emitted by the facility. This air quality analysis amounts to an impact assessment. The analysis must be made available to the public. This preapplication air quality analysis is to be conducted either by the state, local government, or major emitting facility applying for the permit. EPA is to establish regulations requiring the analysis to assess the impact of the source on ambient air quality, climate and meteorology, terrain, soil and vegetation, and visibility at or around the facility.

The air quality impacts must be analyzed using specified EPA models unless the EPA model is shown to be inappropriate due to terrain or meteorological conditions. After August 1978 one year of continuous air quality monitoring data was required as part of PSD permit applications. Such data are to be used to determine whether the facility exceeds maximum allowable increases or concentrations set for pollutants.

Preconditions to Construction of Major Emitting Facilities in PSD Areas

The Clean Air Act forbids the construction of a major emitting facility in classified areas unless several statutory preconditions have been met.

A key construction precondition is that a permit has been issued for the proposed facility setting forth emission limitations that conform with PSD requirements for the designated area classes. Before being granted, the proposed permit must be reviewed, a preapplication analysis must be conducted, and a public hearing must be held on the air quality impacts of the major emitting facility.

In order to be built, the major emitting facility in a PSD area must demonstrate that emissions from its construction or operation will not cause or contribute to air pollution which exceeds any (1) maximum allowable increase or maximum allowable concentration for any pollutant in a PSD area more than one time a year, (2) national ambient air quality standard in any air quality control region, or (3) other applicable emission standard or standard of performance. The proposed facility must use the best available control technology (BACT) for every pollutant regulated by EPA under the Clean Air Act. The Clean Air Act defines BACT as an emission limitation reflecting the maximum degree of emission reduction, which the permitting authority determines, on a case-by-case basis, is achievable, taking into account energy, environmental, and economic impacts and other costs. The BACT may include production processes and other available methods, systems, and techniques, including fuel cleaning or treatment or innovative fuel combustion techniques. EPA approval of BACT technology to be incorporated in a permit is a construction precondition in the case of a major emitting facility that proposes to construct in a Class III area and whose emissions would cause or contribute to exceeding maximum allowable increments in a Class II area and where no standard was promulgated after the enactment of the 1977 amendments.

Another precondition to construction of a major emitting facility is that the provisions with respect to the protection of Class I areas will be complied with by the facility. There must have been an analysis of any air quality impacts projected for the areas as a result of growth associated with the facility. The major emitting facility for which the permit is required must agree to conduct any monitoring regarded as necessary to determine the effect of the facility's emissions on air quality in any area that may be affected by these emissions.

Special Preconstruction Review and Permit Requirements for
Mandatory Class I Federal Areas

The Clean Air Act establishes special requirements for preconstruction review and permits for a source that impacts a mandatory Class I federal area.

EPA must provide notice of any permit application for the construction of a major emitting facility to the appropriate federal land manager and the federal official charged with direct responsibility for management of any lands in a Class I area that may be affected by emissions from the proposed facility. The federal land manager has a responsibility to protect values related to air quality, which include but are not restricted to visibility. Even if a major emitting facility's emissions will not exceed the maximum allowable increases for a Class I area, a permit may not be issued when any emission from the source will have an adverse impact on values related to air quality in the Class I area.

If, however, the federal land manager certifies that emissions will not have an adverse impact on air quality-related values, and if the preconstruction requirements are otherwise met, then the state may authorize EPA to issue a variance from the Class I increments. This variance allows increases of sulfur dioxide and particulate increments similar to those permitted in Class II areas, except in the case of the three-hour sulfur dioxide maximum specified in the act.

The Clean Air Act also provides a sulfur dioxide variance at a level between the Class I and Class II increment concentration in the case of a major emitting facility that has been denied certification because it will cause an increase beyond the 24-hour sulfur dioxide maximum. This variance could be granted by the governor, with the federal land manager's concurrence, or it could be granted at the governor's request over a federal land manager's objection upon a presidential finding that such a variance is in the national interest.

VISIBILITY PROTECTION FOR MANDATORY CLASS I FEDERAL AREAS

A major declared goal of the Clean Air Act is to protect visibility and prevent its impairment from manmade pollutants created by manmade pollutants. Visibility impairment is defined to include the reduction of visual range and atmospheric discoloration.

By February 1978 the Department of the Interior was to identify and list the mandatory Class I federal areas where visibility was an important value. The department's list of these areas is to be revised from time to time. By August 1978 EPA was to list, after consultation with Interior, the mandatory Class I federal areas for which EPA deemed visibility to be an important value. By February 1979, EPA was to complete a study and report to Congress on the methods available for preventing and remedying visibility impairment in the protected Class I areas.

By August 1979 EPA was required to promulgate regulations assuring reasonable progress toward the national goal of preventing visibility impairment and correcting existing visibility impairment in mandatory Class I federal areas. In determining reasonable progress, the EPA's regulation's must consider the economic, energy, and environmental costs of compliance, as well as the remaining useful life of any existing source that will be subject to the visibility requirements.

These visibility protection regulations are to provide guidelines to the states for revisions of implementation plans, taking into account EPA's report to Congress on techniques and methods for implementing the visibility protections. States in which any listed Class I area is located and states whose emissions could impact these areas are required to submit any necessary SIP revisions. These SIP revisions are to contain measures, including emission limitations, which may be necessary to make reasonable progress toward meeting the national goal of visibility protection. In the case of fossil fuel power plants with a generating capacity over 750 megawatts, EPA is to set guidelines for emission standards. The revised SIPs were to provide a long-term (10 to 15 years) strategy for making this progress.

The revised SIPs were to require all existing major stationary sources not in operation prior to August 7, 1962, to install "best available retrofit technology" (BART) for controlling emissions that might impair visibility in a protected area. A major stationary source for purposes of visibility protection refers to 28 statutorily designated sources with the potential to emit 250 tons per year of any regulated pollutant. In determining the best available retrofit technology, the state must take into account the cost of compliance, energy and nonair quality impacts of compliance, any existing pollution control technology at the source, remaining useful life of the source, and degree of improvement in visibility which may reasonably be anticipated to result from use of the BART.

Sources subject to the best available retrofit technology requirements must retrofit as expeditiously as practicable, but not later than five years after the SIP revision has been approved by EPA. EPA may grant an exemption from the best available retrofit technology requirements in the case where EPA determines that the source does not or will not emit an air pollutant that may impair visibility in a mandatory Class I federal area. The exemption does not apply to fossil fuel plants with generating power of 750 megawatts or more unless the owner shows that the plant's distance from a mandatory Class I federal area is great enough not to contribute to visibility impairment.

EPA must provide notice of any application for a PSD permit for construction of a major emitting facility to the federal land manager or any other appropriate federal official charged with responsibility for managing lands within a mandatory

Class I federal area that may be affected by emissions from the proposed source. The permit cannot be issued if the federal land manager determines to the satisfaction of the state that the major emitting facility will have an adverse impact on air quality, including visibility. However, if the federal land manager certifies that the emissions will not adversely affect air quality, including visibility, the state may issue the permit, even if the change in air quality caused by the emissions will cause or contribute to concentrations that exceed the maximum allowable increases for the Class I area.

NONATTAINMENT AREAS

A nonattainment area is any area where a national ambient air quality standard is exceeded for any pollutant. Nonattainment is determined by monitoring data or air quality modeling which demonstrates that a national ambient air quality standard is being exceeded.

Identification of Nonattainment Areas

The states identify and designate the nonattainment areas to EPA, and EPA in turn promulgates the state list of nonattainment areas along with any modifications it considers necessary. The 1977 amendments required states to prepare no later than February 7, 1978, a list of air quality control regions which, as of August 7, 1977, met the national primary ambient air quality standards for sulfur oxides and particulates; did not meet any national primary ambient standard for sulfur dioxides or particulates; did not meet any national secondary ambient air quality standard; could not be identified as attaining any national primary or secondary ambient air quality standard for sulfur dioxides or particulates due to lack of available information; or had air quality that was better than national primary or secondary ambient air quality standards for pollutants other than sulfur oxides or particulates or for which the data were insufficient to determine whether attainment had been achieved for these pollutants.

The state lists are to be revised and resubmitted to EPA from time to time, and EPA is to promulgate the revised lists. These lists are used to designate both the nonattainment and PSD areas.

Nonattainment Plans

SIP Revisions and Requirements for Nonattainment Areas

The 1977 amendments required the states to submit no later than January 1, 1979, revisions to their SIPs to conform with the nonattainment requirements of the act. The 1977 amendments required the states to revise their SIPs by July 1, 1979, to assure that air quality control regions would meet national ambient air quality standards for all pollutants by December 31, 1982, or by December 31, 1987, for photochemical oxidants or carbon monoxide if the 1982 attainment deadline could not be met by using reasonably available measures. For states seeking an extension beyond the 1982 attainment deadline for photochemical oxidants or carbon monoxide, the SIP must contain other measures, including a schedule for implementation of a vehicle emission inspection and maintenance program.

These revised SIPs relating to nonattainment are also sometimes referred to as nonattainment plans. These nonattainment plans must contain emission limitations, schedules, and other measures to assure compliance with attainment deadlines.

The SIP nonattainment revision is important because if not approved by EPA by July 1, 1979, the act would ban the construction or modification of any major stationary source emitting nonattainment pollutants in the nonattainment area. A construction ban is not the only penalty resulting from the failure of a state to revise its SIP to implement the nonattainment requirements by July 1, 1979. These states could lose federal highway funds if transportation control measures would be necessary to achieve attainment. Grants authorized by the Clean Air Act cannot be issued to state or local governments that implement the SIP. Federal agencies are prohibited from taking any action that does not conform with an approved SIP, and that includes providing funds or permits for a project.

A second SIP nonattainment revision from a state had to be submitted by July 1, 1982, for photochemical oxidants or carbon monoxide in areas unable to meet the December 31, 1982, attainment deadline for these pollutants, with the revision to provide the enforcement measures necessary to assure attainment no later than December 31, 1987. Photochemical oxidants and carbon monoxide are primarily from automobiles, and so it should not be surprising that the second revised plan must include a vehicle inspection and maintenance program.

The nonattainment plan must include a comprehensive and current inventory of actual emissions of air pollutants from all existing sources. The emission inventory is to be revised and resubmitted as frequently as necessary to assure reasonable progress toward attainment of national ambient air quality standards in a nonattainment area.

Attainment Requirements for Existing Sources

The nonattainment plan for a nonattainment area must provide, at a minimum, for the use of all reasonably available control measures as expeditiously as practicable. In the interim, the nonattainment plan must require existing sources to make reasonable further progress toward meeting the attainment deadlines. The basic means to be used by existing sources for making reasonable further progress are annual emission incremental reductions which are sufficient to demonstrate attainment with the ambient air quality standards by the statutory 1982 deadline.

The emission reductions of existing sources in the nonattainment areas are to be achieved through the use of reasonably available control technology (RACT). Moreover, existing sources must comply with any other measures required by nonattainment plans to assure reasonable further progress toward attainment.

Growth Allowance (Offset Policy) for New or Modified Major Stationary Sources in Nonattainment Areas

The nonattainment plan must identify and quantify the emissions that will be allowed to result from the construction and operation of major new or modified stationary sources in each nonattainment area. These allowable emissions for new or modified major stationary sources are directly tied to plan requirements which the state must establish for curtailing emissions for existing sources in nonattainment areas. In effect, the nonattainment plan must show that an areawide reduction in a nonattainment area by existing sources will more than offset emissions from new or modified major sources in the area. The plan consequently creates a growth allowance, and this growth allowance can include either an areawide offset policy or a source-by-source offset policy. The nonattainment plan can subject new or modified sources to emission limitations, schedules, and other measures to assure compliance with ambient air quality standards.

Preconstruction Permits for New or Modified Major Stationary Sources in Nonattainment Areas

The nonattainment plan for nonattainment areas must include a permit program for the construction and operation of new or modified major stationary sources that effectuate the offset policy in which new emissions must be offset by emission reductions of existing sources. A source is considered a major source if it emits, or has the potential to emit, 100 tons of any pollutant annually for which attainment is required.

An owner or operator of a new or modified major stationary source in a nonattainment area must acquire a permit in order to construct the source. A permitting agency cannot issue a permit for the construction and operation of a new or modified stationary source if it finds that emissions of a pollutant from the source will cause or contribute to emissions that exceed the allowance for the pollutant. The permitting agency can issue a permit only if it determines that the emissions from the new or modified major emitting facility are more than offset by reductions in existing sources so as to guarantee annual incremental reductions in emissions that will result in the attainment of national ambient air quality standards. Most simply, the new facility must obtain an emission offset. That is, emissions from existing sources must be reduced by an amount that is more than sufficient to offset the new source's emissions.

To obtain a permit the proposed source is required to meet, at a minimum, an emission limitation specifying the "lowest achievable emission rate" (LAER) required by the state or the lowest rate achieved in practice, whichever is more stringent. In no event may emissions from a source subject to LAER be allowed to exceed the level specified in any applicable new source performance standard.

The nonattainment plan that seeks an extension beyond the December 31, 1982, deadline (up to December 31, 1987) for photochemical oxidants and carbon monoxide must require as a precondition to the issuance of preconstruction permits for major emitting facilities that each proposed source conduct an analysis that shows alternative sites, sizes, production processes, and environmental control techniques for the proposed source. These techniques should demonstrate that benefits for the proposed source significantly outweigh the environmental and social costs imposed as a result of its location, construction, or modification.

CLEAN AIR ACT ADMINISTRATIVE POWERS

EPA Rulemaking

EPA is authorized to establish regulations which it considers necessary to carry out the Clean Air Act. The administrator of EPA can delegate its other functions under the Clean Air Act to other EPA officials, but not rulemaking. The Clean Air Act dictates the types of proceedings that are to be followed for specified kinds of rulemaking.

EPA is directed to establish a rulemaking docket for its rulemaking actions. If a rule only applies within a particular state, a second (identical) docket must be simultaneously established in the appropriate regional EPA office in the region where the state is located. Any rule promulgated by EPA may not be based on any information or data that has not been placed on the docket at the time the rule is promulgated. The rulemaking docket is available for public inspection and copying. All written comments and documentary information are to be included in the docket when received. The transcript of any public hearing on a rule must also be included in the docket. The docket is to include drafts of proposed rules submitted by EPA to the Office of Management and Budget (OMB) and all written comments by other federal agencies and EPA's responses to the comments. The record of rulemaking proceedings is to be kept open for 30 days after the completion of a proceeding in order to provide for an opportunity for submission of rebuttal and supplementary information. EPA may supplement the docket with any public comments received after the comment period, as well as other documents that become available after publication of the proposed rule if EPA determines that the documents are of central relevance to rulemaking. These additional materials are to be placed in the docket as soon as possible after they become available.

Notice of proposed rulemaking is to be published in the Federal Register. The notice is to include a statement of the basis and purpose of the proposed rule and to specify the period for public comment. The statement of basis and purpose must contain a summary of the factual data on which the rule is based, the methodology of obtaining and analyzing the data, and the major legal interpretations and policy considerations underlying the proposed rule. The statement must also include a summarization or reference to any findings or comments of the Scientific Review Committee established by the act and of the National Academy of Sciences, and, if the proposed rule deviates significantly from these recommendations, an explanation of the reasons for the difference. The statement of basis and purpose must be placed on the docket on the date of publication of the proposed rule.

Any person may submit written comments, and EPA is required to give interested persons an opportunity for an oral presentation for which EPA is to keep a transcript. Only an objection to a rule or procedure which was raised with reasonable specificity during the period for public comment, including any public hearing, may be raised during judicial review. However, if the person raising an objection can demonstrate to EPA that it was impracticable to raise an objection within the period for public comment or if the grounds for the objection arose after the period of public comment and if the objection is of central relevance to the outcome of the rule, EPA is required to convene a proceeding for reconsidering the rule and to provide the same procedural rights that would have been afforded had the information been available at the time the rule was proposed. If EPA declines to convene a proceeding, a person may seek review of the refusal in the U.S. court of appeals for the appropriate circuit.

Ordinarily, EPA is to promulgate a rule within six months after it is proposed. EPA may extend the promulgation deadline up to six months more if EPA determines that such an extension is necessary to afford the public, and the agency, adequate opportunity to carry out the purposes of the act.

EPA Subpoena Power

In connection with determinations regarding temporary emergency suspension orders or for the purpose of obtaining information on emission standards or regarding fuel or fuel additive prohibitions, EPA may issue subpoenas for the attendance and testimony of witnesses and the production of papers, books, and documents, and EPA may administer oaths in proceedings. An owner or operator of a source whose information is subpoenaed may show that certain information, if made public, would divulge trade secrets or secret processes, and that consequently the information is to be considered confidential and not open to public disclosure. This information will not be regarded as confidential when properly used by federal officials in carrying out the Clean Air Act, EPA proceedings, or for studies by the National Academy of Sciences on the technological feasibility of compliance with EPA emission standards. Federal district courts are empowered to issue orders requiring persons to appear or give testimony before EPA or to appear and produce documents in cases where these persons fail to obey a subpoena.

JUDICIAL REVIEW OF EPA RULEMAKING AND ORDERS

Generally

Federal district courts have jurisdiction for suits concerning interpretations of existing valid regulations, while exclusive jurisdiction is conferred on the federal circuit courts of appeals to review the validity of EPA regulations after they are promulgated.

The District of Columbia Circuit Court of Appeals has exclusive jurisdiction to review EPA actions with regard to the promulgation of the following: ambient air quality standards; emission standards for new sources; emission standards for hazardous air pollutants; motor vehicle or motor vehicle engine emission standards; motor fuel controls or prohibitions; aircraft emissions standards; noncompliance rules or orders; and any other nationally applicable regulations or final action taken by EPA.

Other EPA actions which are of local or regional application, and not national in importance or scope, may be reviewed only in the federal court of appeals for the appropriate circuit. These actions include the following: approval or promulgation of a SIP; approval of emission standards for existing sources; compliance penalty orders; any order or regulation under the Energy Supply and Environmental Conservation Act of 1974; or any other final action of EPA that is of local or regional applicability. If EPA makes and publishes a finding that an agency action is national in scope or effect, then any suit challenging that action must be brought in the District of Columbia Circuit Court.

A challenge filed in a federal circuit court of appeals to the validity of EPA regulations is initiated by a petition for review. The petition must be filed within 60 days from the notice of the promulgation, action, or approval in the Federal Register. There is an exception to the 60-day requirement, and that is when the challenge to EPA's action is based solely on grounds arising after the sixtieth day. Then the petition must be filed within 60 days after such grounds arise.

The sole forum for challenging procedural determinations in EPA rulemaking is the federal circuit court of appeals for the appropriate circuit which at the time is reviewing the substantive provisions of the rule. The court of appeals may invalidate a rule for procedural error only if the errors were so serious and were related to matters of central relevance to the rule that there is a substantial likelihood that the rule would have been substantially changed if such errors had not been made.

Reviews of EPA actions relating to the validity of regulations are not governed by the provisions of the federal Administrative Procedures Act. The judicial review provisions of the Clean Air Act described above do not apply to EPA's interpretative rules, its rules concerning agency organization and other instances, which are governed by the Administrative Procedures Act.

The federal court of appeals that reviews EPA rulemaking may award the costs of litigation, including reasonable attorney and expert witness fees, whenever it determines that such an award is appropriate.

Scope of Judicial Review

The only matters that can be raised for judicial review are those for which an objection was raised with reasonable specificity during the period for public comment, including public hearings.

The grounds on which a federal court may reverse any EPA action are those actions that are arbitrary, capricious, an abuse of discretion, or otherwise not in accordance with the Clean Air Act; contrary to constitutional rights; in excess of statutory jurisdiction, authority, or limitations, or short of statutory right; or without observance of legal procedures, to the extent that the failure of procedural observance is arbitrary or capricious, an objection was properly raised in administrative proceedings, and the procedural error was serious and substantially affected EPA rulemaking or action.

Leave to Adduce Additional Evidence

Any party may ask the court for leave to bring forward new or additional evidence that was not introduced in original EPA proceedings in a federal judicial proceeding concerned with reviewing an EPA determination under the Clean Air Act which is required to be placed on the record and after formal adjudicatory or rulemaking proceedings. A federal court may grant this leave if such evidence is deemed to be material and if there were reasonable grounds for failure to introduce this additional evidence in the original proceedings before EPA. The court may order this additional evidence to be taken before EPA, which may modify its action based on the new evidence.

ENFORCEMENT

EPA Civil Enforcement

EPA may issue a compliance order or bring a civil suit for a permanent or temporary injunction in the case of violations of the following: new source performance standards; hazardous air pollutant standards; primary nonferrous smelter orders; any requirement relating to recordkeeping, reports, inspections, and monitoring; or preconstruction requirements for major stationary sources in nonattainment areas. EPA is required to undertake enforcement, including issuance of an order or seeking injunctive relief, which is necessary to prevent construction of a major emitting facility that does not conform to the PSD requirements of a state implementation plan.

An EPA order cannot take effect until the person to whom it is issued has an opportunity to confer with EPA about the alleged violation. The opportunity to confer is not required in cases of hazardous air pollutants. The order must state with reasonable specificity the nature of the complaint, taking into account the seriousness of the violation and any good faith efforts to comply with applicable requirements. Copies of the compliance orders must be sent to the appropriate state air pollution control agency. When a notice of violation or compliance order is issued to a corporation, a copy of the notice or order must also be issued to appropriate corporate officers.

When EPA finds that a person is in violation of an applicable SIP, EPA must first notify the alleged violator and the appropriate state agency. If the violation continues for more than 30 days after the notification, EPA may either issue a compliance order or bring a civil suit for a permanent or temporary injunction. The 30-day notice requirement is limited to violations of state implementation plans. If EPA finds that violations of an applicable implementation plan are so widespread that the violations appear to result from the failure of the state to effectively enforce the plan, EPA is to notify the state of this finding. If the state's failure to enforce extends beyond 30 days after this notice, EPA must issue public notice of the finding. Until the state satisfies EPA that the implementation plan will be enforced, EPA can enforce any requirement of the plan during this period, which is called a period of federally assumed enforcement.

Civil actions instituted by EPA are to be brought in the U.S. district court for the district in which the violation occurred or the defendant is located, resides, or is doing business. EPA can bring a civil action to obtain a permanent or temporary injunction, or to recover a civil penalty of not more than $25,000 per day for each violation, or both. In establishing the amount of the penalty, the courts are directed to take into account the size of the business and the seriousness of the violation.

EPA is authorized to institute suit in federal district court for injunctive relief with respect to emission standards, warranties, reporting requirements, and recordkeeping in connection with regulation of new motor vehicles and motor vehicle engines. EPA can also seek a $10,000 daily penalty for violations with respect to fuels and fuel additives.

EPA Criminal Enforcement

Criminal prosecution for violations of the Clean Air Act is confined to knowing violations. Responsible corporate officers are expressly included as being subject to the criminal provisions of the law.

A fine of up to $25,000 per day per violation, or imprisonment of up to one year, or both, are the penalties for a knowing violation of the following: an implementation plan during a period of federally assumed enforcement more than 30 days after notification of the violation by EPA; any EPA order to comply with an implementation plan, new source performance standard, or hazardous air pollutant standard; or new source performance standards or hazardous air pollutant standards, regardless of whether an EPA order has been issued. A second or subsequent conviction for any such knowing violation is subject to a fine of up to $50,000 per day, or two years in prison, or both.

A fine of up to $10,000, and imprisonment for up to six months, or both are the penalties for knowingly making false statements, representations, or certification in any document filed or required to be maintained under the Clean Air Act or for knowingly falsifying or tampering with or rendering inaccurate any monitoring device required by the law.

Imminent and Substantial Endangerment

EPA may commence suit in the appropriate federal district court to restrain air pollution that presents an imminent and substantial danger to human health, if the appropriate state or local authorities have not acted to abate this dangerous pollution. If it is not practicable to promptly protect human health from an imminent and substantial danger by instituting litigation in federal court, EPA may issue necessary administrative orders to achieve this protection without prior court action, after consultation with state and local authorities to determine what action they plan. EPA's order is good for no more than 24 hours unless it institutes a suit for an injunction during this period, in which case the order remains effective for 48 hours or for such longer period as the federal court may authorize pending litigation. The knowing violation of an EPA emergency order is punishable by a fine of $5,000 per day.

Noncompliance Penalties

The Clean Air Act requires the states or EPA to administratively assess and collect noncompliance penalties. EPA, or alternatively the state, is to assess a noncompliance penalty which is fixed and determined by regulation, and calculated on the basis of the savings gained by the noncomplying sources from delaying compliance.

A noncompliance penalty can be assessed when: a stationary source is not in compliance with any emission limitation, emission standard, or SIP compliance schedule; a stationary source is not in compliance with new source performance standards or national hazardous air pollutant standards; a primary nonferrous smelter is not in compliance with a primary nonferrous smelter order; or any source is not in compliance with an extension, order, or suspension issued under the act.

Noncompliance penalties are to be in addition to any other enforcement action such as permits, orders, payments, sanctions, or other requirements and are in no way to affect civil or criminal enforcement proceedings under federal, state, or local law. Determinations of noncompliance penalties are considered final actions for the purpose of allowing judicial review. In any action with respect to the promulgation of regulations for noncompliance penalties or the administration or enforcement of noncompliance penalties, courts are prohibited from granting a stay or injunctive relief before final judgment by the court is rendered.

States can administer the noncompliance penalty provisions if EPA approves a state plan that meets the requirements of the act. If the state does not perform the EPA-delegated obligations, then EPA assumes responsibility for collecting noncompliance penalties. EPA may review the decision of a state-imposed noncompliance penalty, and may disapprove a state decision if it is not in accordance with the law. All penalties assessed by the state are to be paid to the state.

EPA is to promulgate regulations that fix and determine noncompliance penalties. EPA in effect establishes the formula for determining noncompliance penalties, while the violator submits a calculation of the penalty that is owed in accordance with the regulatory formula and makes payment to EPA or the state.

As specified in the Clean Air Act, the noncompliance penalty is calculated on the basis of the savings which the noncomplying source gains by delaying compliance. Specifically, the regulations must establish a method of calculating the penalty which takes into account the capital costs of compliance and debt service over a normal amortization period not to exceed ten years, operation and maintenance costs saved by the polluter as a result of noncompliance, and additional economic value of the delay minus a credit for any compliance expenditures during the period of noncompliance. Calculation of the penalty is to be made no less than on a quarterly basis and is to be no less than the quarterly equivalent of the financial savings realized by a violator as a result of noncompliance. The assessed penalty is to be paid in quarterly payments for the period of noncompliance. Government determination of the noncompliance penalty is considered a final decision which is judicially reviewable.

The first payment of the noncompliance penalty is due six months after the date of the notice of noncompliance. Review of the payments is to be made by EPA or the state no later than six months after the source comes into compliance for the purpose of determining whether there has been an overpayment or whether additional payment is due to EPA or the state. Failure to pay the payment on time results in an additional quarterly non-payment penalty equal to 20 percent of the aggregate amount of the violator's penalties and nonpayment penalties which are unpaid as of the beginning of the quarter.

While EPA regulations fix and determine the manner in which noncompliance penalties are to be calculated, it is up to the violator to apply the EPA formula and return the payment due and owing to EPA or the state. After notice of noncompliance is given to the violator, that person calculates his or her own penalties in accordance with EPA regulations and submits that calculation and a proposed payment schedule, together with information necessary to allow independent verification of the calculation, to the state and to EPA. The penalties are to be paid according to a schedule proposed by the noncomplying source.

The state or EPA must give a reasonably specific notice of noncompliance within 30 days of the discovery of noncompliance. EPA is to require payment of the penalty by any person to whom notice of noncompliance has been issued, unless a final determination has been made upholding a challenge to the notice of noncompliance or granting an exemption under the act. Within 45 days of the notice of noncompliance, a person deciding not to accept and pay the penalty can submit a petition challenging the notice or alleging entitlement to an exemption under the act.

The petitioner challenging a noncompliance penalty must be given an adjudicatory hearing on the record, and a decision must be made in accordance with the Administrative Procedures Act or to equivalent state procedures. EPA is to make a decision on a petition, including findings of fact and law not later than 90 days after receiving the petition. The state or EPA is to adjust or readjust from time to time the amount of a penalty assessment calculated or the payment schedule proposed by the source. If, after notice and opportunity for a hearing on the record, EPA finds that the penalty or schedule does not meet the requirements of the law, it is to require a final adjustment of the penalty within 180 days after the source comes into compliance.

EPA or the state may enter into a contract with outside persons to determine the amount of the penalty payment assessment or payment schedule in cases where the violator fails to submit a calculation of the penalty assessment, or where he or she does not submit a timely petition challenging the notice of noncompliance, or where the petition has been denied. The cost of the contract to determine the penalty may be added to the penalty assessment.

The Clean Air Act provides five mandatory exemptions and one discretionary exemption from the noncompliance penalty.

The five mandatory exemptions where the source will not be subject to a noncompliance penalty when it is not in compliance are: (1) conversion by the source from burning petroleum products or natural gas, or both, to the burning of coal pursuant to an enforcement order or to a primary nonferrous smelter order; (2) pursuant to an order prohibiting use of petroleum products or natural gas, or both, under the Energy Supply and Environmental Coordination Act of 1974 and subsequent amendments; (3) use of innovative technology authorized by an enforcement order; (4) inability to comply with a compliance order having the effect of permitting a delay or violation of the law, including a requirement of an implementation plan, where this inability results from reasons beyond the control of the owner or operator of the source; or (5) by reason of a temporary suspension order.

The discretionary situation in which EPA may exempt a source from a noncompliance penalty, after notice and an opportunity for a hearing, is when it finds the particular instance of noncompliance is minimal in nature and duration—in other words a *de minimis* violation. An exemption ceases if the source fails to comply with any interim emission control requirement or schedule of compliance under an extension, order, or suspension for which the exemption was granted in the first place.

CITIZEN SUITS

Any person may bring a civil suit in federal district court against any person, including the United States or any government agency, alleged to be in violation of emission standards or limitations or compliance orders. Any person may bring a civil suit against EPA for failure to perform any nondiscretionary duty under the Clean Air Act. In addition, any person may bring a civil action against any other person who proposes to construct or constructs any new or modified major stationary source without a permit required by the PSD or the nonattainment requirements of the act. EPA, if not a party, may intervene in a citizen suit as a matter of right.

Before a citizen suit may be brought, 60-day notice must be given to EPA and the state in which the violation occurred. As long as EPA or a state is undertaking an appropriate civil action against a violator, a citizen suit is precluded.

Litigation costs may be awarded in citizen suits. In actions for a temporary restraining order or preliminary injunction, the court may require the filing of a bond or equivalent security. The provisions for citizen suits do not restrict any right which any person, or class of persons, may have under any statute or common law to seek enforcement of any emission standard or limitation or to seek any other relief.

EFFECT OF CLEAN AIR ACT ON STATE OR LOCAL LAWS

The Clean Air Act does not preempt state air pollution control. Air pollution control is explicitly recognized as a primary responsibility of state and local governments. Each state has primary responsibility for assuring air quality within the state. EPA establishes the levels of ambient air quality standards to be adopted nationwide, but the states decide the measures to be incorporated in SIPs which dictate the controls imposed on pollution sources to achieve these standards.

Any state or political subdivision can enforce its emission standards or limitations, except that it may not enforce emission standards or limitations that are less stringent than those in effect under an implementation plan, or than a federal new source performance standard or hazardous air pollutant standard.

REGULATION OF FEDERAL FACILITIES

Federal agencies are subject to all federal, state, interstate, and local air pollution control requirements to the same extent as a private party, including those for recordkeeping, reporting, or permits. The president has the authority to exempt a specific federal facility from the requirements of a SIP if it is determined to be in the paramount interest of the nation, except that the exemption does not apply to new source performance standards.

No officer, agent, or employer of the federal government is personally liable for any civil penalty as a result of such a connection to the federal government for which he or she is not otherwise liable.

INSPECTIONS, REPORTS, RECORDS, AND ACCESS TO INFORMATION

EPA has extensive powers to collect data and information to assist it in developing implementation plans, new source performance standards, or hazardous air pollutant standards; in determining whether any person is in violation of implementation plans; or in carrying out any other portion of the Clean Air Act.

To aid in these purposes, EPA may require any person owning or operating an emission source to establish and maintain records, make reports, use and maintain monitoring equipment or methods, sample emissions, and provide other information that may reasonably be needed by EPA. Upon presentation of credentials, EPA officials have the right of entry to premises in which an emission source, or any records required to be maintained, are located. EPA officials may at reasonable times have the right to inspect facilities, copy records, sample emissions, and inspect monitoring equipment.

EPA may delegate to any state the responsibilities for recordkeeping, inspection, monitoring, and entry if the state develops an adequate program to carry out these responsibilities. The delegation to a state does not prevent EPA from enforcing these responsibilities in a state when it chooses.

Records, reports, or information obtained by EPA must be available to the public. Upon satisfactory showing to EPA that disclosure of such records (other than emission data) would divulge trade secrets, EPA may consider such information, or any part of it, to be confidential. However, the records containing the trade secrets may be disclosed to the federal government to carry out the Clean Air Act.

EPA must give notice to the particular state concerned before entry, inspection, or monitoring is undertaken that relates to any emission standard, limitation, or other requirement of a SIP. States are prohibited from informing the person whose property is to be inspected by EPA. If EPA believes the state will improperly inform a person of a forthcoming inspection, notice to the state is not required until EPA determines the state will no longer inform the person. EPA's failure to notify a state cannot be used either as a defense in an enforcement action or as support of a claim of the inadmissibility of evidence obtained by EPA as the result of an inspection.

Manufacturers of motor vehicles or motor vehicle engines must maintain records, make reports, and provide other information necessary to enable EPA to determine whether the manufacturer complies with vehicle emission standards. EPA is also to have access to inspect and copy records of manufacturers of motor vehicles and engines. EPA authorities, upon presentation of appropriate credentials, may at reasonable times enter motor vehicle manufacturing plants to conduct tests of vehicles or engines or to inspect records, processes, and facilities used in conducting tests. The information obtained in an EPA investigation is to be made available to the public; exceptions are trade secrets that are entitled to protection. Information containing trade secrets may be disclosed to federal officials to carry out the Clean Air Act.

It is unlawful for any person to fail or refuse to provide access to records, to make reports or provide information, or to permit entry, testing, or inspection.

Courts may impose a fine of up to $10,000 or imprisonment for up to six months, or both, on any person who knowingly makes a false statement, representation, or certification of any document filed or required under the law or who falsifies, tampers with, or knowingly renders inaccurate monitoring equipment required by the law.

EMPLOYEE SAFEGUARDS

An employee or representative of the employee who is discharged or laid off, or threatened with the same, or whose employment is otherwise adversely affected or threatened to be adversely affected because of the requirements of the Clean Air Act, including state and local requirements, may request EPA to conduct a full investigation. EPA must investigate, and at the written request of any party, EPA must hold a public hearing after notice. EPA is not given the authority to modify or cancel any requirement because it may have an adverse employment effect.

The Clean Air Act prohibits the discharge or discrimination against an employee because of his or her involvement in aiding in the administration or enforcement of the act. Employees who are fired or who experience discrimination because they have participated in or brought a suit under the act may, within 30 days after the firing or discrimination, file a complaint with the Department of Labor. The Department of Labor can order reinstatement, backpay, and compensatory damages. This order is subject to review by a federal circuit court of appeals. To enforce an order, the Department of Labor may institute a civil suit in federal district court. A person on whose behalf an order was issued may also institute suit in federal district court against the person to whom the order was issued to enforce the order.

FEDERAL PROCUREMENT AND ASSISTANCE

Federal agencies are prohibited from entering into contracts for the procurement of goods and services with any person who has been convicted of an offense under the Clean Air Act if the contract is to be performed at the facility where the violation occurred.

The president may exempt any contract, loan, or grant from the provisions of the law when it is determined that the exemption is in the paramount interest of the nation.

EPA is prohibited from approving projects or awarding grants, and the Department of Transportation is barred from approving projects or awarding grants other than for safety, mass transit, or transportation improvement projects related to air quality improvement or maintenance, in any air quality control region in which national ambient primary ambient air quality standards had not been attained, where transportation control measures are needed to achieve attainment, and where the state has not submitted a SIP that will adequately meet the requirements for nonattainment areas. EPA is prohibited from awarding any grants in any area in which the state or local government or regional agency is not implementing any requirement of a SIP. No federal agency can support any activity that does not conform with an EPA-approved SIP. Metropolitan planning agencies designated for the purpose of developing coordinated transportation planning and interstate areas are prohibited from approving any project, program, or plan that does not conform with a SIP.

MOTOR VEHICLE POLLUTION CONTROL

Emission Standards—Generally

EPA is authorized to establish emission standards for new motor vehicles and new motor vehicle engines which the EPA determines cause or contribute to air pollution that may reasonably be anticipated to endanger public health or welfare. The Clean Air Act specifies minimum limits for the amount of emission reductions both for heavy-duty vehicles or engines and for light-duty vehicles and engines. The statute establishes emission limitations for hydrocarbons, carbon monoxide, nitrogen oxides, and particulates from new motor vehicles and motor vehicle engines. Emission standards are to be applicable for the useful life of vehicles or engines.

Key Definitions

A motor vehicle is any self-propelled vehicle designed for transporting people or property on a street or highway. A heavy-duty vehicle is a truck, bus, or other vehicle that has a gross weight of over 6,000 pounds. Off-road vehicles are considered heavy-duty vehicles. EPA is to define by regulation what is considered a light-duty vehicle. Motorcycles and motorcycle engines are to be treated in the same manner as heavy-duty vehicles and engines, unless EPA by regulation requires otherwise. For light-duty vehicles, useful life is defined as at least five years of use, or 50,000 miles, whichever comes first. For heavy-duty vehicles the same period or mileage is used, unless EPA determines that a longer period or greater mileage is appropriate. Useful life can be any period of use which EPA decides to establish.

Light-Duty Motor Vehicle and Engine Emission Standards

In the case of light-duty vehicles or engines, the emission standards for the 1981 model year and beyond is set at 0.41 grams per mile (gpm) for hydrocarbons, 3.40 gpm for carbon monoxide, and 1.00 gpm for nitrogen oxides. A 0.4 gpm standard for nitrogen oxides for light-duty vehicles is specified as a research goal. EPA is directed to promulgate regulations to require each motor vehicle maker that sells at least 0.5 percent of all light-duty vehicles in the United States to build demonstration vehicles that meet the 0.4 gpm nitrogen oxide emission standard. These demonstration vehicles are to be submitted to EPA every year starting with the 1979 model year.

Heavy-Duty Motor Vehicle and Engine Emission Standards

The 1977 amendments authorized the control of emissions from heavy-duty vehicles or engines beginning with the 1979 model year. For the model years 1979 to 1982, EPA was to issue regulations prescribing interim heavy-duty vehicle and vehicle engine emission standards for hydrocarbons, carbon monoxide, and nitrogen oxides which are to reflect the greatest degree of emission reduction achievable through the application of technology that EPA determines would be available for the model year for which the standards are applied. In setting these interim standards, EPA was to give consideration to cost factors as well as to noise, energy, and safety factors.

Statutory emission standards applying to heavy-duty vehicles and heavy-duty vehicle engines for hydrocarbons and carbon monoxide became effective for the 1983 model year, and statutory standards for nitrogen oxides became effective for the 1985 model year. The 1983 hydrocarbon and carbon monoxide standards were to reflect at least a 90 percent reduction from baseline model year standards, and the 1985 nitrogen oxide standard was to reflect at least a 75 percent reduction from the baseline standard. The baseline model year is defined as the model year immediately preceding the year in which the federal standards for a heavy-duty vehicle or engine first applied to the particular pollutant. EPA was required to prescribe particulate emission standards for heavy-duty vehicles or engines beginning in the 1981 model year.

Motorcycle and Motorcycle Engine Emission Standards

Motorcycles and motorcycle engines are to be treated in the same manner as heavy-duty vehicles and engines, unless EPA by rule reclassifies motorcycles as light-duty vehicles or by regulation treats them as a separate class or category.

Gasoline Vapor Emissions from Automobiles and Fueling Vapor Control

EPA is directed to issue regulations that prescribe measuring the gasoline vapor emissions from the vehicle or engine as a whole. The requirement becomes effective for the 1978 model year for light-duty vehicles. For heavy-duty vehicles the measurement of gasoline vapor emissions is to become effective either by the 1978 model year or the earliest model year it becomes feasible.

The 1977 amendments authorized EPA to issue fill pipe standards for new vehicles to assure effective connection with certified gasoline vapor recovery systems for the fueling of automobiles. EPA's issuance of fill pipe standards is preconditioned on EPA's promulgation of regulations applying controls and test procedures for gasoline vapor recovery of uncontrolled emissions from motor vehicle fueling. The fill pipe standards are to prepared in consultation with the Department of Transportation. The 1977 amendments required EPA to consider the use of onboard hydrocarbon control technology as an alternative to using gasoline vapor recovery systems in the fueling of automobiles. EPA was to employ this alternative if considered feasible and desirable.

Certification of New Vehicles and Engines for Conformance with Emission Standards; Emission Testing

No new motor vehicle or new motor vehicle engine can be sold to the public unless EPA certifies there is conformance with emission standards.

A certificate of conformity must be issued for any new motor vehicle or new motor vehicle engine that conforms with the emission standards. In the case of heavy-duty vehicles, engines, or motorcycles, EPA must issue certification even when there is a failure to conform with emission standards, provided the manufacturer pays a nonconformance penalty. The penalty is to be calculated by a formula established by EPA regulations.

EPA is to test, or require to be tested, any new motor vehicle or engine submitted by a manufacturer to determine compliance with emission control regulations. If the vehicle or engine conforms, EPA is to issue a certificate of conformity for up to one year. The manufacturer must indicate by a label or tag permanently affixed to the vehicle or engine that it is covered by a certificate of conformity.

EPA is to determine conformity to standards by tests conducted on new motor vehicles or new motor vehicle engines that are submitted by the manufacturers. EPA is also required to test emission control systems used by motor vehicles or motor vehicle engines that may be submitted by anyone to determine whether the system enables a vehicle or engine to meet emission control standards. If EPA finds from these tests that an emission control system enables the vehicle or engine to meet emission control standards, it must inform automobile makers, the National Academy of Sciences, and the public of the results of the tests. For the purpose of informing prospective automobile buyers, EPA is required to make reports in nontechnical English at the beginning of each model year indicating the results of tests on the automobile models submitted by their companies.

EPA initially bases certification of conformity with emission standards on motor vehicles and engines submitted the manufacturers. In other words, manufacturers submit prototypes in order to obtain a certificate of conformity, not assembly line vehicles or engines. In order to determine whether production vehicles off the assembly line do in fact conform with emission standards for which a certificate of conformity has been issued, EPA may test production line vehicles or engines covered by a certificate of conformity.

EPA may suspend a certificate of conformity in whole or in part if it determines that all or some of the previously certified vehicles or engines do not conform with the requirements on which the certification was based. The suspension or revocation of certification applies to all vehicles still held by the manufacturer, but if EPA finds that, contrary to the tests, any of these vehicles or engines actually conform with emission standards, these particular vehicles or engines are to be certified.

The manufacturer may request a hearing to challenge whether the vehicle or engine tests leading to a suspension or revocation of certification were properly conducted or assessed by EPA. In the event of a challenge, EPA must make its determination on the record. The manufacturer may appeal EPA's decision upholding the revocation or suspension of certification to the federal court of appeals.

EPA is authorized to exempt from certification vehicle or engine makers with projected yearly US. sales of 300 or fewer vehicles or engines.

The dealer of a new light-duty motor vehicle must furnish to each purchaser a certificate that the vehicle conforms with emission standards.

Labeling of Vehicle or Engine Emission Certification; Instructions for Use

A vehicle or engine may not be sold unless a label is affixed indicating it is covered by a certificate of conformance with emission requirements. The manufacturer is required to furnish each new motor vehicle or engine with a set of instructions for proper maintenance and use by the purchaser. The instructions are to include a notice that maintenance, replacement, or repair of emission control devices and systems may be performed by any automotive repair establishment or individual using any automotive part certified by the manufacturer as meeting the emission control requirements of the law.

Automobile Manufacturer Emission Control Warranties

It is unlawful for any automobile manufacturer not to comply with the terms of all the warranties they are required to provide by the act. The manufacturer of any new motor vehicle or motor vehicle engine is required to warrant to purchasers that the vehicle is designed, built, and equipped to conform at the time of sale with all applicable Clean Air Act regulations. This is commonly known as the design warranty. Another warranty which the manufacturer is required to extend is that the vehicle or engine is free from defects in materials and workmanship which can cause the vehicle or engine to fail to conform during its useful life (defined as five years or 50,000 miles) with emission control regulations. The manufacturer is also required to warrant that the emission control device or system of each new motor vehicle or new engine is free of defects in material and workmanship. This latter warranty is sometimes known as the performance warranty.

The performance warranty for emission control devices is limited to 24 months or 24,000 miles. When the performance warranty terminates, the manufacturer's remaining warranty for emission control devices is limited to catalytic converters, thermal reactors, or other components that were installed in the vehicle for the sole or primary purpose of reducing vehicle emissions. This warranty is good for up to 50,000 miles or five years from the date of purchase.

The warranties required by the act run to both the initial purchaser of the new vehicle or engine and each subsequent purchaser during the term of the warranty, but the manufacturer is not required to make good the warranty if the vehicle or engine is not properly maintained or operated.

The owner of a motor vehicle or engine warranted under the act is responsible for its proper maintenance and operation. At any place of the owner's choice he or she must bear the expense of maintaining parts related to emission control but not designated as emission control devices, unless the part is covered by any other warranty covered by the act. The manufacturer is not obligated to pay the cost for the failure of a vehicle or engine to conform with its warranty unless the vehicle is properly maintained and operated and the failure of the vehicle or engine to comply subjected the purchaser to a penalty or other sanctions, including denial of the right to use the vehicle, under state or federal law. If during the warranty period the motor vehicle or engine fails emission testing, the manufacturer is to remedy the nonconformity at no cost to the purchaser. The emission testing may be adopted as part of a SIP and may be used to determine nonconformity from the time of sale to the end of the warranty.

The manufacturer of any light-duty vehicle is required to bear the cost of the replacement of any part, device, or component of any light-duty vehicle that is designed for emission control, that is scheduled for replacement during the useful life of the vehicle according to warranty instructions, and that has an expected retail price that, including installation costs, exceeds 2 percent of the suggested retail price of the vehicle. Dealer costs created by the warranty requirements must be reimbursed by the manufacturer, and the manufacturer is prohibited from transferring any cost obligation to a dealer by a franchise agreement or other agreements.

Certification of Parts; Manufacturers Requiring Use of Brand-name Parts or Particular Repair Services

Manufacturers or rebuilders of motor vehicles or motor vehicle engine parts may certify, in accordance with EPA regulations, that the use of their parts will not cause the vehicle or engine to violate emission standards. The manufacturer cannot require the use of any particular brand, trade, or corporate name or require that the motor vehicle or engine be serviced at a particular establishment, unless the manufacturer satisfies EPA that the vehicle or engine will perform properly only if the particular component or service is used in connection with the vehicle or engine. The manufacturer is prohibited from requiring the use of its parts as a condition of the warranty or from conditioning the warranty upon service to be performed by any person under the manufacturer's control.

Dealer Certification of Emission Standard Compliance

The dealer who sells a new light-duty vehicle is to furnish the purchaser with a certificate that the vehicle conforms with emission standards.

Recalls for Widespread Nonconformity with Emission Standards

The Clean Air Act establishes a procedure that provides EPA with the authority to order automobile manufacturers to recall or repair groups of vehicles or engines that exceed emission standards when in actual use. If EPA determines that a substantial number of any class of properly maintained and used vehicles or engines do not meet emission standards during their useful life (five years or 50,000 miles), it must immediately notify the manufacturer and require it to submit a plan for remedying the nonconformity. The plan must provide that the nonconformity will be remedied at the expense of the manufacturer. Automobile and engine manufacturers have the right to a public hearing for the purpose of contesting EPA's findings that emission standards are not being met. The costs for repairs to vehicles or engines subject to the recall are to be borne by the manufacturer. The manufacturer must provide prompt notification of the nonconformity to dealers, ultimate purchasers, and subsequent purchasers.

Manufacturer Advertising of the Cost of Emission Controls

If a manufacturer includes in an advertisement a statement on the cost or value of emission control devices or systems, then it must set forth in the statement the cost or value which the Bureau of Labor Statistics in the Department of Labor attributes to the devices or systems.

Vehicle and Engine Modifications for High Altitude Areas

Adjustments to emission controls for automobiles or engines in high altitude areas are not prohibited as long as they are performed in accordance with manufacturer's instructions which have been approved by EPA. These

EPA-approved instructions must insure emission control performance for each pollutant that is at least as good as that which would result if no adjustments had not been made. The instructions must also provide for adjustments made for vehicles moving from the high altitude area to low altitude area after initial certification of the vehicle. Instructions relating to high altitude performance adjustments may not require the use of manufacturer's parts covered by the certificate of conformity requirements unless EPA determines that the use of these certified parts is necessary to ensure emission control performance.

High altitude adjustments are permitted only in states designated as high altitude states by EPA regulations which were promulgated prior to August 7, 1977. After January 1, 1981, however, adjustments are further limited to those high altitude states that have implemented inspection and maintenance programs in their nonattainment areas. After the 1984 model year, all light-duty vehicles and engines must comply with EPA emission standards at all the altitudes at which they are sold.

Imported and Exported Vehicles

Individuals and manufacturers are prohibited from importing nonconforming vehicles or engines. A new motor vehicle or engine offered for importation and imported in violation of emission control regulations will be refused admission to the United States. The final determination of the admission of imported vehicles or engines may be deferred, and delivery may be allowed upon terms and conditions which EPA and the Department of Treasury by joint regulation determine to be appropriate for insuring that the vehicles or engines will conform with emission control requirements.

A new motor vehicle or engine intended solely for export and so labeled or tagged for that purpose on the outside of the container and on the vehicle or engine itself is subject to emission control standards, certificate of conformity, and warranties. There is an exception if the importing country has emission standards that differ from EPA's standards, in which case the vehicle or engine must comply with the importing country's standards.

Research Exemptions from Motor Vehicle and Engine Requirements

EPA may exempt any new motor vehicle or engine from the emission control standards, certificate of conformity, and warranties for the purpose of research, investigations, studies, demonstrations, or training, or for reasons of national security.

Effect on State and Local Laws

The federal law explicitly preempts states from enforcing emission standards for new motor vehicles. The states are prohibited from adopting regulations for the control of emissions from new motor vehicles or engines and from requiring approval of emission control measures as a condition to the initial sale, titling, or registration of the vehicle or engine.

There is an exception to federal preemption that applies only to California. The Clean Air Act directs EPA to waive the preemption for any state that has adopted standards, other than crankcase emission standards, for the control of emissions from new motor vehicles or engines prior to March 30, 1966, if such a state determines that these standards are in the aggregate at least as protective of public health and welfare as EPA standards. Since California was the only state with pre–1966 emission standards, it was the only state eligible for the waiver, as was intended.

States or political subdivisions are expressly forbidden and thus preempted from adopting or enforcing parts testing, inspection, or certification programs, except California if it has obtained a waiver.

States and political subdivisions retain the right to otherwise control, regulate, or restrict the use, operation, or movement of registered or licensed motor vehicles.

States are required to develop and maintain emission inspection and testing programs. EPA is authorized is make grants to these state programs.

Tampering with Emission Control Devices

It is unlawful to remove or tamper with emission control devices by anyone, including manufacturers, dealers, repair establishments, leasing operations, or motor vehicle fleet operators.

EPA may exempt vehicles manufactured before the 1974 model year and permit modifications to emission control devices in order to allow use of fuels other than those used in EPA certification testing, provided the automobile maker applicant establishes that the modification will not result in the vehicle or engine violating emission control standards.

A person in the business of repairing, servicing, selling, leasing, or trading motor vehicles or engines or operating a fleet of motor vehicles who tampers with emission control devices is subject to a civil penalty up to $2,500.

Penalties

A civil penalty up to $10,000 may be assessed for violations of emission standards, certificates of conformity, and the information and inspection requirements of the Clean Air Act. Since a nonconforming vehicle constitutes a separate offense, the maximum penalty is $10,000 for each nonconforming vehicle. A person in the business of repairing, servicing, selling, leasing, or trading motor vehicles or engines or operating a fleet of motor vehicles who tampers with air pollution control devices is subject to a civil penalty of up to $2,500. Jurisdiction to restrain violations of provisions of the law relating to motor vehicles or engines is in federal district court.

FUEL AND FUEL ADDITIVE REGULATION

Registration, Testing, and Information Requirements

Any fuel or fuel additive not identified by EPA as suitable for sale by manufacturers or processors may not be introduced into commerce unless EPA has registered the fuel or additive. Before registering a fuel or fuel additive, EPA must require the manufacturer to provide information concerning the commercial name and the name of the manufacturer of any additive contained in the fuel, the concentration range of the additive, and the purpose of the additive. In addition, EPA must require the manufacturer of any additive to notify the agency of the additive's chemical composition. If the manufacturer complies with the requirements of the law regarding the submission of required information, including assurances that EPA will be provided with information concerning changes in the fuel or additive, EPA is to register the fuel or additive.

For the purpose of registration, EPA may require the manufacturer to conduct tests on the fuel or fuel additive to determine its effects on public health, including whether the fuel or additive causes cancer, birth defects, or genetic damage. EPA may also require the manufacturer to provide a description of analytical techniques used to detect and measure any additive in the fuel as well as the recommended range of concentration and purpose of the additive in the fuel. EPA is authorized to require automobile manufacturers to provide information on emissions from automobiles using a particular fuel or additive or the effect of such use on the performance of an emission device or system. EPA may also require other information that may be reasonable and necessary to determine the emissions resulting from the use of the fuel or additive, or their effect on the emission control performance of vehicles.

EPA is required to promulgate regulations for testing and information gathering in connection with the registration of fuel and additives. Any tests required must be conducted in conformance with test procedures established by EPA, and the results of the tests are not considered confidential. EPA may exempt any small business from testing or information requirements or defer or modify the fuel additive regulations for any small business. EPA may exempt any person from testing with respect to a particular fuel or additive if EPA finds this testing would duplicate existing tests.

EPA may provide for cost sharing for fuel or additive testing when the fuel or additive is manufactured or processed by two or more persons, or may provide for their shared testing responsibility to avoid duplication.

Control or Prohibition of Fuels or Fuel Additives

Before a fuel or fuel additive may be regulated, it must be registered. The function of the registration process is information gathering. On the basis of this information, EPA is authorized to issue regulations to control or prohibit the sale of any fuel or fuel additive for use in a motor vehicle or engine if in EPA's judgment the emission products of the fuel or fuel additive are a danger to public health or welfare or if the emission products will impair to a significant degree the performance of any emission control device or system.

EPA's control or prohibition of any fuel or fuel additive is to be based on all relevant medical and scientific data available to it, including consideration of other technologically or economically feasible means of achieving emission standards. EPA cannot control or prohibit a fuel or fuel additive until available scientific and economic data are considered, including a cost-benefit analysis comparing the proposed control measure or prohibition with emission control devices or systems that are or will be in general use. Before prohibiting any fuel or fuel additive, EPA is required to find, and publish the finding, that the prohibition will not cause the use of a replacement fuel or additive producing emissions that will endanger the public health or welfare to the same or greater degree as the prohibited use.

There is a prohibition against the use of gasoline additives in concentrations that impair the effectiveness of emission control systems that have been certified. A strict limit of 0.0625 grams per gallon of gasoline is placed on manganese added to fuel.

EPA may waive any prohibition, except the statutory manganese limit, if it determines that an applicant has established that a particular fuel or additive will not impair an emission control device or system to meet emission standards during the useful life of the vehicle or engine.

No EPA determination regarding the prohibition or control of a fuel or fuel additive, or a waiver of this kind of regulation, can be stayed by any court pending judicial review of this determination.

For the purpose of gathering evidence and data for the control or prohibition of fuel and additives that endanger public health or welfare or impair emission control devices, EPA has the power to subpoena information developed by the manufacturer of the automobile or engine.

Lead Additives

Lead additives in gasoline are controlled. Prior to 1982 EPA was prohibited from reducing the lead content of the gasoline pool of small refineries below specified levels in the act. Since October 1, 1982, EPA has been allowed to reduce lead content of gasoline refined by small refineries including banning lead.

Penalties

A penalty of up to $10,000 is provided for a violation of the fuel or fuel additive regulations for each day of the violation. The penalty may be remitted or mitigated by EPA upon application by the offending party.

Effect on State or Local Laws

The federal fuel regulations preempt state or local controls, unless these controls are identical with those established by EPA. States or local political subdivisions are prohibited from regulating fuel or fuel additives if EPA has found that no control or prohibition is necessary.

The Clean Air Act provides that states with a waiver from regulation of new motor vehicles or engines may establish controls or prohibitions on fuel and additives. This means California, since it is the only state eligible for the waiver. In addition, a state with an EPA-approved SIP that contains provisions on fuel or additive regulation may regulate fuel and additives. EPA is authorized to approve these SIP provisions only if it finds that the state control or prohibition is necessary to achieve national ambient air quality standards.

AIRCRAFT EMISSIONS

The 1970 amendments directed EPA to begin a study and investigation of aircraft emissions on air quality to determine the effect and the technological feasibility of controlling the emissions.

EPA is authorized to issue aircraft emission standards. EPA's regulations are to be developed in consultation with the Department of Transportation, which enforces the aircraft emission standards. Aircraft emission standards issued by EPA may be postponed from taking effect by EPA for the period it determines is needed to develop the requisite technology to achieve compliance, giving appropriate consideration to the cost of compliance during this period.

The president is authorized to disapprove any aircraft emission standards on the basis of a finding by the Department of Transportation that these standards would create a hazard to aircraft safety.

No state or political subdivision may adopt or enforce any aircraft emission standard unless the standard is identical to the federal standard.

OZONE PROTECTION

After a wide range of studies and reports to Congress, EPA has been authorized to establish regulations to control substances, practices, processes, or activities that may reasonably be anticipated to affect the stratosphere, especially ozone in the stratosphere, if EPA reasonably anticipates there may be a danger to public health or welfare. EPA regulations must take into account the feasibility and costs of achieving control.

EPA regulations with regard to protecting the stratosphere may exempt products for medical use which EPA determines have no suitable substitute.

The Clean Air Act provisions on ozone protection do not alter or affect EPA's authority under the act relating to emergency powers or aircraft emission standards or any other provisions of the act. The authority of other federal agencies or departments is unaffected.

States are not preempted from regulating substances, practices, processes, or activities to protect the stratosphere or ozone in the stratosphere except where there are federal regulations, in which case the state or a political subdivision must adopt identical regulations. There is no preemption, however, even where there are federal regulations, in the case of controls on the use of halocarbons as propellants in aerosol spray containers.

3 Toxic Substances Control Act (15 U.S.C. §§ 2601 et. seq.)

ENFORCEMENT
   Unlawful Acts
   Administrative and Criminal Penalties
   Federal Civil Suits and Seizure Actions
   Imminent Hazard Seizure
CITIZEN SUITS
CITIZEN PETITIONS
EMPLOYEE SAFEGUARDS
   Employee Protection
   Employment Effects
EPA ANNUAL TSCA REPORT

GENERALLY

The primary purpose of the Toxic Substances Control Act (TSCA) is to regulate chemical substances that present a hazard to human health or the environment. Among its most important features is its authorization of control over chemicals that pose unreasonable risks to human health or the environment. TSCA greatly expanded federal regulation of chemicals when it was first enacted in 1976. It is intended to control chemical hazards at their source before they can be released into society and the environment to do damage. TSCA performs its objectives by creating new requirements for testing, reporting, and recordkeeping in relation to chemicals.

The key definition in TSCA is "chemical substance" which the act defines to mean any organic or inorganic substance of a particular molecular identity, including any combination of such substances occurring in whole or in part as a result of a chemical reaction or occurring in nature, and any element or uncombined radical. Because of this definition, the major provisions for testing, premarket notification, and recordkeeping in TSCA apply not only to pure chemical substances but also to the impurities of materials, incidental reaction products, contaminants, co-products, and trace materials. Substances that are defined as chemical mixtures are sometimes regulated less strictly than chemical substances for the key requirements of testing, premarket notification, and recordkeeping. TSCA defines a mixture as an artificial combination or two or more substances not resulting from a chemical reaction.

ADMINISTRATION OF TSCA

EPA administers and enforces TSCA. TSCA created the position within EPA of the assistant administrator for toxic substances to take lead responsibility for administering TSCA programs in EPA. TSCA also required EPA to establish an office within EPA to provide technical and other nonfinancial assistance to manufacturers and processors of chemicals.

The regulatory authority given EPA to control chemicals is broad. Any action which EPA takes against a particular chemical substance or mixture can be taken against the category of chemicals to which the substance or mixture belongs.

TESTING OF CHEMICAL SUBSTANCES AND MIXTURES

Generally

The major TSCA provisions for testing are contained in Section 4 of the act. There are two circumstances in which EPA may order testing and the gathering of data by manufacturers of chemical substances or mixtures, and both require as a precondition that there be insufficient information to properly evaluate the substance or the mixture. One circumstance under which EPA is to require testing is when it finds that the possibility of manufacture, processing, distribution, or disposal may pose an unreasonable risk of injury to human health or the environment. The second circumstance under which EPA is to require testing is if it determines that there may be production of the chemical in substantial quantities and either it enters or possibly may enter the environment in substantial quantities or there is or may be significant or substantial human exposure.

TSCA does not require EPA to order the testing of every chemical. Instead, EPA is to order testing of a chemical that is believed to pose an unreasonable risk to human health or the environment or that creates extensive exposure of people or the environment, but only where there is insufficient information to assess the chemical. Testing may also be required for chemical mixtures, but only if testing cannot be achieved more reasonably and efficiently by tests of the individual constituents of the mixture.

EPA is required to publish notice of the data it has received and to make the data available to the public, subject to the confidentiality requirements of TSCA. EPA may impose a filing fee of no more than $2,500 for test data submitted under TSCA to defray its administrative costs. A filing fee limit of $100 is provided for small companies.

Testing Rules and Standards

When EPA determines that there are insufficient data to predict the effects of a chemical substance or mixture that may be hazardous, it must publish a proposed rule requiring testing. After public comments and hearings on the proposed hazardous substance rule, EPA is to publish a final testing rule establishing standards for developing test data and a reasonable time period for submitting the test results to EPA. EPA may also require the submission of preliminary data during the test submission period. The manufacturer or processor must perform any testing required by a testing rule. The agency must review its test standards for adequacy at least once a year and revise them if necessary.

The testing rule may include health and environmental standards for the development of test data which may require testing for toxicity, persistence, and other health and environmental effects, including causing cancer, genetic damage, birth defects, behavioral disorders, cumulative or synergistic effects, and any other effect that may present an unreasonable risk of injury to health or the environment.

The methodologies that may be employed in EPA's testing standards can include epidemiological studies, serial or hierarchical tests, in vitro tests, and whole animal tests. Tests on a substance's epidemiological effects on employees may also be required, but EPA must confer with the National Institute for Occupational Safety and Health before requiring them.

Once EPA requires testing by a rule to determine the safety and effects of a chemical substance or mixture, the manufacturer or processor of the chemical, must develop test data on the chemical and submit them to EPA. The test requirement is also to apply to those manufacturers and processors who distribute or plan to distribute the chemical. The chemical testing may also be done by any qualified outside party, provided that at least two of the three parties required to test, for example, the manufacturer or processor, designate the third party to conduct the testing. This outside party accumulates the data and submits the results to EPA.

An EPA testing rule will expire five years from its effective date, or as otherwise prescribed by EPA. Testing rules are to be made public. EPA must give interested parties an opportunity to submit comments on the testing rules, either orally or in writing. Transcripts are to be made of any oral presentation. EPA is to publish the rule and test data findings together.

A chemical manufacturer or processor who intends to produce a new chemical substance or mixture for which no testing rule has been issued may request EPA to propose test standards. This kind of petition can only be made if the chemical maker or processor is not subject to test data and submission requirements under the act. EPA has 60 days to grant or deny the petition. If granted, EPA must issue standards within 75 days or publish the causes for denial in the Federal Register.

EPA is required to publish notice of the testing data which it has received from a manufacturer or processor of the chemical, and to make the data available to the public, subject to the confidentiality requirements of TSCA.

A filing fee of no more than $2,500 may be imposed by EPA for test data submitted under TSCA to defray its administrative costs. A filing fee limit of $100 is provided for small companies.

Exemption from Testing Requirements: Reimbursement for Testing Done Previously by Others

Persons required to conduct testing and to submit the testing data under an EPA testing rule may apply to the agency for an exemption by claiming that data are being developed or have been previously submitted which are equivalent to or duplicate the data required. If an exemption is requested on the basis that another person is already developing test data and EPA determines that the testing requirements are not being met, it may cancel all related exemptions by written notice after opportunity for a hearing.

If EPA determines that duplication of testing exists and grants the exemption, the party granted the exemption must agree with the chemical firm that developed the data to fairly share the costs with them, as well as other applicants who had previously obtained an exemption and been required to contribute prior reimbursements. EPA will set an amount for "fair and equitable" reimbursement if the parties cannot agree on a cost-sharing arrangement.

In determining a reasonable reimbursement amount, EPA after consultation with the Justice Department and the Federal Trade Commission, must consider all relevant factors, including the effect of the reimbursing party's competitive position in the market relative to the party being reimbursed, and the market share which the chemical substance or mixture represents for the reimbursing party relative to the reimbursed party.

The reimbursement period during which one may be reimbursed for the costs of required testing for which another has received an exemption is the period beginning on the day the data are submitted to EPA and ending five years later or at the end of a period which EPA determines to be sufficient for the development of the testing data.

EPA decisions on reimbursement orders are considered final agency actions for purposes of judicial review.

Chemical Testing Priority List

The act established a federal interagency committee of eight officials whose agencies have scientific or regulatory responsibilities to compile a priority list of chemicals for which testing is considered necessary. The committee must list the substances in the order which it thinks EPA should issue testing rules.

In making its determination on the priority ranking of chemicals for testing, the committee must consider the following factors: (1) the quantities in which the chemical substance or mixture is or will be manufactured, and the amount in which it will enter the environment; (2) the number of humans who are or will be exposed to the substance or mixture in their workplaces, the duration of the exposure, and the extent of human exposure; (3) the extent to which the substance or mixture relates to a chemical known to pose an unreasonable risk of injury to human health or the environment; (5) the extent to which testing of the chemical will result in the development of data on which the chemical's effects on human health or the environment can be determined or predicted; and (6) the reasonably foreseeable availability of testing facilities and personnel for performance of tests on the chemical.

In formulating the list, the committee is to give priority to those substances suspected of causing cancer, mutations, or birth defects. No more than 50 substances or mixtures may be listed for a designated 12-month period, and the committee must revise the list every 6 months. Within 12 months after a chemical is listed, EPA must either initiate testing rules for it or publish in the Federal Register its reasons for not taking action.

PREMARKET NOTIFICATION

Generally

With certain exceptions, TSCA requires manufacturers and processors of chemicals to provide advance notice of the manufacturing or processing of any new chemical substance or any chemical substance that is being put to a significant new use. Section 5 of TSCA contains most of the requirements for this kind of premarket notification. TSCA authorizes EPA to impose delays or restrictions on the making of a chemical substance for which a premarket notification is required if there is inadequate information to evaluate the health or environmental effects of the substance and if, in the absence of such information, the substance may cause or significantly contribute to an unreasonable risk to health or the environment.

EPA is required to publish an inventory list of chemicals known to be made in the country. If the chemical is not listed, it is to be regulated as a new chemical and its planned production must be reported to EPA by a premarket notification.

TSCA requires manufacturers of new chemical substances and manufacturers and processors of chemicals to be put in significant new uses to notify EPA 90 days in advance of commercial production. EPA may extend the notice period for an additional 90 days. No later than five days after EPA receives a premarket notification of a new chemical or significant new use, EPA is to publish a notice in the Federal Register identifying the chemical substance, its uses or intended uses, and describing tests and testing data. A generic identification of the substance in the EPA notice is sufficient unless EPA determines that a more specific identification is in the public interest.

At the beginning of each month, EPA is to publish a list in the Federal Register of all substances for which premarket notification has been received and the substances for which the notification period has expired and has not expired.

EPA determines what constitutes a new use. In determining whether the use of a chemical is a significant new use, EPA is to consider the following factors: (1) the projected volume of manufacturing and processing of the chemical; (2) the extent to which a use changes the type or form of human and environmental exposure to the substance; (3) the extent to which a use increases the magnitude and duration of human exposure; and (4) the reasonably anticipated manner and methods of manufacturing, processing, distribution, and disposal of the chemical substance.

The premarket notification to EPA is to contain the following information: (1) the chemical's common or trade name, chemical identity, and molecular structure; (2) the chemical's use or proposed use category; (3)

reasonable estimates of the total amount of each substance or mixture to be manufactured or processed, the amount manufactured or processed for each category of use, and reasonable estimates of the amounts manufactured or processed for each category of use; (4) a description of the byproducts from the manufacture, processing, use, or disposal of each substance or mixture; (5) all existing environmental and health data on the substance or mixture; (6) reasonable estimates of the people exposed to such a substance or mixture in their place of work and the duration of that exposure; (7) the manner and method of disposal of the substance or mixture; (8) test data which the manufacturer, processor, or distributor possesses on the effects of the substance or mixture on the environment from manufacturing, processing, and disposal and its effects on health; and (9) a description of any other data concerning the environmental or health effects of the chemical.

If a person is required to submit premarket notification to EPA for the manufacture of a new chemical or for a significant new use chemical, and the person is also required to submit Section 4 hazardous substance testing data to EPA, then both the test data and premarket notification may be submitted to EPA at the same time.

EPA may, by rulemaking, compile a list of suspect substances which, in manufacture, processing, distribution, use or disposal, may create an unreasonable risk of injury to health or the environment. In classifying a substance as an unreasonable risk, EPA must consider its effects on health, the degree of exposure to the substance, its effects on the environment, and the degree of environmental exposure. If no testing rules have been issued for a substance on the unreasonable risk chemical list, then the chemical firm must, in addition to submitting premarket notification, also submit test results that the new chemical or significant new use will not present an unreasonable risk in order to make, process, distribute, use, or dispose of the chemical. All the test data submitted to EPA in support of a claim that there is no unreasonable risk is to be made available to the public, subject to the confidentiality requirements of federal law.

When a person is required to submit premarket notification for a new chemical or significant new use, but has been exempted from testing requirements by EPA before submission of the notice is required, the manufacturing or processing of the chemical cannot begin until the expiration of the 90-day notice period. Parties, who are subject to premarket notification but who are not required to submit test data, must submit information showing that an unreasonable risk of injury to health or the environment will not be presented by the new chemical or significant new use in question in order to make, process, distribute, or dispose of the chemical. This information is to be made available to the public, subject to the confidentiality requirements of federal law.

Regulation of a Chemical Subject to Premarket Notification by Orders to Protect Against Unreasonable Risks, Substantial Production, or Substantial Human Exposure Caused by the Chemical, Pending Data Development

If EPA determines from a premarket notification that it has insufficient information on which to make a safety judgment and the substance might present an unreasonable risk to health or the environment or will be produced in substantial quantities, or may result in substantial human exposure, then the agency may propose an order to restrict or prohibit the manufacture, processing, marketing, use, or disposal of the chemical.

The proposed order must be issued at least 45 days before the expiration of the premarket notification period. The proposed order may not be issued unless EPA has already notified the manufacturer in writing of the determination which is the basis for the proposed order. The proposed order will take effect when the premarket notification period has expired unless the manufacturer of the chemical files an objection within 30 days of receiving notice of the proposed order.

If an objection is made to a proposed order, the order does not take effect and EPA must request an immediate injunction in federal district court against the manufacturer, processing, distribution, use, or disposal of the chemical unless the objections filed with EPA convince it that an injunction is unnecessary. To get an injunction, EPA must demonstrate to the court the presence of the same factors that led the agency to propose a ban or limitations on manufacture, processing, distribution, use, or disposal. The federal district court may also issue a temporary restraining order if the court finds that the premarket notification period will expire before an injunction action can be completed. A federal injunction remains in effect until EPA has received sufficient information to evaluate the effects of the substance. The injunction will be dissolved on a petition by EPA. However, if EPA has classified the chemical as a hazardous substance to be restricted under Section 6(a) of TSCA, then the injunction will remain in place until the issuance of the Section 6(a) hazardous substance rule by EPA.

Protection Against Unreasonable Risks for a Chemical Subject to Premarket Notification Prior to Issuance of a Section 6(a) Hazardous Substance Rule

If EPA finds that the manufacturing or processing of a chemical requiring premarket notification may pose an unreasonable risk to health or the environment before a hazardous substance rule can be promulgated to protect against the risk, EPA may undertake several actions before the expiration of the premarket notification period: (1) impose a limit on the amount of the chemical which may be manufactured, processed, or distributed in commerce; (2) impose any requirement or combination of requirements restricting or prohibiting a hazardous substance under a Section 6(a) hazardous substance rule of TSCA; (3) issue a proposed order prohibiting the manufacturing, processing, or distribution in commerce of the substance, effective at the end of the premarket notification period; or (4) apply for an injunction to the federal district court to prohibit the manufacture, processing, or distribution of the substance.

Both a court injunction and an EPA proposed order are subject to the same terms mentioned in the previous section for orders and injunctions relating to the regulation of a chemical substance pending data development. If an objection is filed to an EPA proposed order to ban a toxic substance, EPA must seek an injunction against the chemical unless it determines that the objection is correct that the chemical will not pose an unreasonable risk of injury to health or the environment.

Statement of Reasons for Not Taking Action to Control or Prohibit a Chemical Subject to Premarket Notification

If EPA has not initiated any action to prohibit or limit the manufacture, processing, distribution, use, or disposal of a chemical that is subject to premarket notification requirements prior to the expiration of the premarket notification period, EPA must publish its reasons for not acting in the Federal Register before the end of this notice period.

Exemptions from Premarket Notification

Mixtures are exempt from the premarket notification provisions of TSCA, since they only refer to chemical substances.

For test marketing purposes, a manufacturer or processor of a chemical may apply to EPA for an exemption to premarket notification and testing by showing that a test product will not present an unreasonable risk to health or the environment. EPA may impose restrictions on any test market exemption it grants.

Premarket notification and test data requirements are not required for chemicals manufactured or processed for scientific experimentation or analysis or for chemical research or analysis, including research and analysis for product development. This exemption will not be allowed unless all the persons involved in the experiment, research, or analysis are notified of the risk to health which the manufacture, processor, or EPA has reason to believe may be associated with the chemical substance.

EPA may grant an exemption from any of the premarket notification and testing requirements to a manufacturer of a new chemical substance upon a satisfactory showing that the manufacturer, processing, disposal, or distribution of the substance will not present an unreasonable risk to health or the environment.

EPA may also grant an exemption from the premarket notification and test data submission requirements for a substance that exists temporarily because of a chemical reaction in the manufacturing or processing of another chemical substance or mixture, and for which there will be no human or environmental exposure.

As described in a previous section, parties subject to premarket notification, but not required to submit test data, must submit data showing there is no unreasonable risk of injury to health or the environment in order to make, process, use, distribute, or dispose of the chemical. If EPA determines that a chemical subject to this data submission requirement is equivalent to one for which data have already been submitted and additional data would be duplicative, EPA may grant an exemption from this data submission requirement and require reimbursement to the original data developers by the party benefiting from their earlier data development.

SECTION 6 HAZARDOUS SUBSTANCE RESTRICTIONS

Section 6(a) Hazardous Substance Rule

EPA has the authority under Section 6 to regulate chemical substances and mixtures to protect against unreasonable risks to health or the environment.

When EPA determines that the manufacture, processing, distribution, disposal, or use of a chemical substance or mixture will present an unreasonable risk to health or the environment, it is empowered to issue a rule that can employ a wide variety of control measures to protect against the hazardous chemical. Such a rule to protect against hazardous substances is commonly known as a Section 6(a) hazardous substance rule, referring to the TSCA provision authorizing these requirements.

In a Section 6(a) hazardous substance rule, EPA may apply one or more of the following control measures, and must use that measure(s) which is the least burdensome in the situation: (1) prohibit or limit the manufacture, processing, or distribution of a chemical substance or mixture; (2) prohibit or limit the manufacture, processing, or distribution of a substance or mixture for a particular use, or for a particular use in a concentration above a level imposed by EPA; (3) require that the chemical (or any article containing it) be marked with or accompanied by clear and adequate warnings and instructions for its use, distribution, or disposal, or any combination of these activities; (4) require manufacturers and processors to establish and maintain records of the processes used to make or process the chemical, and require them to monitor or conduct tests to assure compliance with an EPA rule; (5) prohibit or otherwise regulate the manner or method of commercial use of the chemical; (6) prohibit or regulate the disposal of the chemical or any article containing the chemical, and require the parties disposing of the chemical or article to inform any local government affected; and (7) require manufacturers and processors to notify distributors and others in possession of or exposed to the substance of its hazardousness, to give public notice of the risk of injury, and to replace or repurchase the chemical at the option of the manufacturer or processor.

Quality Control Requirements

EPA has the authority to regulate quality control procedures used in manufacturing or processing chemical substances or mixtures.

EPA can require descriptions of quality control procedures followed in manufacturing or processing when it has a reasonable basis to believe that a chemical is being manufactured or processed in a manner that unintentionally causes the substance or mixture to present an unreasonable risk of injury to health or the environment. If EPA determines that the quality control measures reported by the manufacturer or processor are inadequate to prevent the risk of harm by a chemical, EPA can require that the procedures be changed to correct the inadequacy. In addition, if EPA determines that the quality control procedure has resulted in the distribution of a chemical that is a risk to health or the environment, EPA can require the manufacturer to give notice of the risk to processors, distributors, and others in possession of or exposed to the chemical, to provide public notice of the hazard, and to replace or repurchase the chemical to the extent necessary to protect health or the environment.

Promulgation of Hazardous Substance Rules

When promulgating a rule imposing a control measure for a chemical to protect against an unreasonable risk, EPA is to publish a statement on the chemical's effects on health and the magnitude of human exposure, the effects on the environment and the magnitude of environmental exposure, the benefits of the chemical for various uses and the availability of substitutes, and the reasonably ascertainable economic consequences of the rule, taking into consideration the effect on the national economy, small business, technological innovation, environment, and public health.

If EPA determines that a risk of injury to health or the environment could be eliminated or reduced by action under another federal law administered wholly or partially by EPA, then EPA may not promulgate a Section 6(a) hazardous substance rule to protect against a chemical risk, with the exception where EPA finds it is in the public interest to protect against the risk by such a rule. In deciding whether to proceed with a Section 6(a) hazardous substance rule, EPA must consider all relevant aspects of the risk, compare the estimated costs of compliance under TSCA as opposed to other applicable federal statutes, and consider the relative efficiency of action under TSCA compared to these other statutes.

EPA is to publish notice of a proposed Section 6(a) hazardous substance rulemaking; state the particular reason for the proposed rulemaking; allow public submissions and examination of comments, data, and arguments; provide an opportunity for an informal hearing; promulgate, if appropriate, a final rule based on the rulemaking record; and publish with the rule a finding of unreasonable risk of injury to health or the environment.

The informal hearings for rulemaking conducted by EPA are to allow interested parties to present their position orally or by written submission, or in both forms. If EPA determines that there are disputed issues that must be resolved, interested parties can also present rebuttal submissions and conduct such cross-examination which EPA determines is appropriate and necessary.

EPA can make rules and issue rulings on procedures in an informal hearing to avoid unnecessary costs or delay. These rules and rulings may impose time limits on the presentations and submissions by interested parties and may require that any cross-examination to which an interested party may be entitled may be conducted by EPA.

If a group of persons with common interests cannot agree at an informal hearing on a single representative to conduct their cross-examination, EPA may limit their representation and the manner in which cross-examination is conducted. A person who has been unable to agree on group representation with other interested parties may be allowed to conduct a cross-examination by showing EPA that a good faith effort was made toward agreement on a representative and that the group representative does not adequately represent all substantial and relevant issues.

EPA may provide compensation for reasonable attorney's fees, expert witness fees, and other costs of participating in the Section 6(a) hazardous substance rulemaking to any person who represents an interest that would substantially contribute to a fair determination of the issues to be resolved in the proceeding. In order to be entitled to compensation, the person's economic interest must be smaller than the actual costs of that person's participation in the proceeding, or the person must prove to EPA that he or she does not have adequate resources to participate in the proceeding without compensation.

In determining whether compensation will be paid to a party for participating in rulemaking proceedings, EPA is to consider the financial burden incurred by the interested person in participating in the proceedings. EPA must ensure that the total compensation paid in a fiscal year to persons receiving compensation for any one Section 6(a) hazardous substance rulemaking does not exceed 25 percent of the total compensation paid to all persons in that fiscal year.

A Section 6(a) hazardous substance rule must specifically state its effective date, and that date must be as soon as feasible. Ordinarily, the effective date is several months after EPA has proposed the rule. However, EPA may also make a rule effective immediately upon its publication as a proposed rule in the Federal Register until final action is taken on the rule. EPA may make a proposed rule immediately effective only when it has determined that the manufacture, processing, distribution, or disposal of the chemical poses an unreasonable risk of serious or widespread injury to health or the environment before the final action on the rule becomes effective and that making the proposed rule immediately effective in the meantime is necessary to protect the public interest. If the immediately effective proposed rule seeks to ban a chemical substance or mixture, a federal court must have first granted an injunction declaring it an imminent hazard.

When a proposed rule is made immediately effective upon publication in the Federal Register, EPA must notify interested persons of the action, allow a reasonable opportunity for a public hearing on the rule, and either promulgate or revoke the rule. If a hearing is requested, it must be commenced within five days of the request date, unless a later date is agreed on. EPA must take final action on the immediately effective proposed rule within ten days of the completion of the hearing by either promulgating the rule or revoking it.

PCB RESTRICTIONS AND RULES

By July 1, 1977, EPA was to establish rules governing the disposal of polychlorinated biphenyls (PCBs). By this date EPA rules were to require all PCBs to be marked with clear and adequate warnings and instructions with respect to their processing, distribution in commerce, use, and disposal.

By January 1, 1978, PCBs could not be produced or used except in a totally enclosed system, unless specifically authorized by an EPA rule that finds an exempted activity will not present an unreasonable risk of injury to health or the environment.

An exemption is allowed for the PCB production ban if a manufacturer upon petition leads EPA to find that no unreasonable risk of injury to health or the environment would result and good faith efforts have been made to develop a PCB substitute that does not pose an unreasonable risk.

The processing or distribution of PCBs in commerce has been prohibited since July 1, 1979. However, the ban on PCB distribution does not apply to any PCB sold for the purpose of resale prior to July 1, 1979.

The PCB provisions in TSCA do not limit the authority of EPA and TSCA, or any other federal law, to take action regarding any PCB.

REPORTING AND RECORDKEEPING

Generally

EPA is required to promulgate regulations for reports and recordkeeping by manufacturers and processors of commercial chemicals. EPA is also required to compile, keep updated, and publish a list of all chemicals manufactured or processed in the United States.

The reporting rules that must be adopted by EPA differ for large and small manufacturers and processors, with processors subject to considerably less extensive requirements. Standards for determining who qualifies as small manufacturers and processors are set by EPA after consultation with the Small Business Administration.

Reporting—Large Manufacturers

Large manufacturers and processors of chemicals are to maintain records and submit reports that are required by EPA. When these large chemical makers and processors utilize small quantities of chemicals for research, they are required to maintain records and submit reports only to the extent to which EPA determines it is necessary for effective enforcement of TSCA.

EPA may require records and reports to include these items: (1) common or trade name, chemical identity, and molecular structure; (2) categories or proposed categories of use; (3) the total amount manufactured or processed, reasonable estimates of the total amount manufactured or processed for each category of use, and reasonable estimates of the amount to be manufactured or processed for each category or proposed category; (4) a description of the byproducts resulting from manufacture, processing, use, or disposal; (5) all existing data concerning environmental and health effects; (6) the number of individuals exposed to the chemical, and reasonable estimates of the number who will be exposed, in their places of employment and the duration of the exposure; (7) in the initial report, the manner or method of disposing of chemicals, and in any subsequent report, any change in such manner or method.

Reporting—Small Manufacturers

EPA recordkeeping and reporting rules do not apply to small manufacturers and processors, but EPA may establish regulations requiring them to submit information which the agency needs to compile and publish the first chemical inventory. EPA may also require information from small chemical makers and processors who have been granted relief pursuant to the premarket notification or the imminent hazard provisions of TSCA. EPA may by rule require a small chemical maker or processor to maintain records and submit reports for chemicals that are subject to the Section 4 testing rules, listed as a suspect substance under Section 5(b) (4), subject to rules or orders issued pending the development of data for a chemical subject to premarket notification, or subject to Section 6 hazardous substance restrictions.

Records of Adverse Health and Environmental Reactions

Recordkeeping requirements apply to all chemical makers, processors, and distributors, whether large or small. They are required to keep records of significant adverse reactions to health or the environment alleged to be caused by a chemical for five years. Records of significant adverse reactions to employees must be maintained for 30 years. The records on adverse reactions to health and environment are to include records of consumer allegations of personal injury or harm to health, reports of occupational disease or injury, and reports or complaints of injury to the environment submitted by any source to the chemical maker, processor, or distributor. On EPA request all these records on health and environmental reactions must be made available for inspection, and copies must be submitted to EPA.

Notice of Substantial Health or Environmental Risks

Any chemical maker, processor, or distributor is required to inform EPA immediately when it obtains information that the chemical presents a substantial risk to human health or the environment. The exception to the requirement is actual knowledge that EPA has been adequately informed of the substantial risk.

National Chemical Inventory

EPA is required to compile and keep an up-to-date inventory of chemicals made or processed in the United States. The list of chemical substances is to include all substances contained in reports sent to EPA. EPA may exempt chemicals made or processed in small amounts for research or product development. A substance not on the list is considered a new chemical substance, and is subject to the premarket notification requirement before production begins.

Health and Safety Studies

EPA is to issue rules requiring the submission of lists and copies of health and safety studies by chemical makers, processors, and distributors. The health and safety studies to be submitted include those conducted or initiated by the chemical maker, processor, or distributor, or those known to or reasonably ascertainable by them. EPA may exclude types of studies from submission requirements which the agency finds are unnecessary to carry out the purposes of TSCA.

RESEARCH AND USE OF INFORMATION

EPA Research, Data Gathering, and Monitoring

EPA can conduct such research, data gathering, and monitoring as is necessary to carry out the purposes of TSCA. In carrying out these responsibilities, EPA must consult and cooperate with other federal agencies.

EPA is to establish, administer, and be responsible for an interagency committee whose purpose is to design, establish, and coordinate an efficient and effective system for collection, dissemination to other federal departments and agencies, and use of data submitted to EPA.

Another data system is to be developed by EPA, in consultation with other federal departments and agencies, for the retrieval of toxicological and other scientific data that could be useful in carrying out TSCA.

EPA must establish research programs to develop and improve the fundamental scientific basis of screening and monitoring techniques for chemical substances.

A system for the exchange of research and development results among federal, state, and local authorities is to be established and coordinated by EPA. This system is to include a system to facilitate and promote the development of a standard data format and analysis and consistent testing procedures.

Confidentiality and Disclosure of Information

Privileged and confidential information, including trade secrets and commercial or financial data, reported to or acquired by EPA cannot be disclosed by EPA except under four circumstances: (1) disclosure is to a federal official requiring the information in connection with official duties under any law to protect health or the environment or for specific law enforcement purposes; (2) disclosure is to a contractor with the federal government and its employees when EPA determines that the disclosure is necessary for the satisfactory performance by the contractor of work in connection with TSCA; (3) disclosure is to the public if EPA determines that it is necessary to protect health or the environment against an unreasonable risk of injury to health or the environment; or (4) disclosure of the information is relevant for any proceeding under the act, except that the disclosure is to be made in such a manner as to preserve confidentiality to the extent practicable without impairing the proceeding.

The disclosure prohibition does not apply to any health or safety study that pertains to (1) any chemical which, on the date it is to be disclosed, has been distributed commercially or (2) any chemical substance for which hazardous substance testing is required under Section 4 of TSCA or for which premarket notification is required. However, information from a study which may be released is not to include data on processes used in the manufacturing or processing of a chemical substance or mixture, or in the case of a mixture, the release of data disclosing the portion of the mixture made by any of the chemical substances in that mixture.

If a request is made to EPA for information that it is not prohibited from releasing, the request cannot be denied on the grounds that the information is confidential or prohibited.

In submitting data under TSCA, a manufacturer, processor, or distributor may designate the information which it believes is entitled to confidential treatment and is to submit this information or material separately from other data submitted under the act. The request for confidential treatment is to be made in writing and in the manner prescribed by EPA.

If EPA proposes to release information designated as confidential, it must notify the party that submitted the data of its intent to release the data. If the release of information requested is made pursuant to the federal Administrative Procedure Act, notice must be given immediately upon approval of the request and the information cannot be released until 30 days after receipt of the notice. Notice is not required for information disclosable to a federal employee, by a contractor, or in a proceeding under TSCA. When the information is needed to protect against an unreasonable risk of injury to health or the environment, notice must be given the person submitting the information within 15 days before the release, except where EPA determines that the release of the information is necessary to protect against an imminent unreasonable risk of injury to health or the environment. In the case of an imminent unreasonable risk, notice must be given by the means EPA determines will provide notice at least 24 hours before release of the information.

Criminal Penalty for Wrongful Disclosure

Any present or former official or employee of the federal government who discloses information whose revelation is prohibited to a person not entitled to receive it is guilty of a misdemeanor and may be fined up to $5,000 or imprisoned for more than one year, or both. A contractor with the federal government given otherwise nondisclosable information is to be treated like a federal employee if he or she discloses information to any person not entitled to receive it.

Congressional Access to Information

A duly authorized committee of Congress is entitled to any information reported to or acquired by EPA.

EXPORTS AND IMPORTS

Generally

Imported chemicals are subject to all the requirements of TSCA. Exports, with some exceptions, are not.

Export Restrictions

Chemical substances, mixtures, or articles that have been manufactured, processed, or distributed in commerce for export from the United States and bear an export stamp are not generally subject to TSCA. Exported chemicals, however, are not exempted from TSCA's reporting and record-keeping requirements. Moreover, the export exemption is lost for chemicals designated for export which EPA finds will pose an unreasonable risk of injury to health or the environment in the United States. EPA may require testing of the chemical under Section 4 of TSCA to determine whether it poses an unreasonable risk to health or the environment.

A person exporting or intending to export a chemical that is subject to testing requirements under TSCA's provisions for testing rules or premarket notification must notify EPA of the exporting activity. The same requirement of notification to EPA applies to an exported chemical for which EPA proposes regulatory action under TSCA. EPA must notify the foreign government in the country receiving the chemical of the regulatory action against it.

Import Restrictions

The Treasury Department, after consultation with EPA, is responsible for promulgating the regulations governing the entry of chemicals into the United States.

TSCA directs the Treasury Department to prevent entry into the United States of any chemical substance, mixture, or article that does not comply with TSCA's provisions or rules or orders issued under the statute.

If entry is denied, the Treasury Department is to notify the consignee of the denial. The Treasury Department is to release the chemical to the consignee but will either dispose of the chemical or store it if it has not been exported by the consignee within 90 days of receiving the notice of refusal of entry. An exception is allowed for releasing the chemical to the consignee when, pending review by EPA of entry refusal, the consignee posts a bond equal to the full invoice amount and the duty on the chemical. The consignee or owner of the chemical must pay all charges for storage, transportation, and labor or for disposal of the chemical refused entry. Default on payment of the charges constitutes a lien against any future importation of chemicals by the defaulting owner or consignee.

JUDICIAL REVIEW

Generally

A petition for judicial review of a rule issued by EPA must be filed within 60 days in a federal court of appeals in the case of a rule for testing requirements, notification of a significant new use, listing of any unreasonable risk chemicals, restriction or prohibition on a chemical, regarding PCBs or reporting or recordkeeping. The judicial review petition must be filed with the District of Columbia Court of Appeals or the court of appeals for the federal circuit where the petitioner resides or has his or her principal place of business. Exclusive jurisdiction for judicial review of these rules is vested in the federal court of appeals; consequently, federal judicial review cannot occur in the federal district courts. The federal courts of appeals also have exclusive jurisdiction for judicial review of quality control revision orders and public notification orders.

In a suit for judicial review of a rule, either the petitioner or EPA can request the court to permit additional oral submissions or written presentations. The federal court may order additional oral submissions and written presentations if the party can show that additional matters would be material and that there were reasonable grounds for it and the failure to present it in the rulemaking proceedings before EPA. It is up to EPA then to modify or set aside the rule under review in light of the additional submissions and to file the new or modified rule with the additional submissions. The court is then to review the new or modified rule.

Rulemaking Record

Judicial review focuses on the rulemaking record. The rulemaking record is to include: (1) the rule presently under judicial review; (2) in the case of a Section 4 testing rule, the finding of an unreasonable risk injury to health or the environment which the chemical subject to testing presents; (3) in the case of placing a chemical on the unreasonable risk chemical list, the finding of unreasonable risk of injury to human health or the environment caused by the chemical; (4) in the case of a Section 6(a) restriction or prohibition on a hazardous chemical substance, the finding of an unreasonable risk of injury to health or the environment and a statement of the extent and magnitude of effects on humans and environment and benefits and economic effects; (5) in the case of a polychlorinated biphenyl rule, the finding of qualification for an exemption from a PCB ban: (6) any required transcript of oral presentations made in rule promulgation proceedings; (7) any written submission by interested parties relative to the promulgation of the rule; and (8) any other information which EPA considers relevant in rulemaking and which it has identified in the Federal Register notice published prior to the rule.

Standard of Review

Upon the filing of a petition for judicial review of a rule, the court acquires jurisdiction to grant any appropriate relief, including interim relief, and to review the rule. The court must hold unlawful and set aside a rule not supported by substantial evidence in the rulemaking record regarded as a whole. For review of a Section 6(a) hazardous substance rule restricting or prohibiting a chemical because it poses an unreasonable risk, the court must find the rule unlawful and set aside the rule, if it finds that EPA's denial or limitation of a person's privilege to conduct a cross-examination or present rebuttal submissions or oral views precluded disclosure of disputed materials that were necessary to the fair determination of the rulemaking proceeding taken as a whole. Federal courts are barred from reviewing the contents or adequacy of any required statement of EPA regarding the health, environmental, beneficial, or economic effects or any statement of basis or purpose required by federal law to be incorporated in the rule by EPA.

The judgment of a federal court of appeals under the judicial review provisions is final and reviewable only by the U.S. Supreme Court. Both the courts of appeals and the Supreme Court may awarded costs and reasonable fees for attorneys and expert witnesses.

RELATIONSHIP TO STATE AND FEDERAL LAWS

Relationship to Other Federal Laws

TSCA addresses the relationship between EPA's administration of TSCA and different laws that EPA and other federal agencies administer and enforce to control hazardous substances.

If EPA determines that a chemical posing an unreasonable risk of injury to health or the environment can be better prevented or controlled under a law administered by another federal agency, EPA must submit a report to that agency describing the risk and the activities that create the risk. EPA's report must request the other federal agency to determine whether or not it can undertake effective action to prevent or reduce the chemical risk under its legal authority and whether or not it will take such action and issue an order on the matter and a response to EPA on the subject. The other federal agency receiving a request from EPA to utilize its legal authority for controlling the chemical risk must make a determination, issue the requested order, and respond to EPA within the time specified by the report, but in no event less than 90 days.

If EPA notifies and makes a report to another agency concerning a chemical risk and the other agency declares by an order that the chemical does not present the risk described in the report or does not initiate within 90 days actions to protect against the risk, EPA may initiate action by issuing a Section 6 hazardous substance rule or by utilizing the imminent hazard measures under Section 7. If EPA has initiated an action by way of a TSCA hazardous substance rule or imminent hazard order for a chemical that was a subject of an EPA report to another agency requesting action, the other agency is required for the purposes of avoiding duplication of federal action to consult with EPA before taking action under other laws to protect against the chemical risk.

If a chemical risk arises under a law administered by EPA other than TSCA, EPA is to determine whether the law or TSCA allows the most effective action. EPA is to resort to TSCA if it finds the public interest is served by taking action under TSCA. TSCA is expressly to be construed as not relieving EPA of any requirement imposed on the agency by other federal laws.

TSCA clearly indicates that the authority of EPA under the act is not to be construed as a limitation on the authority established under the Occupational Safety and Health Act of 1970 to regulate occupational safety and health.

Relationship to State Laws and Preemption

TSCA provides two instances in which it preempts state laws. In one instance, if EPA requires Section 4 testing of a chemical, then the states are barred from imposing a similar testing requirement. In the second instance of preemption, state laws and rules are preempted in cases where EPA has rules that involve the control of hazardous substances or that affect manufacturers of toxic substances, except for disposal for toxic substances. This second type of preemption does not apply when a law or regulation from a state or a political subdivision is identical to EPA's, or is promulgated under another federal law, or bars the use of the substance in the state or political subdivision (other than its use in manufacturing or processing of other substances or mixtures).

EPA may exempt a state or local requirement from federal preemption if compliance with this requirement does not cause the manufacturer, processor, or distributor of the chemical or its use to violate federal law. In order to quality for the exemption, the state or local requirement must provide a significantly higher degree of protection from the substance than does the federal requirement and must not place an undue burden on interstate commerce.

NATIONAL DEFENSE WAIVER

If the president determines that a waiver of a provision of TSCA is necessary for national defense, EPA is to waive the measure.

EPA INSPECTIONS AND SUBPOENAS

Inspections

TSCA provides EPA with broad inspection authority. EPA may inspect any establishment, facility, or other premises in which chemicals are manufactured, processed, stored, or held before or after their distribution in commerce. In order for an inspection to be made, written notice must be provided and the inspector must present appropriate credentials. A separate notice must be given for each inspection. However, the initial notice is all that is needed for each entry made during the period covered by the inspection. Inspections must be made with reasonable promptness and be conducted at reasonable limits, and in a reasonable manner.

Inspections can extend to everything on the premises or the conveyances inspected, but not to financial, sales (other than for shipment), pricing, personnel, or research data, unless the nature and extent of this kind of data are described with reasonable specificity in the written notice of inspection.

Subpoenas

EPA has broad subpoena power to require the attendance and testimony of witnesses and the production of documents. In the event of the failure or refusal of any person to obey a subpoena, a federal district court has jurisdiction to order compliance.

ENFORCEMENT

Unlawful Acts

TSCA specifies the actions that are unlawful under the act. These include: (1) noncompliance with a Section 4 testing rule, any premarket notification requirement prescribed by Section 5 or hazardous substance requirement prescribed by Section 6, or any Section 5 or 6 rule or order; (2) commercial use of a chemical with knowledge or having reason to know it was made, processed, or distributed in violation of the act or a rule or order under the act; (3) failure or refusal to establish or maintain records, submit reports, notice, or other information, or permit access or copy of records as required by TSCA or a rule under the act; (4) failure or refusal to permit entry or inspection as required by TSCA.

Administrative and Criminal Penalties

A civil penalty of up to $25,000 for each violation per day is provided for violating TSCA. EPA is authorized to assess a civil penalty administratively. The EPA penalty is assessed by an order made on the record after providing an opportunity for a hearing. Before issuing the order for a civil penalty, EPA is to provide the alleged violator with written notice of the proposed order and to offer an opportunity for a hearing. The request for the hearing must be made within 15 days after the alleged violator receives the EPA notice.

In determining the amount of administrative penalty, EPA is to take into account the notice, circumstances, extent, and gravity of the violation, the alleged violator's ability to pay, the effect on the violator's ability to stay in business, any prior history of violations, degree of culpability, and any other matter which justice may require to be considered. EPA can compromise, modify, and remit, with or without conditions, any penalty which it assesses.

A person on whom EPA has imposed an order assessing an administrative penalty may seek judicial review of the penalty order in the District of Columbia Court of Appeals or in any other circuit where the person resides or transacts business. The petition can be filed only during the 30-day period beginning on the day the EPA issued the assessment order.

The federal government may bring a suit in federal district court to recover an EPA administrative penalty after a final order has been issued and no judicial review petition has been filed, or after judicial review has resulted in a decision for EPA. The penalty will not be subject to a review by the federal district court in a recovery action.

Criminal penalties consisting of a fine of up to $25,000 per day and imprisonment of up to one year, or both, can be imposed on any person who knowingly or willingly performs an unlawful act. These criminal penalties may be in addition to or in place of a civil penalty.

Federal Civil Suits and Seizure Actions

Federal district courts have jurisdiction in civil suits brought by the federal government to enforce TSCA. The district courts have jurisdiction over civil actions to restrain any unlawful act; restrain persons from prohibited acts or violation of orders or rules under premarket notification requirements or hazardous substance control requirements; compel the taking of any action required by TSCA; or direct any manufacturer or processor of a chemical in violation of premarket notification or hazardous substance control requirements to give notice to persons in possession of the chemical, to give public notice of the risk of injury, or to replace or repurchase the chemical.

Any chemical made, processed, or distributed in violation of the act or rule or order under it is subject to seizure or condemnation by a federal district court order issued in an EPA civil suit. Proceedings for seizure or condemnation in federal district court must conform as nearly as possible to proceedings *in rem* in admiralty.

Imminent Hazard Seizure

EPA can institute an action in federal district court to protect the public and the environment from chemical substances and mixtures and any article containing them that present an imminent hazard. This kind of action is available for imminently hazardous chemicals or mixtures that are likely to seriously endanger health or the environment before EPA can initiate a Section 6 hazardous substance rule to restrict or prohibit a hazardous substance.

An imminent hazard action allows EPA to obtain a judicial order to seize the chemical or hazard. Judicial relief is available against any person who manufactures, processes, distributes, or uses or disposes of an imminently hazardous chemical or mixture or any article containing the dangerous materials. An imminent hazard action may be for both seizure of the offending material and relief against parties involved with it.

EPA may bring an imminent hazard action even if EPA has not issued rules for premarket notification, testing requirements, or hazardous substance restrictions or prohibition or a regulatory order against an unreasonable chemical risk. The imminent hazard action can also be initiated despite a pending administrative or judicial proceeding under TSCA.

If an EPA civil seizure action is brought against the manufacturer, processor, or distributor of the chemical or article, then the judicial relief available includes, along with seizure, a mandatory order requiring notification to purchasers known to the defendant, public notice of the risk, the recall, replacement, or repurchase of the chemical or article, or any combination of these remedies. When appropriate, EPA must institute a Section 6 hazardous substance regulation for controlling a hazardous substance either concurrently with the filing of an imminent hazard action or as soon as practicable afterwards.

CITIZEN SUITS

TSCA has a citizen suit provision that allows any person to bring a civil action in federal district court against anyone, including federal agencies and EPA, who is alleged to be in violation of the act. This kind of action is to be brought in the federal district court where the violation occurred or where the defendant resides or has the principal place of business. A citizen suit may be brought against EPA to force it to perform any mandatory act or duty under TSCA. Such a suit is to be brought in the Federal District Court for the District of Columbia or in the federal district court for the district in which the plaintiff lives. Federal district courts have exclusive jurisdiction over all citizen suits.

When two or more citizen suits are instituted, all of which involve the same defendants and the same issues or violations pending in two or more judicial districts, the suits may be consolidated in one judicial district if the defendant applies for the consolidation and the court grants it.

EPA, if not a party already, may intervene in any citizen action as a matter of right. The court may award costs and reasonable fees for attorney and expert witness costs in citizen suits.

The citizen suit provision expressly does not restrict the right of any person under any other statute or under common law to seek enforcement of TSCA, or any rule or order under TSCA, or to seek any other relief that may be available.

TSCA imposes limitations on citizen suits. A sixty-day notice must be given to EPA or the alleged violator before a citizen suit can be commenced against either defendant to restrain a violation of TSCA or a rule or order under TSCA. Sixty-day notice also must be provided to bring a suit against EPA to compel performance of a discretionary duty under TSCA, and the notice is to inform EPA of its failure to perform the duty. In citizen suits against EPA alleging failure to file an imminent hazard action, the action must await the expiration of a 10-day period following the 60-day notice period to EPA. A citizen suit is barred if EPA or the Justice Department has commenced or is diligently prosecuting a suit in a federal court to require compliance with TSCA or a rule or order under it. However, in this situation where a citizen suit is barred, a party is allowed to intervene as a matter of right if the proceeding or civil action instituted by the federal government is begun after the party has given notice of the violation.

CITIZEN PETITIONS

TSCA allows citizens to petition EPA directly to issue, amend, or repeal certain kinds of rules or orders issued under TSCA. EPA may be petitioned to issue, amend, or repeal a chemical testing rule, a hazardous substance regulation, or a reporting and recordkeeping rule; or to issue an order for premarket notification requirements; or to impose hazardous chemical quality control measures. The petition must specify the facts claimed to establish the necessity to issue, amend, or repeal a rule or order under TSCA.

EPA has 90 days to grant or deny the petition after it is filed. If EPA either denies the petition or fails to grant or deny the petition within the

90-day period, the petitioner may file a civil suit in federal district court to compel EPA to initiate the action sought in the citizen petition. The civil action must be filed within 60 days of EPA's denial of the petition or, if EPA does not act on the petition, within 60 days following expiration of the initial 90-day period for EPA action on the petition.

In a civil suit to compel EPA to undertake action because of denial of a citizen petition or failure to act on it, the petitioner is given the opportunity to have the petition considered by the court in a *de novo* proceeding. The *de novo* proceeding is available if the petitioner demonstrates to the court's satisfaction that EPA has insufficient information to permit a reasonable evaluation of the health and environmental effects of the chemical that is subject to a testing rule or a premarket notification order. An additional requirement to obtain a *de novo* proceeding regarding a testing rule or premarket notification order is that the petitioner must show that, because of insufficient information on health and environmental effects, the chemical substance may pose an unreasonable risk to health or the environment, or will or may be produced or enter the environment in substantial quantities, or there may be or is significant exposure to the chemical. In the case of a petition to initiate a proceeding for a hazardous substance rule, a reporting or recordkeeping requirement, or an order concerning hazardous chemical quality control requirements, then the petitioner must show the court that there is a reasonable basis to conclude that the issuance of the rule or order is necessary to protect human health or the environment against an unreasonable risk of injury.

The court is to order EPA to initiate the action requested by a petitioner who makes a satisfactory showing to the court for the granting of the petition. If the court finds that the extent of the risk to health and the environment alleged by the petitioner is less than the extent of risks for which EPA is acting under TSCA, and there are insufficient resources available to EPA to take action sought by the petitioner, the court may allow EPA to defer action or the petitioner's request until such time as the court establishes.

The court may award costs and reasonable fees for attorneys and expert witnesses in citizen petition suits. Finally, the remedies available under the citizen petition provisions are in addition to, not in place of, any other remedies provided by law.

EMPLOYEE SAFEGUARDS

Employee Protection

TSCA protects employees who assist in carrying out the act. The protection of TSCA does not extend to employees who, acting without the direction of their employer or employer's agents, deliberately cause a violation of TSCA. Employers are prohibited from discharging or discriminating against an employee who initiates, participates, or assists in a proceeding or any other action to carry out the provisions of TSCA.

An employee may file a complaint with the Department of Labor for an alleged unlawful discharge or discriminatory action. The complaint must be filed within 30 days of the alleged violation. The Department of Labor must conduct and complete an investigation of the matter within 30 days after the complaint is received. Within 90 days after receiving the complaint, the Department of Labor must issue an order providing relief to the employee or denying the complaint, unless the complaint has been terminated by the Department of Labor on the basis of a settlement entered into by the Department of Labor and the employer. The Department of Labor cannot enter into a settlement terminating a proceeding without the participation and consent of the employee.

If the Department of Labor determines that the employer has acted unlawfully against the employee, it is to order: (1) the persons who committed the violation to abate the violation; (2) reinstatement of the employee to the former position together with compensation (including backpay), terms, conditions, and privileges of employment; (3) compensatory damages; and (4) where appropriate, exemplary damages. If an order is issued by the Department of Labor, it can also assess costs and expenses (including attorney's fees) incurred by the employee in bringing the complaint.

An employee or employer against whom the Department of Labor has issued an order may file for judicial review in a federal circuit court of appeals. The petition for judicial review must be filed within 60 days from the issuance of the Department of Labor's order.

When an employer has failed to comply with an order, the Department of Labor is to file a civil action for enforcement in federal district court.

Employment Effects

EPA is required to continually evaluate the potential effects on employment (including reductions in or loss of employment from threatened plant disclosures) resulting from the issuance of testing rules or orders, premarket notification requirements, or hazardous substance restrictions or prohibitions.

An employee or employee representative may request EPA to conduct an investigation of an actual or threatened discharge or layoff of an employee or of adverse or threatened adverse effects on employment resulting from testing rules or orders, premarket notification requirements, or hazardous substance restrictions or prohibitions. The investigation must be in writing, stating the particular grounds for the request, and must be signed by the employee or employer representative making the request.

If hearings are requested in an investigation request, EPA must conduct a public hearing within 45 days of the hearing request, unless EPA determines that there are no reasonable grounds for the hearing. If the request for a hearing is denied, EPA must notify the person requesting the hearing of the denial and the reasons for the denial, which are also to be published in the Federal Register.

If public hearings are to be held, five days' notice of the hearings must be given to the person requesting the investigation and anyone named in the request. All the employees involved in the investigation request and the employers are required to present information on the threatened or actual employment effects, together with the basis for the information.

At the completion of the investigation, EPA is to make findings of fact and any recommendation which EPA considers appropriate.

The provisions of TSCA regarding employment effects are expressly not to be construed by EPA to amend or repeal any rule or order in effect under TSCA.

EPA ANNUAL TSCA REPORT

Each year EPA is to prepare and submit to the president and to Congress a comprehensive report on the administration of TSCA during the preceding fiscal year. The contents of the annual report are to include: (1) a list of the chemical testing rules during the year of the report and an estimate of the costs incurred during that year by persons required to conduct the tests; (2) the number of premarketing notices received during the year, the number of premarketing notices received during the year for substances subject to testing rules, and a summary of Federal Register statements which explain why EPA has not taken any action on a chemical substance under the hazardous substances or imminent hazard provisions prior to the expiration of a premarket notification processing period; (3) a list of hazardous chemical rules; (4) a list, with a brief statement of issues, of completed or pending judicial actions under TSCA and all administrative penalty actions during the year; (5) a summary of the major problems encountered in administration of the act; and (6) any recommendations for additional legislation which EPA feels necessary to carry out the purposes of TSCA.

4   Safe Drinking Water Act (42 U.S.C. §§ 300f et. seq.)

OVERVIEW

DRINKING WATER REGULATIONS

National Primary Drinking Water Regulations

Establishment of National Primary Drinking Water Regulations

Variances and Exceptions from Primary Drinking Water Standards

Variances

Exemptions

Secondary Drinking Water Regulations

Filtration of Surface Water Supplies

Disinfection by Drinking Water Systems

Administration and Enforcement of Drinking Water Regulations by EPA and the States

OVERVIEW

The Safe Drinking Water Act (SDWA) was first enacted in 1974 and directed EPA to establish regulations to protect drinking water sources. Congress enacted the Safe Drinking Water Act Amendments of 1986 to correct several major shortcomings in the original legislation. Under SDWA, EPA is required to establish drinking water standards for public water supplies for both bacterial and chemical contaminants and to regulate underground injection of contaminants into groundwater sources that are public drinking water supplies.

SDWA provides for two types of drinking water standards. One type is the primary drinking water standard, which is intended to control contaminants for the purpose of protecting human health. The other type is the secondary drinking water standard, which is intended to control contaminants that affect odor or appearance or otherwise adversely affect public welfare. Most simply, the primary drinking water regulations are meant to protect public health, and the secondary drinking water regulations are intended to protect public welfare. The SDWA Amendments of 1986 also established regulatory programs for the filtration and disinfection of public water supplies.

The states are given primary enforcement responsibility for protecting drinking water supplies and implementing EPA regulations, but EPA is provided with backup enforcement authority if a state does not perform its enforcement responsibilities under SDWA.

DRINKING WATER REGULATIONS

National Primary Drinking Water Regulations

Establishment of National Primary Drinking Water Regulations

EPA is directed to establish national primary drinking water regulations for public water systems that specify the maximum levels of contaminants and measures for reducing the contaminants. The primary drinking water regulations are aimed at controlling those contaminants in public water systems that may have an adverse effect on human health.

Primary drinking water regulations cover public water systems. A public water system is defined as a system that provides the public with piped water for human consumption, if the system has at least 15 service connections or regularly serves at least 25 individuals. A public water system includes the collection, treatment, storage, and distribution facilities under control of the operator of the system and used primarily in connection with the system, as well as any collection or pretreatment facilities not under the control of the operator of the system but used primarily in connection with the system.

A public water system is excluded from primary drinking water regulations if it possesses the following four characteristics: (1) it consists only of distribution and storage facilities; (2) it obtains all its water from, but is not owned or operated by, a public water system that is subject to the primary drinking water regulations; (3) it does not sell water to any person; and (4) it is not a passenger carrier in interstate commerce, such as passenger trains or buses.

SDWA as enacted in 1974 specified an overly complicated and time-consuming procedure for EPA to follow in establishing national primary drinking water standards that when added to EPA procrastination resulted in slow progress and long delays in its promulgation of these standards. The original 1974 legislation required EPA first to establish national interim primary drinking water standards, followed by establishing revised national primary drinking water regulations, with these regulations being based on participation by the National Academy of Sciences (NAS) through its role of conducting studies meant to determine maximum drinking water contaminant levels. The maximum drinking water contaminant levels were levels which NAS deemed would protect against known or anticipated adverse human health effects. An assortment of statutory deadlines were established by the original 1974 SDWA provisions for EPA to follow in ultimately setting national primary drinking water regulations. These deadlines were consistently missed, and EPA ended up adopting few national primary drinking water regulations for dangerous drinking water contaminants.

The SDWA Amendments of 1986 streamlined and accelerated the process for establishing national primary drinking water standards. As a beginning, the legislation immediately converted each national interim and revised national primary drinking water regulations that were in existence at the time of the enactment of the SDWA Amendments of 1986 into national primary drinking water regulations. The 1986 amendments also immediately converted maximum contaminant levels published prior to the enactment of the legislation into maximum contaminant-level goals. Under this new legislation, the national primary drinking water standards were thereafter to be set as close to maximum contaminant goals as was feasible. Maximum contaminant-level goals are creations of the SDWA Amendments of 1986. The maximum contaminant-level goals sought to be attained by the primary standards are to be fixed at the levels that do not allow known or anticipated adverse effects of human health and involves an adequate margin of safety protective of human health.

EPA has sole responsibility for establishing national primary drinking water regulations. Whenever EPA proposes a national primary drinking water regulation for a contaminant, it must simultaneously propose a maximum contaminant-level goal. Whenever a national primary drinking water regulation is promulgated for a contaminant EPA must also simultaneously promulgate the maximum contaminant goal for the contaminant. EPA must publish maximum contaminant-level goals and establish national primary drinking water regulations for any contaminant which it determines might adversely affect human health or which is known or anticipated to occur in public water systems.

Prior to the enactment of the SDWA Amendments of 1986, EPA had delayed establishing enforceable national primary drinking water regulations for 82 contaminants for which it had proposed to establish maximum contaminant-level goals and national primary drinking water standards.

The SDWA Amendments established a staggered schedule for EPA's promulgation of maximum contaminant-level goals and national primary drinking water regulations for the list of 82 contaminants for which EPA had long delayed establishing national primary drinking water standards. By no later than June 19, 1987, EPA was to establish maximum contaminant-level goals and national primary drinking water regulations for at least nine contaminants it chose from the list. EPA must set maximum contaminant-level goals and national primary drinking water regulations for no less than 40 more of the listed contaminants by June 19, 1989, and do likewise for the remaining 33 contaminants on the list.

EPA has a limited option to substitute contaminants on the list. Prior to June 19, 1988, EPA can make up to seven substitutions on the contaminant list. EPA, however, can only make a substitution in cases in which it determines that setting standards for the substituted contaminants would provide greater public health protection than setting standards for the contaminants that are bumped from the list by the substitutions. Any contaminant bumped from the EPA statutory list must be included, no later than January 1, 1988, on the priority contaminant list which EPA must establish, as is described below.

EPA must establish a priority list of contaminants known or anticipated to occur in public water systems. The priority list must be updated by EPA every three years after January 1, 1988. EPA's consideration of contaminants to be included on the priority list is to include substances regarded as hazardous under Comprehensive Environmental Response, Compensation, and Liability Act (CERCLA) or regulated as pesticides under the Federal Insecticide, Fungicide, and Rodenticide Act (FIFRA).

EPA is subject to deadlines by which it must propose and set maximum contaminant-level goals and national primary drinking water regulations for priority listed contaminants. No later than January 1, 1991, EPA must propose maximum contaminant-level goals and national primary drinking water regulations for at least 25 contaminants to be included on the first priority list. EPA must establish final maximum contaminant-level goals and national primary drinking water regulations no later than 12 months after it has proposed them. Thus, no later than January 1, 1992, EPA must establish final maximum contaminant-level goals and national primary drinking water standards for at least 25 contaminants on the first priority list.

As noted before, EPA is required to publish maximum contaminant-level goals and to establish national primary drinking water regulations for any contaminant which it determines might adversely affect human health or which is known or anticipated to occur in public water systems. As also noted earlier, whenever EPA proposes a national primary drinking water regulation for a contaminant it must simultaneously propose a maximum contaminant-level goal, and when a primary drinking water regulation is finally promulgated it must likewise be simultaneously accompanied by a maximum contaminant-level goal.

The SDWA Amendments of 1986 tied national primary drinking water regulations to maximum contaminant-level goals, with the regulations meant to attain the goals. The link between the two is the concept of feasibility. National primary drinking water regulations are to be set as close to the maximum contaminant-level goals as is feasible.

In requiring primary drinking water standards to come as close to the maximum contaminant-level goals as feasible, the legislation defines "feasible" to mean with the use of the best technology, treatment techniques, and other means EPA finds are available. The concept of availability requires EPA to take cost into consideration. As a result, EPA's primary drinking water standards can be called "best available technology" standards, which simply means that EPA is required to set national primary drinking water standards as close to the maximum contaminant-level goals as the best available technology allows it. Because cost is a factor in determining availability (and thus feasibility), the criterion of best available technology necessitates technology that is generally affordable, and by negative implication precludes EPA from setting a standard necessitating the use of a technology that is unaffordable since it would not be feasible as that term is used in the legislation. It would perhaps be appropriate to say that the legislation requires EPA to adopt "best affordable technology" standards. Finally, in determining the feasibility of primary drinking water standards to attain maximum contaminant-level goals, EPA is to examine their effectiveness under field conditions and not solely under idealized laboratory conditions.

The specific technology of granular-activated carbon is designated as feasible by the legislation for the control of synthetic organic compounds. Hence, primary drinking water standards could be based on the degree to which granular-activated carbon filters can remove synthetic organic compounds. Any other methods of treatment which EPA might designate as the best available technology or measure for the control of synthetic organic compounds must be at least as effective as granular-activated carbon.

In establishing national primary drinking water standards, EPA cannot generally require a specified kind of technology to comply with a standard.

As described earlier, EPA establishes national primary drinking water standards set at a level that comes as close as feasible to maximum contaminant-level goals, but leaves it up to the public water system to choose itself a particular technology or measure to comply with the EPA standard. While EPA cannot generally impose a technology or control measure, EPA is to list the technology and control measures which it finds to be feasible to reach a primary drinking water standard. There is one situation in which EPA may prescribe a specific treatment technology. EPA may issue a primary drinking water standard that requires a specific treatment technique, rather being based on the feasibility of the degree to which a maximum contaminant level can be attained, in the situation where EPA finds it is not economically or technologically possible to determine the level of the contaminant in the water. Whatever specified technology might be imposed, EPA may grant a variance for it.

EPA has a duty to amend the primary drinking water regulations whenever technology, treatment techniques, and other means permit greater protection of human health. EPA must review primary drinking water regulations every three years.

Variances and Exceptions from Primary Drinking Water Standards

Variances. SDWA allows four major variances from primary drinking water regulations.

The first variance occurs when the characteristics of reasonably available raw water sources make compliance impossible. The variance can be granted by a state with primary enforcement responsibility or by EPA in a state without primary enforcement responsibility. EPA or the state must also find that the variance does not result in an unreasonable risk to health. For such a variance a schedule must be established to bring the water system into eventual compliance.

The second variance is available to a water system that can demonstrate that the quality of the raw water source makes the use of a required treatment technique unnecessary to protect public health. This variance can be granted by either the state with primary enforcement authority or by EPA in a state without primary enforcement responsibility.

Only EPA can grant a third type of variance. This variance is allowed for a treatment technique requirement when the public water system can show that an alternative treatment technique not included in the primary drinking water regulations is at least as efficient in lowering the level of the contaminant for which the requirement applies.

The fourth variance relates to EPA's authority in limited instances to require a specified technology as the means for complying with a national primary drinking water regulation. EPA is authorized to grant a variance from any such specified treatment technology.

Exemptions. States with primary enforcement responsibility or EPA in a state without that responsibility may grant an exemption from primary drinking water regulations upon a finding that due to compelling factors, which may include economic factors, a public water system is unable to comply with a contaminant-level or reduction treatment technique required by the primary drinking water regulation. A system is not eligible for the exemption unless it was in operation prior to the effective date of the regulation. A system that was not in operation prior to the regulation is not eligible for the exemption unless there is no reasonable alternative source of drinking water available to the new system. Finally, an exemption cannot be granted if it will create an unreasonable risk to health. Another requirement is that a schedule of compliance be prescribed at the time the exemption is granted which will bring the system into compliance with the primary drinking water regulations as expeditiously as practicable.

Secondary Drinking Water Regulations

EPA must establish, and from time to time revise, secondary drinking water regulations which EPA determines are necessary to protect public welfare. These regulations are directed at drinking water contaminants which may adversely affect the odor or appearance, or any other aspect of water quality that may affect public welfare. Secondary drinking water regulations may only use maximum contaminant levels as the means of control, and may not impose specific reduction treatment techniques as is the case for national primary drinking water regulations. Furthermore, secondary drinking water regulations are not, unlike primary drinking water regulations, obligated to be feasible when established. Finally, while primary drinking water regulations are uniformly national in coverage, secondary drinking water regulations may vary according to geographic and other circumstances.

Filtration of Surface Water Supplies

By December 19, 1987, EPA must establish criteria for determining which public water systems utilizing surface water supplies would have to be required to filter their water. Within 18 months after establishing these criteria, no later than June 19, 1989, a state with primary enforcement authority must adopt regulations needed to implement a filtration program. Within 12 months of adoption of these regulations, no later than June 19, 1990, the state is to determine which public water systems should have filtration. If the state determines that filtration is required, it must prescribe a schedule for compliance by the public water system with the filtration requirement. The schedule must institute compliance within 18 months after the state or

EPA has determined that the filtration system is required. In other words a public water system can be given up to 18 months to install a filtration system.

In states without primary enforcement authority, EPA takes responsibility for administering and enforcing filtration requirements.

Disinfection by Drinking Water Systems

EPA has until June 19, 1989, to issue primary drinking water regulations for requiring public water systems to disinfect their water, and must simultaneously issue criteria for granting variances from the disinfection requirement.

Administration and Enforcement of Drinking Water Regulations by EPA and the States

Establishment of State Primary Enforcement Authority

EPA and the states share responsibility for enforcing drinking water regulations. EPA initially has the authority to enforce drinking water regulations in any state. A state may obtain primary enforcement responsibility by applying for it to EPA and satisfying criteria specified by the SDWA. Once EPA has determined that the state satisfies the statutory criteria, EPA loses primary enforcement responsibility for the drinking water regulations and it is transferred to the state.

The state must satisfy five statutory criteria in order to obtain primary enforcement authority in place of EPA: (1) the state has adopted drinking water regulations that are no less stringent than EPA's national primary drinking water regulations; (2) the state has adopted adequate procedures for enforcement of the state drinking water regulations, including monitoring and inspection activities which may be required by EPA regulations; (3) the state will maintain records and make reports on drinking water control which may be required by EPA regulations; (4) variances and exemptions which the state may allow for the drinking water regulations are no less stringent than allowed by SDWA; and (5) the state has adopted a plan for providing safe drinking water in an emergency.

Primary Enforcement Authority Retained by EPA or Revoked from a State

There are four circumstances under which EPA may either revoke or bypass primary enforcement authority for a state and reestablish this responsibility for EPA.

The first circumstance is when EPA determines that any of the specific criteria under which the state was granted primary enforcement authority is no longer being satisfied. EPA is required to specify a procedure by which it determines whether the specific criteria for state primary enforcement authority are no longer being met. SDWA specifies that a state has a primary enforcement responsibility only when EPA determines that the specific qualifying criteria are satisfied. Consequently, when EPA finds that a state no longer complies with any of the criteria, EPA may revoke the state primary enforcement responsibility and take the duty over itself.

The second circumstance in which EPA regains enforcement authority is when the state fails to assure adequate enforcement. EPA must first find that a public water system is not complying with federal primary drinking water regulations and has not received a variance or exception for the noncompliance, or that a public water system has been granted a variance or exception but is not complying with the requirements imposed with the variance or exception, in which case EPA is required to notify the state and the public water system of the noncompliance and may also provide advice and technical assistance. SDWA provides for swift federal enforcement when the state has failed to act promptly after it has received notice of noncompliance. If the state has not commenced an appropriate enforcement action within 30 days after EPA's notification of the public water system's noncompliance, EPA must issue an administrative order requiring the public water system to come into compliance, or it must commence a civil action in federal court. Most simply put, EPA is required to take enforcement action when a public water system is in violation for 30 days and the state has not taken enforcement action.

EPA may also provide advice and technical assistance in the case where it finds a public water system is in noncompliance and the state has not engaged in adequate and prompt enforcement. EPA is authorized to hold a public hearing for the purpose of gathering information from experts, public officials, representatives and customers of the public water system, and other interested persons on the ways the system can by the earliest feasible time be brought into compliance and the means to be used for maximum feasible protection of the public health while the system is not in compliance. On the basis of the hearings, EPA is to issue recommendations to the state and the public water system, which are also to be made available to the public and the media.

The third situation in which EPA regains enforcement authority is when EPA enforcement is requested by the governor of the state with the non-complying public water system or the state agency with jurisdiction for enforcing the drinking water regulations. In this case, EPA is not required to wait 60 days to assume enforcement authority. EPA may institute the enforcement action in federal district court.

The fourth situation in which EPA retains enforcement authority is in emergencies. EPA may take immediate action, and need not wait 60 days for state action, when it receives information that a contaminant likely to enter a public water system may present an imminent and substantial danger to public health and the state and local governments have not acted to protect human life or health.

EPA Enforcement of Primary Drinking Water Standards

EPA's authority to undertake enforcement action when a state fails to do so is restricted to noncompliance with national primary drinking water regulations and variances and exception granted for the primary drinking water regulations. EPA does not have enforcement authority for federal secondary drinking water regulations which are not being enforced by an EPA-approved state program.

When EPA has primary enforcement responsibility, then EPA must undertake enforcement action for violation of primary drinking water regulations or violations of requirements imposed with a variance or exception to a primary drinking water standard. EPA has the choice either to issue an administrative order requiring that the public water system comply or to bring a civil suit in federal court.

When a state with primary enforcement authority has failed to take adequate enforcement action or request EPA to undertake enforcement, EPA may bring a suit in federal district court for enforcement in the case of violations of national primary drinking water regulations, administrative compliance orders, or variances or exceptions to primary drinking water regulations.

The federal district court in suits brought by EPA can enter orders to protect public health to the extent it considers necessary, taking into consideration the time to comply and the availability of alternative water supplies. If the court determines that there has been a violation, it may impose a civil penalty of up to $25,000 for each day of the violation, taking into account the seriousness of the violation, the population at risk, and other appropriate factors. EPA has the authority to enforce drinking water regulations without going to court. In any case where EPA may bring a civil action in federal court to enforce drinking water requirements, compliance schedules, or other requirements, it may also issue an administrative compliance order. Violation of an administrative compliance order subjects the violator to a civil penalty of up to $25,000 per day.

When a contaminant threatening a public water system poses an imminent and substantial danger to public health, EPA is not limited to instituting a civil action in federal district court. EPA emergency enforcement choices include, but are not limited to, issuing immediate administrative compliance orders as may be necessary to protect the users of the system, as well as bringing civil action for relief, including a restraining order or injunction. An EPA administrative order may require those causing the endangerment to provide alternative water supplies. Civil penalties for emergency enforcement actions brought in federal district courts are limited to willful violation of EPA orders, and the courts can impose a fine of up to $5,000 for each day the violation occurs or continues.

Enforcement of Secondary Drinking Water Standards

EPA's authority to undertake enforcement authority when the state fails to do so is restricted to noncompliance with national primary drinking water regulations and variances and exceptions granted from the primary drinking water regulations. Secondary drinking water regulations are not federally enforceable but are guidelines for the states which represent reasonable standards for drinking water quality. EPA is to notify the state, and is required to do no more, when it finds that one or more public water systems do not comply with secondary drinking water regulations and this noncompliance results from the state's failure to assure compliance.

Public Notification of Drinking Water Violations

SDWA requires that notice be given to the public by public water systems that fail to comply with the major regulatory provisions of the law. The public water system must give notice to its customers if the system fails to comply with a national primary drinking water regulation, to perform monitoring required by EPA, or to comply with a requirement associated with a variance or exemption granted to the water system.

EPA is to promulgate regulations providing for different types and frequencies of notice based on the difference between violations that are intermittent or infrequent and those that are continuous or frequent. Notice of a violation of a maximum contaminant level or any violation designated as posing a serious potential health risk must be given as soon as possible, but cannot be later than 14 days after the violation. Notice of a continuous violation of a regulation other than a maximum contaminant level must be given no less frequently than every three months. Yearly notice at the very least is required for violations that are less serious. EPA can also require that public water systems give notice to their customers of contaminant levels of unregulated contaminants which EPA nevertheless requires to be monitored under SDWA. A violation of the public notice requirement is subject to a civil penalty of up to $25,000.

LEAD-FREE WATER PROTECTION

SDWA prohibits lead-containing pipe, solder, or flux in public water systems or in plumbing of residential or nonresidential facilities that provide water for human consumption and are connected to a public water system. The restriction does not apply to leaded joints that are necessary for the repair of cast iron pipes. Federal Housing Administration and Veterans Administration mortgages cannot be made available to newly constructed houses that do not comply with the lead-free restrictions for plumbing. Public water systems with customers who may be at risk because of lead in the drinking water have to provide notification to these customers. The notice must provide a clear and readily understandable notification of potential sources of lead in the drinking water, potentially adverse effects, reasonably available methods of mitigating the lead contamination, steps the system is undertaking to mitigate the lead problem, and the necessity, if any, of seeking alternative water supplies.

Enforcement of the lead-free protection requirements of SDWA is put in the hands of the states. The states must establish a proper enforcement program no later than June 19, 1988, and its enforcement program may be implemented by state or local plumbing codes, or other appropriate means. If a state fails to enforce the lead-free program, EPA may withhold up to 5 percent of the federal grants available for public water systems in the state.

UNDERGROUND INJECTION CONTROL

Generally

SDWA establishes a regulatory program to protect underground sources of drinking water. EPA is directed to issue regulations for state underground injection control programs to prevent underground injection of contaminating fluids that endanger drinking water sources. States are allowed to secure primary enforcement responsibility for underground injection control regulations with EPA approval.

The underground injection that endangers a drinking water source and that is to be regulated is injection that may result in the contamination of groundwater that will adversely affect public health or result in the water system's failure to comply with any national primary drinking water regulation. The term *underground injection* is defined in SDWA as the subsurface emplacement of fluids by well injection, but does not include natural gas injection for the purpose of storage.

State Primary Enforcement Responsibility

Primary enforcement responsibility is extended to states for underground injection control programs. EPA is to list the states which it determines need an underground injection control program to protect drinking water sources. Each state designated by EPA has the opportunity to develop an underground injection control program that conforms to EPA's regulations.

If EPA approves a state's underground injection control program, the state acquires primary enforcement responsibility for underground water sources, until EPA determines that the state's program does not conform with the federal regulations.

The regulations issued by EPA for adoption by state programs must contain minimum requirements to prevent underground injection which endangers drinking water sources. The regulations require that in order to be granted primary enforcement responsibility, a state must do the following: (1) prohibit all underground injection which is not authorized by state rules or regulations; (2) require authorization either by rule or permit for any underground injection but not allow injection that endangers drinking water sources; (3) include inspection, monitoring, recordkeeping and reporting requirements; and (4) apply state regulation to underground injection by federal agencies. The federal regulations are prohibited from prescribing any requirement that will interfere with the injection of fluids to recover oil or gas, unless the requirement is essential for protecting underground sources of drinking water.

EPA's regulations for state programs must allow for consideration of varying geological, hydrological, or historical conditions in different states and in different areas within a state. EPA regulations are not to unnecessarily disrupt existing state underground injection control programs as long as the state programs assure that underground injection will not endanger underground sources of drinking water. An unnecessary disruption is considered to be a situation in which it is infeasible to comply with both EPA's regulations and the existing state underground injection control program.

Any state that develops an EPA-approved underground injection control program acquires primary enforcement responsibility for regulation underground drinking water sources. EPA is to create an underground injection control program and to take over primary enforcement responsibility in a state that does not develop an approved program or that has lost a previously approved program because it no longer complies with EPA requirements.

Protection of Sole Source Acquifers

SDWA provides for EPA's interim control of underground injection in a sole source acquifer area until a fully developed state control program is in effect.

SDWA allows any person to petition EPA to designate an area that is a sole source acquifer in which no new underground injection may occur without an EPA permit until an underground injection control program governing the area has been approved by EPA. EPA may grant this designation if it finds that the area has one acquifer that is the sole or principal drinking water source for the area and that if contaminated by underground injection would create a significant public health hazard. If the area is designated as a sole source acquifer area, no commitment of federal grants, contracts, or loan guarantees may be used in support of any underground injection system that may contaminate the area's sole acquifer through a recharge zone if the system poses a significant hazard to public health.

Until an underground injection program covering a protected sole source acquifer area is approved by EPA, all permit applications for new underground injection must be resubmitted to EPA. After notice and opportunity for an agency hearing, EPA may issue a permit if it finds that the underground injection will not result in contamination of the acquifer that is a significant hazard to public health. If a permit is granted, EPA may impose any control measure in the permit which it regards as appropriate to prevent the creation of a significant health hazard.

Anyone who operates an unauthorized underground injection system in an area designated for interim protection is subject to a civil penalty of up to $5,000 for each day the violation occurs, unless the violation is willful, in which case a penalty of up to $10,000 per day is allowed. EPA may seek injunctive relief in federal district court to enforce interim control of sole source acquifers against any violator.

The SDWA Amendments of 1986 established a demonstration program that would allow any state, municipal, or local government or appropriate governmental planning entity to protect critical acquifer areas. In order to be eligible for protection, the area must have been designated as a sole source acquifer under SDWA prior to June 19, 1988. EPA must establish criteria by June 19, 1987, for identifying critical acquifer protection areas. In order to be eligible for a demonstration program and grants for it, a governmental body must meet the requirements that it direct the applicant to outline of the boundaries of the critical area, designate a planning agency to develop a comprehensive plan for the area, establish procedures to include public participation in the planning process, conduct a hydrogeological assessment of the area, include a comprehensive management plan for the proposed protection area, and indicate the measures and schedule for carrying out the plan.

EPA has 120 days to approve or disapprove of an application. EPA may provide a matching grant of up to 50 percent to governmental bodies to carry out approved plans, but no more than $4 million can be provided for a single acquifer during a fiscal year.

Wellhead Protection

SDWA directs the states to adopt wellhead protection programs. A wellhead protection area is defined as the surface and subsurface area surrounding a water well or wellfield that supplies a public water system through which contaminants are reasonably likely to move and reach.

States have until June 19, 1989, to adopt and submit to EPA a plan to protect wellhead areas from contaminants that would adversely affect human health in order to obtain EPA grants. The state must make every reasonable effort to implement its wellhead area protection program within two years after submitting it to EPA.

Enforcement

Whenever EPA finds a violation of the underground injection regulations in a state with an approved program, it must notify the state and the person violating the requirement. EPA must take enforcement action in cases where the violation extends beyond 30 days after the notification and the state has not taken adequate enforcement action. EPA can either issue an administrative order requiring compliance or institute a civil suit for injunctive relief or damages.

If EPA discovers a violation in a state in which it and not the state has primary enforcement responsibility, it need not give notice to the state and can immediately issue an administrative compliance order or commence a civil suit in federal district court for injunctive relief or damages. When EPA brings a civil action the federal district court has the latitude to provide whatever relief is necessary to protect public health. The court is empowered to require compliance with any requirement of the underground injection program or an administrative compliance order issued by EPA. For a violation the district court may impose a civil penalty of up to $25,000 daily. If the violation is willful, the court may in lieu of the civil penalty impose a prison term of up to three years, or a criminal fine, or both. For violations relating to other than underground injection for oil and gas production, an EPA administrative order may assess a civil penalty of up to $10,000 daily for any past or current violation, up to a maximum of $125,000. For a violation relating to underground injection for oil and gas production, an EPA administrative order may assess a civil penalty of up to $5,000 daily, up to a maximum of $125,000.

RECORDKEEPING, MONITORING, AND INSPECTIONS

EPA may establish regulations that require parties regulated by SDWA to keep and maintain records, make reports, conduct monitoring, and provide other information which EPA considers necessary.

SDWA requires monitoring by public water systems for unregulated contaminants. EPA is required to establish regulations governing the monitoring of unregulated contaminants. The agency may vary the frequency and schedule of monitoring for public water systems based on the number of persons served, the source of supply, and the contaminants likely to be found. However, each system is required to monitor at least once every five years. EPA monitoring regulations must include a list of unregulated contaminants to be monitored by public water systems. States can petition EPA to delete or add contaminants from the designated list through a show cause procedure. States may also delete contaminants to be monitored for an individual water system in accordance with any EPA criteria established to allow it. Public water systems must make their monitoring results available to their customers.

EPA must establish regulations requiring operators of Class I injection wells to undertake monitoring that can provide the earliest possible detection for the migration of injected substances into or in the direction of an underground drinking water source. Class I injection wells are deep wells and are sometimes used to inject hazardous wastes.

Upon the appropriate presentation of credentials and written notice, EPA officials may enter facilities and conduct inspections in order to ensure compliance with SDWA. In states with primary enforcement, EPA may give the state notice of the intended inspections. In determining whether an inspection is appropriate, EPA is to consider the state's showing that a federal inspection will be detrimental to the state's primary enforcement program. However, the state does not have the power to prevent federal inspection if EPA decides it is necessary. The state given notice by EPA of an inspection is prohibited from informing or warning the person whose property is to be inspected. If the state does give such a warning, EPA need not give the state notice of inspection thereafter until such time as the agency determines the state has provided satisfactory assurances that it will no longer give warnings of EPA inspections.

Any person who violates the recordkeeping, inspection, or monitoring requirements is subject to a fine of up to $25,000.

CONFIDENTIAL PROTECTION OF TRADE SECRETS OR SECRET PROCESSES

EPA may protect as confidential and not disclose to the public information that is required under SDWA, upon a satisfactory showing by the person from whom the information is required that to make it public would divulge trade secrets or secret processes. The trade secret or secret process confidentiality protection is not available for disclosure of information to federal government officials who are carrying out SDWA. This protection of confidentiality is also not available to the extent public disclosure is concerned with information on the levels of contaminants in drinking water.

IMMINENT AND SUBSTANTIAL DANGERS

EPA may undertake immediate action when it receives information that a contaminant that is already in or is likely to enter a public water system or an underground source of drinking water may present an imminent and substantial danger to human health and that the state and local governments have not acted to protect human health. EPA is authorized to issue administrative orders (including orders requiring that alternative water supplies be supplied by those causing or contributing to the endangerment) or to bring a civil action for appropriate relief, including a restraining order or permanent or temporary injunction.

Any person who willfully violates or refuses to comply with an order to abate an imminent and substantial danger may be subject to a civil penalty by a federal district court for up to $5,000 for each day the violation occurs.

TAMPERING WITH PUBLIC WATER SUPPLIES

SDWA provides for criminal and civil penalties for tampering with public water systems. Tampering is defined as introducing a contaminant into a public water system or otherwise interfering with the system with the intention of harming people. Tampering with a public water system is punishable by imprisonment for not more than five years or a federal criminal fine. Threatening or attempting to tamper with a public drinking water system is punishable by imprisonment of not more than three years or a federal criminal fine. EPA may bring a civil action in federal district court for actual, threatened, or attempted tampering, and the court may impose a fine of up to $50,000 for actual tampering and up to $20,000 for attempted or threatened tampering.

CITIZEN SUITS

Any person may commence a civil suit against a party alleged to be in violation of an SDWA requirement. Such a citizen suit can also be brought against EPA when it has failed to perform a nondiscretionary duty required by SDWA. Jurisdiction for citizen suits is the federal district court.

A citizen suit cannot be brought for a violation of SDWA until a 60-day notice of intent to sue is given to EPA, the violator, and the state of the violation. The citizen suit is also precluded where EPA, the Justice Department, or the state has commenced and is diligently prosecuting a civil action. However, the citizen may intervene as a matter of right. Furthermore, EPA or the Justice Department may intervene as a matter of right in a citizen suit.

The federal court may award court costs and reasonable fees for attorneys and expert witnesses in the issuance of any final order regarding a citizen's petition. If a temporary restraining order or preliminary injunction is sought, the court may require the posting of a bond or equivalent security.

The remedies available under the citizen suit provisions are in addition to, not precluded by or in lieu of, any other remedies provided by statutory or common law.

JUDICIAL REVIEW

SDWA provides for judicial review of EPA and state determinations or actions made pursuant to the act. For EPA actions regarding the establishment of national primary drinking water regulations, including maximum contaminant-level goals, judicial review is allowed only in the U.S. Court of Appeals for the District of Columbia. Judicial review of other EPA actions pursuant to SDWA is under the jurisdiction of the federal courts of appeals for the appropriate circuit. SDWA provides for judicial review of decisions to grant or deny variances and exceptions, and jurisdiction for those actions is in federal district courts. A decision by EPA to make the substitutions to the contaminants list as allowed by SDWA is not subject to judicial review.

EMPLOYEE SAFEGUARDS

Employers are prohibited from discharging or otherwise discriminating against employees who bring or cause to be brought a proceeding for the administration or enforcement of drinking water regulations or state underground injection control programs, testify or are about to testify in such a proceeding, or assist or participate in or are about to assist or participate in such a proceeding or in any other action to carry out the purpose of SDWA.

Any employee who believes that he or she has been discharged or otherwise discriminated against may, within 30 days after the violation occurs, file a complaint with the Department of Labor. The Department of Labor must conduct an investigation within 30 days after receiving the complaint. Within 90 days after receiving the complaint, the department must issue an order either providing for appropriate relief or denying the complaint. The department need not act within the 90-day period if it and the alleged violator have terminated the proceeding by coming to a settlement. The Department of Labor may not enter into such a settlement without the participation and consent of the complainant. A Department of Labor order is to be made on the record after notice and opportunity for an agency hearing.

Any person adversely affected or aggrieved by an order may obtain judicial review in the federal courts of appeals.

Whenever a person has failed to comply with an order, the Department of Labor may file a civil action to enforce the order in the federal district court in the district in which the violation occurred. The district court can grant all appropriate relief, including but not limited to, injunctive relief and compensatory and punitive damages.

5 Federal Insecticide, Fungicide, and Rodenticide Act (7 U.S.C. §§ 136 et. seq.)

ENFORCEMENT

  Unlawful Acts

  Exemptions from FIFRA Prohibitions

  Notice and Warning of Violations

  Inspections and Seizure Warrants

  Orders for Stop Sale, Use, Removal, and Seizure of Pesticides or Devices

  State Enforcement

PENALTIES

  Civil Penalties

  Criminal Penalties

JUDICIAL JURISDICTION AND REVIEW

  Jurisdiction for Federal Enforcement

  Judicial Review

MISCELLANEOUS EPA AUTHORITY

NATIONAL PESTICIDE MONITORING PLAN

IDENTIFICATION OF PESTS

GENERALLY

The Federal Insecticide, Fungicide, and Rodenticide Act (FIFRA) was originally enacted in 1947 and began the application of significant federal authority to regulate the production, storage, distribution, sale, use, and disposal of pesticides. FIFRA has been amended several times since its 1947 enactment, and the subsequent statutory provisions continue to be commonly referred to as FIFRA. The provisions of the pesticide law are also known as the Federal Environmental Pesticide Control Act, which was enacted in 1972 and amended FIFRA in every major respect. The Federal Environmental Pesticide Control Act of 1972 was in turn amended by the Federal Environmental Pesticide Control Act Amendments of 1978.

When enacted in 1947, FIFRA was primarily a pesticide labeling law. The 1972 legislation went beyond labeling to require the registration of all pesticides, which constituted premarket clearance for the sale of pesticides into public commerce. Registration is now the cornerstone of FIFRA because, in order to approve registration, EPA must find that the pesticide will not adversely affect the environment or people. In making this finding, EPA must determine that the benefits of using the pesticide outweigh the risks associated with its use. EPA can cancel the registration of a pesticide whose widespread and common means of use adversely affects the environment.

FIFRA divides pesticides into two classifications—general use and restricted use by qualified applicators. EPA has the authority to determine whether the continued registration of a pesticide presents an imminent hazard to human health and the option of suspending the registration of such a pesticide. Pesticide manufacturers and retailers are entitled to federal indemnity payments if EPA removes their product from the market as an imminent hazard.

The other major areas covered by FIFRA include provisions for the certification of users of restricted use pesticides, informative and accurate labeling of pesticide products, and enforcement to ensure proper pesticide practices.

STATE RESPONSIBILITIES UNDER FIFRA

State Enforcement

A state is given primary responsibility for the enforcement of pesticide use violations under FIFRA if the state enters into a cooperative agreement with EPA for undertaking this responsibility or meets the statutory requirements for primary enforcement responsibility. EPA retains primary enforcement responsibility when a state has not complied with statutory requirements.

EPA may rescind state primary enforcement responsibility if it determines that the state is not adequately carrying out its enforcement duties or cannot do so because of inadequate legal authority.

State Regulatory and Registration Powers

FIFRA imposes restrictions on the extent to which states can regulate pesticides. States can regulate the sale or use of any federally registered pesticide or device within the state, but only when and to the extent EPA does not prohibit any sale or use of the pesticide. States may provide for the registration for additional uses of EPA registered pesticides within their boundaries to meet local needs, but only when in accord with FIFRA and if the state registered use has not been previously denied, disapproved, or canceled by EPA. This state registration for special local needs is regarded as registration for purposes of FIFRA, but it only authorizes distribution and use within the state and nowhere else. EPA may disapprove a state registration and suspend state authority to register pesticide use for local needs. State registration of a pesticide is barred for use on food or feed unless a tolerance level or exemption has been issued earlier by the Food and Drug Administration under the Federal Food, Drug and Cosmetic Act.

PESTICIDE REGISTRATION

Generally

Unless exempted by FIFRA and unless it has been registered with EPA, no pesticide can be sold or distributed in intrastate or interstate commerce. After receiving an application for registration, EPA must review the data that are submitted. After review of the data submitted with the pesticide registration application, EPA must, as expeditiously as possible, either register the pesticide or notify the registrant that the registration will be denied.

EPA is to register a pesticide if it determines, when considered along with any restrictions that may accompany the classification of the pesticide for general use or restricted use as a result of the registration, that the following factors are satisfied: (1) the composition is such to warrant the proposed claims for it; (2) its labeling and other materials comply with the act; (3) it will perform its intended function without unreasonable risks to people and the environment, taking into account the economic, social, and environmental costs and benefits of the use of the pesticide; and (4) when used in accordance with widespread and commonly recognized practice it will not generally cause unreasonable risk to people and the environment, taking into account the economic, social, and environmental costs and benefits of the use of the pesticides.

Registration of Several Products as a Single Pesticide

The registration requirement applies to any person who distributes, sells, offers for sale, holds for sale, ships, delivers for shipment, or receives and delivers or offers to deliver a pesticide to another person. Products with the same formulation and claims may be registered as a single pesticide when manufactured by the same person, the labeling of which contains the same claims, and the labels of which bear a designation identifying the product as the same pesticide. In the case of such products registered as single pesticides, additional names and labels must be added to the registration by supplemental statements.

Application Statement

An applicant for registration of a pesticide must file with EPA a statement that includes: (1) the name and address of the applicant and of any other person whose name will appear on the labeling; (2) the name of the pesticide; (3) a complete copy of the labeling of the pesticide, a statement of all claims made for the pesticide, and any instructions for its use; (4) the complete formula of the pesticide; (5) a request that the pesticide be classified for general use, for restricted use, or both; and (6) if requested by EPA, a full description of the tests made and their results on which claims are based, which the applicant may cite from public literature or which has been previously submitted to EPA, provided that the exclusive use and data compensation requirements of FIFRA are met.

EPA must publish a notice of the Federal Register if a registration application is for a pesticide that contains any new active ingredient or would entail a changed pattern of use. The notice must provide for a period of 30 days during which time any federal agency or any other interested person may comment.

Data in Support of Registration

Generally

EPA is to publish guidelines specifying the kinds of information or data required to support the registration of a pesticide and to revise the guidelines from time to time.

An applicant must submit any additional data which EPA requests as necessary to support an existing registration of a pesticide.

An applicant who proposes to purchase a registered pesticide from another producer in order to formulate the purchased pesticide into an end-use product need not submit or cite data relating to the safety of the purchased product, but does have to provide data relating to the safety of the end-use product.

EPA may waive data requirements pertaining to the effectiveness of the pesticide in considering an application for registration. If the pesticide is found to be effective by any state in accordance with FIFRA requirements, a presumption is established that EPA should waive the efficacy require-ments for the pesticide's use in this state.

In establishing standards for the registration of pesticides intended for minor uses, EPA must make the standards commensurate with the antici-pated extent of the use, pattern of use, and level and degree of potential exposure of people and the environment to the pesticide. In developing these minor use data requirements, EPA must also consider the economic factors of the potential volume of use, extent of distribution, and the impact of the cost of meeting the requirements on the incentives for any potential registrant to develop the required data.

Use of Another Applicant's Previously Submitted Data

FIFRA allows EPA to consider the data developed and submitted by a previous applicant in support of a new application for registration, but only if either (1) the prior applicant who submitted the data gives permission to the new applicant to use the data, or (2) the new applicant makes a specific offer to pay the prior applicant reasonable compensation for the use of the data and evidence of delivery of the offer is provided to EPA.

Original data on the active ingredients of a pesticide submitted after Sep-tember 30, 1978, either in an application for the initial registration of the pesticide or for a new use registration of the pesticide, cannot be used by another person after such registration without permission of the data's orig-inator. This gives ten years of exclusive use of data to the original registrant after the new chemical is first registered. No one else can use the data in a registration application without the original registrant's permission.

Data submitted from 1970 onwards by an applicant or registrant in support of an application for registration, an experimental use permit, and an amend-ment adding a new use to an existing registration, or to support or maintain an existing registration, may be considered by EPA without the written permission of the original data submitter under certain conditions: when the present applicant uses the data within 15 years after the data are originally submitted and provided the applicant offers to pay compensation. An ap-plicant for registration of a pesticide who proposes to purchase a registered pesticide from another producer in order to use the purchased pesticide to formulate another end-use product is exempt from the requirement that compensation be offered before EPA grants registration. If the present and previous registrants cannot agree on fair compensation, the dispute will be settled by binding arbitration.

A specific offer of compensation must be made directly to the data origin-ator, and this offer of compensation must also be submitted to EPA. The data originator and the subsequent applicant must reach an agreement fixing the amount and terms of compensation or procedures for reaching such an agreement within 90 days of delivery of the applicant's offer of compensation.

If no joint data development arrangement is made within the 90-day period, either party may initiate binding arbitration by requesting the ap-pointment of an arbitrator by the Federal Mediation and Conciliation Ser-vice. The parties to arbitration are to share equally in the payment of the arbitrator's fees and expenses. The findings and determination of the arbi-trator are final and conclusive and may not be appealed further except when there is a fraud, misrepresentation, or misconduct by one of the parties or the arbitrator, and there is a verified complaint with supporting affidavits attesting to specific instances of any of these grounds.

If EPA determines that the original data submitter failed to participate in compensation negotiations or arbitration, or failed to comply with the terms of an agreement or arbitration decision, then the original data submitter forfeits the right of compensation. If the subsequent applicant engages in the same conduct, EPA is to deny the application or cancel the registration of the pesticide without further hearing. Before forfeiting compensation or denying or canceling a registration, EPA must provide the affected person, by certified mail, with notice of intent to take such an action and is to allow the party 15 days to respond.

After expiration of the 10-year exclusive use period or the 15-year com-pensation period, EPA may consider the previously submitted data in sup-port of an application by any other applicant without the permission of the originator of the data and without need to receive a compensation offer from a subsequent applicant.

Additional Data to Support Existing Registration—Shared Data Development

If EPA determines that additional test data are required to maintain an existing pesticide registration, it must notify all existing registrants of that pesticide and provide a list of these registrants to all interested persons. EPA must allow registrants a sufficient amount of time to obtain additional information. Within 90 days after receiving notification, the registrant of the pesticide must indicate that it is taking appropriate steps to secure the additional data.

Two or more registrants are allowed to agree to develop jointly or share the cost of developing the additional data which EPA requires to maintain an existing pesticide registration. The parties agreeing to joint data devel-opment must advise EPA of the intent to engage in this activity within 90 days of being notified by EPA of the need for the additional information.

A registrant who agrees to share the cost of producing data is entitled to examine and rely on the previously submitted data of the other parties in support of the continuance of his or her registration. The additional data submitted in support of an existing registration are subject to the compensation provisions of FIFRA in which subsequent applicants must offer compensation to data originators in order to rely on these data. If the data are submitted jointly by two or more registrants, they must agree on an agent at the time the data are jointly submitted to handle any compensation matters.

Arbitration is provided when the parties engaged in the joint development of data cannot agree. If the registrants cannot agree on the terms of a data development arrangement or on a procedure for reaching an agreement within 60 days of advising EPA of their intent to do so, then any one of the registrants may initiate binding arbitration by requesting appointment of an arbitrator by the Federal Mediation and Conciliation Service. The findings and determination of the arbitrator are final and conclusive and may not be further appealed to federal officials or courts except for fraud, misrepresentation, or misconduct by one of the parties or by the arbitrator, where there is a verified complaint with supporting affidavits attesting to specific instances of any of these kinds of misconduct. The parties to the arbitration are to share equally in the payment of the arbitrator's fees and expenses.

Conditional Registration or Amendment of Registration

EPA may conditionally register a pesticide product under special circumstances when certain data that are required may not have been submitted or comprehensively evaluated by EPA. A conditional registration allows registration when the submission of EPA's review of certain supporting data has been deferred to a future date. A conditional or amended registration may be granted only if EPA determines that the pesticide will not adversely affect the environment.

EPA can conditionally register or amend the registration of a pesticide if it determines that (1) the pesticide and proposed use are identical or substantially similar to any currently registered pesticide and use, or differ only in ways that would not significantly increase the risk of unreasonable adverse environmental impacts, and (2) approving the registration or amendment in the manner proposed by the applicant would not significantly increase the risk of unreasonable adverse environmental impacts.

An applicant seeking conditional or amended registration must submit data that would be sufficient to obtain registration of a similar pesticide. However, if the applicant is unable to submit an item of data because it has not yet been developed, EPA may register or amend the registration of the pesticide with conditions requiring the submission of the missing data no later than the time for submission for such data that are required for similar pesticides already registered under FIFRA.

EPA may conditionally register a pesticide containing an active ingredient not contained in a currently registered pesticide for a period reasonably sufficient to generate and submit the required data. This kind of conditional registration is to be granted on the condition that by the end of the period EPA will receive the data and the data do not meet or exceed EPA's risk criteria, and any other conditions EPA may prescribe. However, this kind of conditional registration will be granted only if EPA determines that the use of the pesticide during the period required to generate and submit data will not cause any unreasonable risk to people and the environment, taking into account costs and benefits, and that the use of the pesticide is in the public interest.

Denial of Registration

After receiving an application for registration, EPA must review the data that are submitted.

After review of the data submitted with the pesticide registration application, EPA must, as expeditiously as possible, either register the pesticide or notify the registrant that the registration will be denied.

If an applicant for a pesticide registration is denied by EPA, the applicant must be notified of this determination, setting forth the reasons and factual basis for it. The applicant has 30 days from the date EPA's notice is received to correct the conditions that were the basis for the denial.

If the corrections are not made in time, EPA may refuse to register the pesticide and must promptly publish notice of the refusal, along with reasons and its factual basis, in the Federal Register. Within 30 days after publication of the notice in the Federal Register, the applicant may seek an EPA hearing and administrative review on the refusal or denial of the registration.

CLASSIFICATION OF PESTICIDES—GENERAL USE OR RESTRICTED USE

As part of the registration process, EPA must determine whether to classify the uses of the pesticide for general or restricted use, or general use for some uses and restricted use for other uses.

EPA will classify a pesticide for general use if it determines that the pesticide will generally not adversely affect the environment when applied in accordance with its directions for use, warnings, and cautions and for the uses for which it is registered, or for one or more such uses, or in accordance with widespread and commonly recognized practice. In determining whether there are adverse environmental impacts, EPA is to examine any unreasonable risk to people and the environment, taking into account the economic, social, and environmental costs and benefits of the use of the pesticide.

EPA will classify a pesticide for restricted use if it determines that the pesticide may generally cause, without additional regulatory restrictions, unreasonable adverse effects on the environment, including injury to the pesticide applicator, even when applied in accordance with directions for the pesticide's use, warnings, and cautions and for the uses for which it is registered, or for one or more such uses, or in accordance with widespread and commonly recognized practice. In sum, a pesticide is classified and regulated for restricted use because of hazards it might pose to applicators, other persons, and the environment.

If EPA determines that some of the uses for which the pesticide is registered should be for general use and that other uses for which it is registered should be for restricted use, it is to classify the pesticide for both general and restricted use. If some of the uses of the pesticide are classified for general use and other uses are classified for restricted use, the directions for its general use must be clearly separated and distinguished from the directions for restricted use. EPA may require that the pesticide's packaging and labeling for restricted uses must be clearly distinguishable from the packaging and labeling for general use.

When a pesticide is classified for restricted use because of hazards to the applicator or other persons, the pesticide can be applied only by, or under the direct supervision of, an EPA certified applicator. Where a pesticide is classified for restricted use because of its unreasonable adverse environmental effects, it can be applied only by, or under the direct supervision of, an EPA certified applicator, or under other restrictions which EPA may impose by regulation. Any such regulation is reviewable by an appropriate federal court of appeals upon petition of a person adversely affected which is filed within 60 days of the publication of the final regulation.

CANCELLATION AND SUSPENSION OF REGISTRATION; CHANGE OF CLASSIFICATION

Five-Year Review of Pesticide Registration

A pesticide registration is reviewed every five years. Registration is cancelled every five years unless continuation of the registration is requested. EPA can re-register the pesticide only if it determines that the pesticide will not cause unreasonable adverse effects to the environment. EPA can approve the continued sale and use of existing stocks of pesticide whose registration has not been renewed, to such an extent, under such conditions, and for such uses that will not unreasonably adversely affect the environment. EPA must publish in the Federal Register, 30 days prior to the end of the five-year period, notice of the impending cancellation in the event there is no request for renewal of the registration.

Cancellation of Registration and Change in Classification

EPA can issue a notice of cancellation for a pesticide registration or change in a pesticide classification, or can hold a hearing to decide whether to do so, if it appears to EPA that the pesticide or its labeling or other material requested to be submitted does not comply with the law, or if it appears that the pesticide generally causes unreasonable adverse effects to the environment when used in accordance with widespread and commonly recognized practice. EPA must consider restricting a pesticide's use as an alternative to cancellation. The agency must consult with the Department of Agriculture before issuing a notice of cancellation or change in classification. Upon receiving notice of the change in classification or cancellation, the registrant can either correct the problem or request a hearing to review the notice.

The notice of cancellation or change in classification must be sent to the registrant, be made public, and state the reasons, including the factual basis for the proposed cancellation or change in classification. The proposed action will not become final and effective until the end of 30 days from the receipt of notice by the registrant, or publication of the notice, whichever is later, unless within that time either the registrant makes the necessary corrections or a request for a hearing is made by a person adversely affected by the notice. The decision of a hearing held by EPA is final.

If EPA determines that it is necessary to change a pesticide classification from general use to restricted use in order to prevent unreasonable adverse effects to the environment, it must notify the registrant of this determination at least 45 days before making the change and must publish the change in the Federal Register. The registrant is entitled to a hearing on the change in classification.

The registrant of any pesticide with one or more uses classified for restricted use may petition EPA to change the classification from restricted use to general use. The petition must demonstrate that the restricted use classification is unnecessary because classification of the pesticide for general use would not cause unreasonable adverse effects to the environment. Within 60 days after receiving the petition, EPA is to notify the registrant as to whether the request for the classification change from restricted to general use has been granted or denied.

Suspension of Existing Registration for Which Additional Data are Required

EPA is allowed to issue a notice of intent to suspend the registration of the pesticide for which additional data are required if the agency determines that the registrant has not taken appropriate steps to obtain the data, has not participated in procedures for reaching an agreement on the joint development of data or in an arbitration proceeding to establish a joint data development arrangement, or has not complied with a joint data development agreement or arbitration decision concerning joint data development. The notice of intent may include provisions on the continued sale and use of any existing stocks of the pesticide.

The suspension becomes final and effective at the end of 30 days from the registrant's receipt of the notice from EPA of intent to suspend, unless the registrant has satisfied EPA that the registrant has complied with the requirements in the notice of intent to suspend, or the person adversely affected by the notice of intent to suspend requests a hearing.

If a hearing is requested, a determination must be made within 75 days after the request. The hearing is to be confined to matters of whether the registrant failed to take the action that served as the basis for the notice of intent to suspend the registration for which additional data are required, and whether EPA's determination as to the disposition of existing stocks of the pesticide is consistent with FIFRA provisions. The decision reached at the hearing is final. A registration suspended for not complying with the additional data requirements of EPA must be reinstated if EPA determines that the registrant has fully complied with the requirements that served as the basis for the suspension.

Imminent Hazard Suspension of Registration

If EPA determines that the continued registration of a pesticide presents an imminent hazard to the environment or human health during the time required for proceedings relating to cancellation or a change of classification, it may order the immediate suspension of the pesticide's registration. For such a suspension, the imminent hazard must be likely to result in unreasonable adverse effects to the environment or involve an unreasonable hazard to the survival of an endangered species.

There are two kind of imminent hazard suspensions under FIFRA—an ordinary suspension that will not take effect until the decision is rendered in an expedited hearing, and an emergency suspension that takes effect immediately and is not postponed until the conclusion of an expedited hearing. No order for an ordinary suspension may be issued unless EPA has issued, or at the same time issues, notice of its intent to cancel the registration or change the classification of the pesticide. The notice of suspension must include EPA findings pertaining to the question of imminent hazard. If such a suspension order is issued, a registrant can request an expedited hearing to review the finding of imminent hazard before a final order of suspension takes effect. If EPA finds that an emergency exists, it can issue a suspension

order immediately, prior to an expedited hearing, which will be in effect
until the decision of the expedited hearing.

Administrative Review of Refusal, Cancellation, or Suspension of Registration and Change of Classification

FIFRA provides for administrative hearings with regard to the refusal,
cancellation, or suspension of the registration of pesticides, and the change
of classification of pesticides. Upon notification of refusal of a registration,
FIFRA makes administrative review available to the applicant or any other
interested person with the concurrence of the applicant. EPA may hold
hearings to determine whether or not to cancel the registration of a pesticide,
or to change its classification, if it appears that the pesticide, or its labeling
or other material required to be submitted, does not comply with FIFRA
or if it appears that the pesticide generally causes unreasonable adverse
effects to the environment even when used in accordance with widespread
and commonly recognized practice.

FIFRA provides for expedited hearings at the request of the registrant
upon the initiation of proceedings to immediately suspend the registration
of a pesticide because it presents an imminent hazard while EPA proceedings
are pending for the cancellation of the registration. The request for an expedited hearing must be filed with EPA within five days of the registrant's
receipt of EPA notice of intention to suspend. If no request for an expedited
hearing concerning a suspension order is submitted within the five-day period, the suspension order may be issued and will be effective and is not
reviewable by a court.

Prohibition of Interim Risk-Benefit Administrative Review of a Pesticide Prior to Action for Cancellation, Suspension, or Denial of Registration

EPA is prohibited from initiating a public interim administrative review
process for the purpose of developing a risk-benefit analysis of the ingredients
of a pesticide or any of its uses prior to taking a formal action to cancel,
suspend, or deny the registration of the pesticide, unless the interim administrative review process is based on a validated test or other significant
evidence raising prudent concerns of unreasonable adverse impacts on the
environment.

Federal Indemnity for Losses Resulting from Cancellation or Suspension of Registration

EPA is to pay an indemnity to any person owning a quantity of pesticide
who experiences losses because of the suspension or cancellation of the

pesticide's registration. EPA does not pay an indemnity to the person who had knowledge of facts that showed the pesticide did not meet registration requirements but nevertheless continued to produce the pesticide without providing EPA with timely notice of these facts.

International Notice of Registration, Cancellation, or Suspension of Registration

When a registration, cancellation, or suspension of a pesticide registration becomes effective, or ceases to be effective, EPA must transmit through the State Department notification, which is to be made available to foreign governments and to appropriate international agencies. The notification must include, upon request, all information related to the cancellation or suspension of the registration of the pesticide and information concerning other pesticides that are registered and that could be used in the place of the registered, cancelled, or suspended pesticide.

Storage or Disposal of Cancelled Pesticides or Pesticide Uses

EPA is required, after consultation with other federal agencies, to establish regulations for the disposal of a pesticide whose registration has been cancelled after having been suspended to prevent an imminent danger if requested by the owner of the pesticide. For any pesticide whose registration is cancelled for posing an imminent hazard, EPA is required, after consultation with other interested federal agencies and when requested by an owner of the pesticide, to establish procedures and regulations for the disposal or storage of pesticide packages and containers and for disposal or storage of pesticide wastes, and to accept at convenient locations for safe disposal any excess quantities of the pesticide. Notification of the cancellation of any pesticide must include specific provisions for the disposal of unused quantities of the cancelled pesticide.

EXPERIMENTAL USE PERMITS

EPA can issue experimental use permits in order to allow an applicant to develop the information necessary to register a pesticide. EPA may also issue an experimental use permit to public or private agricultural research agencies or educational institutions. The permit may be issued for no more than one year, or such other period as EPA may dictate. The pesticide may be used only by the research agency or educational institution for experimentation purposes.

If EPA determines that the use of a pesticide may reasonably be expected to result in residue in food or feed, it may establish a temporary tolerance level for the pesticide residue before issuing the experimental use permit.

EPA must complete the review of an application of an experimental use permit within 120 days of receiving the application and all supporting data, and either must issue the experimental use permit or notify the applicant of a denial and the reasons for it. If the application for an experimental use permit is denied, the applicant may correct it or request a waiver of the conditions of the permit within 30 days of receiving notification of the denial.

When an experimental use permit is issued for a pesticide containing any chemical or combination of chemicals which has not been included in any previously registered pesticide, EPA may require that studies be conducted to determine whether the use of the pesticide under the permit could cause unreasonable adverse effects on the environment. The studies must be submitted to EPA before the pesticide can be registered.

EPA is authorized to supervise the use of a pesticide under an experimental use permit and subject the pesticide use to the terms and conditions it has required for the permit.

EPA may revoke an experimental use permit if it finds that the terms and conditions of the permit are being violated or are inadequate to prevent adverse effects on the environment.

EPA may authorize a state to issue experimental use permits. The criteria for EPA approval of state applicator certification plans apply to state plans establishing a program to issue experimental use permits.

LABELING

A copy of the label for the pesticide must be part of the registration application. Compliance with the labeling requirements of FIFRA is a prerequisite to approval of a registration application by EPA. EPA may require that labeling for restricted uses be clearly distinguishable from labeling from general uses. The registration must be amended if the labeling is changed. Detachment, alteration, defacement, or destruction of labels and misbranding of pesticides or devices are unlawful acts under FIFRA.

CERTIFICATION OF RESTRICTED USE PESTICIDES

Generally

When a pesticide is classified for restricted use because of hazards to the applicator or other persons, the pesticide can be applied only by, or under the supervision of, an EPA certified applicator. Where a pesticide is classified for restricted use because of unreasonable adverse effects on the environment, the pesticide may be subject to any other restrictions which EPA might prescribe by regulation, in addition to the requirement that application be by or under the supervision of an EPA certified applicator. A certified applicator is any individual authorized under EPA standards to use or supervise the use of any pesticide classified for restricted use.

EPA is directed, when establishing or approving standards for licensing or certification, to establish separate standards for commercial and private applicators. Private applicators are certified applicators who use or supervise the use of any pesticide that is classified for restricted use for purposes of producing any agricultural commodity on property which they or their employer own or operate or (if applied without compensation other than the trading of personal services between farmers) on the property of another person. Most simply, farmers and farm workers are private applicators. A private applicator may not be required to take an examination to establish his or her competency in the use of the pesticide. A commercial applicator is an applicator (whether or not a private applicator for some uses) who uses or supervises the use of any pesticide that is classified for restricted use for any purpose or on any property other than for use as a private applicator.

Unless restricted by its labeling, a pesticide is considered to be applied under the direct supervision of a certified applicator if it is applied by a competent person acting under the instructions and control of a certified applicator who is available if and when needed, even though the certified applicator is not personally present at the time and place the pesticide is applied.

In a state where EPA conducts a pesticide applicator certification program, EPA may require persons engaging in the commercial application, sale, or distribution of a pesticide that has been classified for restricted use to maintain records and submit reports concerning these activities in accordance with regulations which EPA might establish. EPA is prohibited from requiring any private applicator to maintain any records or file any reports or other documents.

State Certification Programs

A state may assume responsibility to certify pesticide applicators if EPA has approved a plan for applicator certification. If EPA rejects a state plan, it must provide due notice and opportunity for a hearing to the state beforehand. The state certification program must be conducted in accordance with the plan approved by EPA.

In order to be approved by EPA, a state plan for certification of pesticide applicators, or any modifications to the plan, must meet the following criteria: it must designate a state agency to be responsible for administering the plan; it must be assured that the state agency possesses adequate legal authority, funding, and qualified personnel to carry out the plan; it must require reports to EPA in the form and containing such information as EPA may require from time to time; and it must be satisfied that state standards for the certification of pesticide applicators conform with EPA standards.

EPA may withdraw approval of a state certification program if it is not being administered in accordance with the EPA-approved state plan. EPA must notify the state of its intention to withdraw approval and provide a hearing at the request of the state. If the state does not take appropriate corrective action within a reasonable time, but not later than 90 days, EPA must withdraw approval.

Federal Certification

EPA must administer a certification program in any state that does not have an EPA-approved certification plan. The EPA program must be conducted in consultation with the governor of the state.

Notice and a public hearing are required before implementation of a federal certification program in a state. EPA must publish a summary of the federal plan in the Federal Register for review and comment, and must make copies of the plan available to the state. If within 30 days following EPA's publication of the summarized federal plan, the governor of the state requests a hearing, EPA must hold the hearing within 30 days of this request.

In a state where EPA conducts a certification program, EPA may require persons engaging in the commercial application, sale, or distribution of a pesticide that has been classified for restricted use to maintain records and submit reports concerning these activities in accordance with regulations which EPA might establish. EPA is prohibited from requiring any private applicator to maintain any records or file any reports or other documents.

REGISTRATION OF ESTABLISHMENTS THAT PRODUCE PESTICIDES

FIFRA provides for the registration and inspection of establishments that produce pesticides. These establishments must maintain records as to the types and amount of pesticides produced and the shipping destination of pesticides. EPA is to register any establishment that produces a pesticide or an active ingredient used in producing a pesticide.

The registration application of any establishment must include the name and address of the establishment and of the producer who operates the establishment. Whenever EPA receives an application for registration of an establishment producing pesticides, it must register the establishment and assign it an establishment number.

Any producer operating a registered establishment must inform EPA within 30 days after it is registered of the types and amounts of pesticides and, if applicable, the active ingredients used in producing pesticides which it is actually producing, produced during the past year, and sold or distributed during the past year. Upon EPA request for the purpose of issuing a "stop sale" order under FIFRA, the producer must inform EPA of the name and address of any person receiving a pesticide produced in the registered establishment.

The information submitted to EPA as part of the pesticide establishment registration other than the names of the pesticides or active ingredients used in pesticides produced, sold, or distributed at the establishment must be considered confidential and is subject to the provisions of FIFRA protecting trade secrets, or commercial or financial information.

EPA RULEMAKING

Generally

EPA is authorized to establish regulations to carry out FIFRA. These regulations must take into account the differences between various classes of pesticides, differences in environmental risks for various pesticides, and the appropriate data for evaluating these risks between agricultural and nonagricultural pesticides. Copies of the regulations are to be given to various congressional committees. EPA, before publishing FIFRA regulations, must solicit the views of the secretary of agriculture.

Congressional Veto of Regulations

No rule or regulation under FIFRA may become effective if within 90 days of continuous session after the date of promulgation both houses of Congress adopt a concurrent resolution of disapproval. However, if within 60 calendar days of continuous session after the day of promulgation a committee of either house of Congress has reported or discharged from further consideration a concurrent resolution of disapproval or either house adopts such a concurrent resolution, the rule or regulation cannot go into effect before 90 calendar days of continuous session unless Congress has adopted a joint resolution of disapproval. If within 60 calendar days of continuous session after the date of promulgation no committee of either house has reported or discharged from further consideration of a concurrent resolution of disapproval, the rule or regulation may go into effect immediately.

EXEMPTION FROM FIFRA CONTROL

EPA may exempt from the requirements of FIFRA, by regulation, any pesticide which it determines either to be adequately regulated by another federal agency, or to be of a character where it is unnecessary to employ FIFRA to carry out the purposes of this statute. As an exemption the law also allows the transfer of a pesticide that is not EPA registered if: (1) the transfer is from one registered establishment to another operated by the same producer solely for packaging at the second establishment or for use as an ingredient in another pesticide made at the second establishment, or (2) the transfer is done as part of an experimental use permit under which FIFRA allows the sale, distribution, or use of a pesticide not previously registered in accordance with FIFRA restrictions.

EPA may exempt a federal or state agency from the requirements of FIFRA if it determines that certain emergency conditions requiring an exemption exists. EPA, in determining whether the emergency condition exists, must consult with the department of agriculture and the governor of any state concerned if they request such a determination.

INSPECTIONS AND RECORDKEEPING

Recordkeeping

EPA is authorized to issue regulations requiring pesticide producers to keep records on their operations and the pesticides and devices that are produced. However, the records which EPA may require do not extend to financial data, pricing data, personnel data, and research data (other than data relating to registered pesticides or to a pesticide for which an application for registration has been filed).

Inspection of Records

EPA's inspection authority over pesticides extends to (1) all records showing the delivery, movement, or holding of a pesticide or device, including the quantity, the date of shipment and receipt, and the name of the consignor and consignee; or (2) in the case where a person is unable to produce records containing the foregoing information, all other records and information pertaining to the delivery, movement, or holding of the pesticide or device.

The inspection of these records and information cannot extend to financial data, sales data other than shipment data, pricing data, personnel data, and research data (other than data relating to registered pesticides or to a pesticide for which an application for registration has been filed). Before conducting an inspection, EPA officials must present appropriate credentials and a written statement of the reason for the inspection, including a statement on whether a violation of the law is suspected. If a violation is not suspected, an alternative and sufficient reason must be furnished.

Inspection of Pesticide Establishments

To enforce FIFRA, EPA may enter at reasonable times any establishment or other place where pesticides or devices are held for distribution or sale for the purpose of inspection or taking samples of pesticides or devices. Before undertaking the inspection of a pesticide establishment, EPA officials must present appropriate credentials and a written statement of the reason for the inspection, including a statement as to whether a violation of law is suspected. If no violation is suspected, an alternate and sufficient reason must be furnished in writing. The inspection must be begun and completed with reasonable promptness. If the EPA official obtains any samples, before leaving the premises, he or she must give the owner, operator, or agent in charge a receipt describing the samples obtained, and, if requested, a portion of each sample that is equal in volume or weight to the portion retained. If an analysis is made of the samples, a copy must be promptly furnished to the inspected plant.

INFORMATION PROTECTION AND DISCLOSURE

Protection of Trade Secrets and Other Information Submitted to EPA

Except where such disclosure is authorized by FIFRA, EPA is prohibited from making public any information which it judges contains or relates to trade secrets or commercial or financial information obtained from a person and which is privileged and confidential information. In submitting data required under FIFRA, an applicant for registration may clearly mark any portions of the data which in his or her opinion are trade secrets or protected commercial or financial information and submit the marked material separately from other data.

When necessary to carry out FIFRA, information relating to the formulas of products which EPA acquired under FIFRA authorization may be revealed to any federal agency which EPA might consult, and may be revealed at a public hearing or in the finding of facts issued by EPA.

Federal employees are subject to criminal penalties for willfully disclosing information known to be subject to confidential protection as a trade secret, as well as any civil remedy under state or federal law for wrongful disclosure of trade secrets.

If an applicant or registrant has indicated a belief that certain information should be protected from disclosure, he or she is entitled to 30-day notice if EPA intends to release the information. During this period the applicant or registrant may institute an action in federal district court on the issue of whether the information is entitled to protection.

Limitations on Disclosure

Generally

EPA must make available for public disclosure all information concerning the objectives, methodology, results, or significance of any test or experiment performed on or with a registered or previously registered pesticide or its separate ingredients, impurities, or degradation products, and any information concerning the effects of the pesticide on organisms in the environment, including but not limited to data on safety to fish and wildlife, humans, and other mammals, plants, animals, and soil, and studies on persistence, movement, and fate in the environment, and metabolism. However, unless EPA has first determined that the disclosure is necessary to protect against the unreasonable risk of injury to health or the environment, the requirement to disclose the aforementioned kinds of information does not authorize the disclosure of certain kinds of information. The kinds of information protected are those that pertain to manufacturing or quality control processes, to details of any methods for testing, detecting, or measuring the quantity of any deliberately added inert ingredient of a pesticide, or to the identity or percentage quantity of any deliberately added inert ingredient of a pesticide.

EPA must notify the person submitting information by certified mail if it proposes to disclose information relating to (1) manufacturing or quality control processes, details of any methods for testing, detecting, or measuring the quantity of any deliberately added inert ingredient of a pesticide, or the identity or percentage quantity of any deliberately added ingredient of a pesticide, or (2) the production, distribution, sale, or inventories of a pesticide otherwise entitled to confidentiality as a trade secret. EPA must not disclose the information without the consent of the party submitting it, until 30 days after this party has been provided with notice of EPA's intention to disclose.

However, if EPA finds that disclosure is necessary to avoid or lessen an immediate substantial risk to the public health, it may fix a shorter period for notice, not less than ten days, and provide for an appropriate method of notice.

During the 30-day period, the party submitting the data may institute an action in federal district court to enjoin or limit the proposed disclosure. The federal district court must give expedited attention to the suit.

Disclosure to Contractors of the Federal Government

The information otherwise protected from public disclosure by FIFRA can be disclosed to contractors with the federal government if EPA finds that the disclosure is necessary for the satisfactory performance of work in connection with the provisions of FIFRA and under conditions specified by EPA.

Disclosure to Foreign and Multinational Pesticide Producers

EPA is prohibited, without the consent of the applicant or registrant, from knowingly disclosing information submitted to it to firms making pesticides in foreign countries.

Any person who intends to inspect data submitted by an applicant or registrant under FIFRA must affirm that he or she does not seek the data for the purpose of delivering or selling it to a foreign or multinational pesticide producer, and that he or she will not purposefully deliver or negligently cause the data to be given to these foreign producers. A false or fraudulent affirmation will expose the violator to federal civil or criminal penalties.

EPA is required to maintain records of the names of all persons to whom data are disclosed and the persons or organizations they represent, and must inform the applicant or registrant of the names and affiliations of these persons.

PESTICIDE IMPORTS AND EXPORTS

FIFRA generally does not apply to pesticides, devices, or active ingredients used in producing pesticides solely for export if they are prepared according to the specifications of the foreign producer. However, the producers of these pesticides, devices, or active ingredients are subject to FIFRA provisions for labeling, misbranding, registration of pesticide establishments, and recordkeeping.

For pesticides that are not registered or that are sold by permission of EPA after cancellation, any foreign buyer must sign, before export, a statement acknowledging that he or she understands that the pesticide is not registered for use in the United States or cannot be sold in this country. The acknowledgment statement must be sent to the government of the importing country. EPA must also give notice to the State Department to transmit to foreign countries notice about whenever a registration or cancellation or suspension of registration becomes effective, or ceases to be effective. If requested by a foreign country, the notification is to include all information relating to the cancellation or suspension of the registration of the pesticide and information on other pesticides that are registered and could be used in place of the canceled or suspended pesticide.

The Treasury Department must notify EPA of pesticides and devices imported into the United States. The Treasury Department must give samples of imported pesticides or devices to EPA, upon EPA request, giving notice to the owner or consignee, who may appear before EPA and has the right to introduce testimony. If the sample appears to be adulterated, misbranded, or otherwise violates FIFRA, or is injurious to health or the environment, the pesticide or device may be refused entry into the country. The Treasury Department must refuse delivery to the consignee and destroy the pesticide or device refused admission within 90 days' notice of the refusal. However, the consignee may execute a bond for the full value of the pesticide or sample, in which case the Treasury Department may deliver the pesticide or device pending examination and a decision on the matter. The full amount of the bond is forfeited if the consignee refuses to return the pesticide or device to the Treasury Department when demanded. The consignee or owner is also liable for storage, cartage, and labor on pesticides refused admission or delivery, and default by any one of them is a lien against future importation of pesticides or devices.

ENFORCEMENT

Unlawful Acts

FIFRA prohibits an extensive number of activities in violation of the act.

It is unlawful, unless specifically exempted by FIFRA, to sell, ship, deliver for shipment, or receive and deliver or offer to deliver: any unregistered pesticide, except insofar as EPA may allow the continued sale and use of an existing stock of a canceled pesticide; any registered pesticide for which claims made for it during distribution or sale differ from the claims in its registration application statement; any registered pesticide whose composition at the time of distribution or sale differs from that described in its registration application statement; any pesticide that has not been colored or discolored as required by EPA regulations; and any pesticide that is adulterated or misbranded, or any device that is misbranded.

FIFRA also makes it unlawful to engage in the following acts: detach, alter, deface, or destroy labeling required by EPA; refuse to keep required records, refuse an EPA inspection of records or an establishment, or refuse to allow EPA to take pesticide samples; give a false guaranty for the purpose of obtaining an exemption from a prohibition of the act; use for ones' own advantage or to reveal information acquired by the authority of FIFRA which is confidential, other than to reveal the information to EPA or other federal agencies, or to the courts, physicians, pharmacists, and other qualified people for the performance of their duties; advertise a restricted use product without giving the restricted classification assigned to the product; make available for use, or utilize, a restricted use pesticide for purposes other than its restricted uses; use any registered pesticide in a manner inconsistent with its labeling; use any pesticide contrary to an experimental use permit for it; violate any stop sale, use, or removal order; violate any pesticide registration order; violate any registration cancellation; violate the requirements for the registration of pesticide production establishments; knowingly falsify applications, information submitted to EPA, required records and reports, or information submitted to EPA as confidential; fail to file reports required by FIFRA; add or delete a substance from any pesticide in a manner to defeat the purpose of FIFRA; or use any pesticide in tests on human beings unless they are fully informed of the nature of the test and any reasonably foreseeable mental or physical health consequences and they freely volunteer to participate in the test.

Exemptions from FIFRA Prohibitions

FIFRA penalties for the commission of unlawful acts do not apply to the following: a person who holds a guaranty from the registrant or a person from whom he or she received the pesticide in good faith in the same unbroken package, to the effect that the pesticide is lawfully registered at the time of sale and deliver, and that it otherwise complies with FIFRA; any carrier lawfully transporting a pesticide or device, if the carrier allows EPA officials, at their request, to copy all its records concerning the pesticide or device; any public official engaged in the performance of his or her official duties; any person using or possessing a pesticide in accordance with its special use permit; or any person who ships a substance being put through tests for the sole purpose of determining its value as a pesticide or its toxicity or other properties and from which the user does not expect to receive any benefit in pest control from its use.

Notice and Warning of Violations

EPA is required to notify persons against whom criminal or civil proceedings are considered when pesticides or devices show a failure to comply with FIFRA. The notice must also provide an opportunity to be heard, either orally or in writing, prior to the institution of civil or criminal proceedings. EPA's notice of the contemplated proceedings and the opportunity to be heard are not prerequisites to the bringing of any proceeding by the Justice Department, just EPA.

EPA has the option, in lieu of instituting proceedings for minor violations, to give a written warning when it believes the public interest will be adequately protected by the warning.

Inspections and Seizure Warrants

EPA can obtain and execute warrants to enforce FIFRA upon a showing to a court that there is reason to believe the act has been violated. The use of the warrant is authorized for (1) entry for the purpose of inspection; (2) inspection of records and the name of the consignor or consignee of any pesticide or device found in violation of FIFRA, and in the case of the inability of a party to produce records containing this information, all other records and information relating to the delivery, movement, or holding of the pesticide or device; and (3) the seizure of any pesticide or device in violation of FIFRA.

Orders for Stop Sale, Use, Removal, and Seizure of Pesticides or Devices

EPA may issue a written "stop sale, use, or removal order" if upon inspection or tests it finds that the pesticide or device is in violation of FIFRA, or that the pesticide or device has been distributed or sold in violation of FIFRA, or if the registration of the pesticide has been canceled or suspended.

FIFRA provides for seizure and condemnation proceedings in federal district court of pesticides or devices in the circumstances specified in the act. The seizure and condemnation orders apply to a pesticide if it is adulterated or misbranded, if it is not registered, if its labeling fails to bear information required by FIFRA, if it is not colored or discolored when required under FIFRA, or if any claims made for it or any directions for its use differ in substance from representations made in connection with its registration or when the pesticide causes unreasonable adverse effects. Seizure and condemnation orders apply to a device if it is misbranded, to a pesticide or device that causes unreasonable adverse effects to the environment, and to any plant regulators, defoliant, or dessicant.

State Enforcement

The state is given primary responsibility for enforcing pesticide use violations under FIFRA if the state enters into a cooperative agreement with EPA for this purpose or meets the statutory requirements for state primary enforcement responsibility. EPA retains primary enforcement responsibility when a state has not complied with statutory requirements.

The state's primary enforcement authority may be rescinded if EPA determines that the state is not adequately carrying out its enforcement duties or cannot do so because of inadequate legal authority.

PENALTIES

Civil Penalties

EPA may assess a civil penalty of not more than $5,000 per offense for violation of FIFRA by any registrant, commercial applicator, wholesaler, dealer, or other distributor. A private applicator or any other person not mentioned above who violates FIFRA after receiving a written warning from EPA or following a citation for a previous violation is subject to an EPA-assessed penalty of not more than $1,000 per offense. An exception to the maximum $1,000 per offense penalty applies to any private applicator or to any person who holds or applies registered pesticides or uses dilutions of registered pesticides only for the purpose of providing pest control services and not delivering the unapplied pesticide to the person provided with the pest control services, in which case a violation of FIFRA is subject to an EPA-assessed fine of no more than $500 for the first offense and thereafter not more than $1,000 for each subsequent offense.

EPA must give a person charged with a FIFRA violation notice and opportunity for a hearing before a civil penalty may be assessed.

EPA may issue a warning instead of assessing a penalty when it finds that the violation occurred despite the exercise of due care or did not cause significant harm to health or the environment. In determining the amount of the civil penalty, EPA must take into account the appropriateness of the penalty to the size of the business of the person charged, the effect on the person's ability to remain in business, and the gravity of the violation.

Criminal Penalties

Any registrant, commercial applicator, wholesaler, dealer, retailer, or other distributor who knowingly violates FIFRA commits a misdemeanor and is subject to a fine of up to $25,000 or a jail term of up to one year, or both. Any private applicator or other person not mentioned above who knowingly violates FIFRA commits a misdemeanor and is subject to a fine of not more than $1,000 or a jail term of not more than 30 days, or both. Any person who, with an intent to defraud, uses or reveals information relating to formulas of products acquired under the authority of the FIFRA registration provision is subject to a fine of not more than $10,000 or a jail term of up to three years, or both.

JUDICIAL JURISDICTION AND REVIEW

Jurisdiction for Federal Enforcement

Federal district courts have the jurisdiction to enforce and prevent violations of FIFRA.

EPA is required to publish notice of all judgments in actions instituted under the authority of FIFRA.

Judicial Review

EPA's final orders with respect to the registration and classification of pesticides are subject to judicial review.

Suspension orders that are granted by expedited hearings while proceedings are pending for cancellation or change of classification are subject to judicial review, and so are emergency suspension orders. However, suspension orders issued when an expedited hearing has not been requested are reviewable by the courts.

Federal district courts have jurisdiction to review EPA refusals to cancel or suspend registrations or change of classifications not following a hearing and other final EPA actions that are nondiscretionary. An actual controversy as to the validity of an order issued by EPA following a public hearing may be challenged in a federal court of appeals by a person who was a party to the proceedings and who will be adversely affected by the order. The party challenging the order must petition the court of appeals for judicial review within 60 days after the order has been entered.

Appeals of EPA orders to the court of appeals must be advanced on the docket, and disposition of the appeal must be expedited. The commencement of proceedings for appeal of an EPA order to the court of appeals does not operate as a stay of an order, unless specifically stayed by the court.

The court of appeals must consider all evidence on the record, and EPA's order must be sustained if it is supported by substantial evidence when considered on the record as a whole.

The judgment of the court of appeals is final and subject to review by the Supreme Court by certiorari or certification.

MISCELLANEOUS EPA AUTHORITY

EPA has the authority, after notice and opportunity for a hearing, to do the following: (1) declare as a pest any form of plant or animal life (other than human or other than any bacteria, virus, and other microorganism on or living in people or other living animals) which is injurious to health or the environment; (2) identify any pesticide that contains any substance in quantities highly toxic to people; (3) establish standards consistent with those established under the Poison Prevention Packaging Act for pesticide containers to protect people from serious injury or illness from the accidental ingestion or contact with pesticides or devices regulated under FIFRA; (4) specify the classes of devices which are to be subject to FIFRA provisions with respect to the registration of establishments or disposal or storage of pesticides; (5) establish regulations requiring the coloring or discoloring of a pesticide if deemed feasible and necessary to protect health or the environment; and (6) determine and establish suitable names to be used in the ingredient statement.

NATIONAL PESTICIDE MONITORING PLAN

FIFRA provides for a national plan for monitoring pesticides. FIFRA also requires EPA to establish procedures for monitoring exposure to people, animals, and the environment.

IDENTIFICATION OF PESTS

EPA is required, in coordination with the Department of Agriculture, to identify those pests that must be brought under control.

6 Resource Conservation and Recovery Act (Solid Waste Disposal Act) (42 U.S.C. §§ 6901 et. seq.)

State Programs

Underground Tank Notification

Corrective Action (Cleanup) Response Program and Leaking Underground Storage Tank Trust Fund for Petroleum Releases

Information, Inspections, Monitoring, and Testing

Enforcement

Federal Facilities

OVERVIEW

In 1976 Congress enacted the Resource Conservation Recovery Act (RCRA). RCRA substantially revamped federal regulation of solid waste disposal and created the first comprehensive federal regulatory program for the systematic control of hazardous waste. RCRA is also sometimes referred to by the name of the legislation it amended, the Solid Waste Disposal Act.

RCRA revised the Solid Waste Disposal Act of 1965 in its entirety. The Solid Waste Disposal Act of 1965 was the first federal legislation dealing directly with the solid waste problem and was aimed primarily at establishing a national research and development program for new and better methods to properly dispose of solid waste. The Resource Recovery Act of 1970 amended the Solid Waste Disposal Act to include the promotion of resource recovery programs and added provisions for grants to these programs. It required the now defunct Department of Health, Education, and Welfare to submit a report to Congress on the feasibility of a system of national disposal sites for the storage and disposal of hazardous wastes.

When enacted in 1976 RCRA dealt with hazardous waste control and solid waste control in two different subtitles, Subtitle C and Subtitle D, respectively.

Subtitle D makes regulation of nonhazardous solid waste primarily the responsibility of the states. EPA is directed to develop guidelines that will serve as minimum standards by which states will evaluate and regulate solid waste land disposal operations. Those solid waste land disposal sites that do not comply with EPA guidelines are to be designated as "open dumps" and prohibited. EPA is also directed to establish guidelines for the development of state solid waste plans. These plans are to identify open dumps, prohibit the establishment of new ones, and require that all nonhazardous solid wastes either be used for resource recovery or disposed in secure sanitary landfills. Any existing open dumps that cannot be upgraded to meet the criteria for an acceptable sanitary landfill must be closed.

Subtitle C of RCRA directed EPA to establish a comprehensive "cradle to grave" system for regulating hazardous waste from the generator, through storage and transportation, and to final treatment or disposal. The comprehensive regulation of hazardous waste is to be achieved through six elements: (1) EPA identification of wastes that are hazardous and thus to be subjected to regulation; (2) EPA standards governing hazardous waste generators, and including a manifest system to track wastes from "cradle to grave" to assure they end up at a proper disposal site; (3) EPA standards for hazardous waste transportation: (4) EPA standards for owners and operators of facilities that store, treat, or dispose of hazardous waste; (5) establishment of a permit program for hazardous waste facilities; and (6) EPA guidelines for authorization of state hazardous waste control programs.

In 1984 Congress enacted amendments to RCRA which reauthorized this legislation and expanded and tightened controls on the handling and disposal of hazardous wastes. The amendments, among other things, created for the first time explicit federal legislation for the regulation of relatively small quantities of hazardous waste, set deadlines on EPA to make decisions as to whether specific types of hazardous wastes could be disposed of safely on land and automatically banned such land disposal if EPA did not meet the deadlines, required EPA to establish a regulatory program for underground petroleum storage tanks, and provided for federal intervention in the control of solid waste landfills if states failed to provide additional measures to control them.

SOLID WASTES AND SANITARY LANDFILLS

Definition of Solid Waste

RCRA defines the term *solid waste* to mean any garbage, refuse, sludge from a treatment plant, water supply treatment plant, or air pollution control facility and other discarded material, including solid, liquid, semisolid, or contained gaseous material resulting from industrial, commercial, mining, and agricultural operations, and from community activities. Excluded from the definition of solid waste and hazardous waste (and thus not subject to RCRA regulation) are discharges requiring NPDES permits under the Federal Water Pollution Control Act and nuclear wastes regulated pursuant to the Atomic Energy Act of 1954.

Sanitary Landfill Criteria

EPA is to promulgate regulations establishing criteria for determining which facilities are to be classified as sanitary landfills and which are open dumps. At a minimum, the criteria must provide that a facility may be classified as a sanitary landfill and not an open dump only if there is no reasonable probability of adverse effects to health or the environment from disposal at the facility. EPA's regulations may provide for the classification of sanitary landfills.

No later than November 8, 1987, EPA must submit a report to Congress determining whether its sanitary landfill criteria are adequate to protect human health and the environment from groundwater contamination and recommending whether additional measures are needed to enforce them. Not later than March 31, 1988, EPA must revise the criteria for facilities that may receive hazardous household waste or hazardous waste from small-quantity generators. The generators create hazardous waste in amounts greater than 100 kilograms but less than 1,000 kilograms during a calendar month. The criteria must protect human health and the environment and take into the account the practicability of the facilities. At a minimum the

EPA sanitary landfill criteria should require groundwater monitoring, establish location standards, and provide for corrective action at sites when appropriate.

Sanitary Landfill Requirement

All land disposal of solid waste must be at sanitary landfills. At a minimum a site can be classified as a sanitary landfill only if there is no reasonable probability of adverse effects on health or the environment from the disposal of solid waste at the site.

Open Dump Prohibition

RCRA prohibits disposal at open dumps. An open dump is defined as an area where solid waste is disposed other than a sanitary landfill that meets EPA sanitary landfill criteria and is not a hazardous waste disposal facility. EPA is to promulgate regulations containing the sanitary landfill criteria for determining what facilities constitute open dumps and what facilities are sanitary landfills. RCRA requires the states to see that all existing facilities or sites that are open dumps are eliminated. RCRA provided for the phased upgrading or closing of open dumps by the states leading to compliance with the prohibition on open dumping within a reasonable time, but not to exceed five years after EPA promulgated criteria for sanitary landfills. EPA, in cooperation with the Bureau of the Census, is required to establish and publish an inventory of all open dumps in the nation.

State Permit Programs for Sanitary Landfills (Including for Small-Quantity and Household Hazardous Waste Disposal in Sanitary Landfills)

By November 8, 1987, each state must develop a permit program or other system of prior review to ensure that sanitary landfills comply with EPA's criteria for them. Within 18 months after EPA revises protective sanitary landfill criteria for facilities receiving hazardous household waste or hazardous waste from small generators, the state must develop an adequate permit program or other prior approval review program to assure compliance with the criteria. If the state fails to do so, then EPA may enforce the sanitary landfill criteria.

State or Regional Solid Waste Management and Plans: Regulatory Activities

According to RCRA, the objectives of solid waste management are to assist states in developing methods of disposal of discarded materials that are environmentally sound and to maximize the utilization of valuable resources that encourage resource conservation. The objectives are to be accomplished through federal financial and technical assistance, comprehensive planning, and cooperation among all levels of government.

Key instruments for achieving the objectives of solid waste management under RCRA are the comprehensive solid waste management plans which the legislation authorizes the states to establish. RCRA establishes a procedure for states, as well as regions within states or interstate regions, to develop a comprehensive plan for solid wastes. To be approved, these plans must meet guidelines published by EPA.

The EPA guidelines, after consultation with appropriate state and local governments, are to identify those areas that have common solid waste problems and are appropriate units for planning the management of these problems. The guidelines are to consider the size and location of areas included, the volume of solid wastes which should be included, and the available means to coordinate the plan with other regions and the state plan. By April 21, 1977, and after consultation with appropriate federal, state, and local authorities, EPA was to issue guidelines to assist the states in developing and implementing their solid waste management plans. These guidelines are to be revised from time to time, but not less frequently than every three years.

In developing state plan guidelines, EPA must consider 11 factors: (1) regional, geographic, hydrologic, climatic, and other conditions, and circumstances under which practices regarding discarded material are operated and reasonable protection of the quality of ground and surface waters from leachate contamination can be obtained; (2) characteristics and conditions of collecting, storing, processing, and disposing of solid wastes and the location of such facilities and operations; (3) methods of closing and upgrading open dumps for the purposes of eliminating health hazards; (4) population density; (5) geographic, geologic, climatic, and hydrologic characteristics; (6) the types and locations of transportation systems within the states; (7) constituents and generation of waste within the state; (8) political, economic, organizational, and financial problems effecting solid waste management; (9) types of resource recovery facilities that would be appropriate; and (10) available new and additional markets for recovered materials.

The state plan must contain certain minimum requirements, including: directing solid waste disposal activities to utilize better management methods; requiring that all nonhazardous solid wastes either be used for resource recovery or disposal in secure sanitary landfills, or in an environmentally sound manner; and establishing regulatory powers necessary to carry out the solid waste plan.

A major focus of the state plan is the open dump. Each state plan must contain a requirement that all existing facilities or sites that are open dumps be eliminated. The plan must prohibit any new open dumps and establish a strategy to close or upgrade all existing open dumps. RCRA provided for the phased upgrading or closing of open dumps leading to compliance with the prohibition on open dumping within a reasonable time, but not to exceed five years after EPA promulgated criteria for sanitary landfills.

In order to be approved by EPA, the state plan must meet the following other minimum criteria: identify state, local, and regional authorities for planning and implementing the state plan; assure that the distribution of federal funds to the state is reallocated among the state, local, and regional authorities according to the responsibility at each level of government; provide a means of coordinating regional and local plans with state plans; provide for the establishment of state regulatory powers necessary to implement the plan; and provide for such resource conservation or recovery and sanitary landfill disposal or any combination of these practices which may be necessary to protect the environment.

EPA Report to Congress on Extending Sanitary Landfill Life

By October 1, 1986, EPA was to submit a report to Congress for extending the useful life of sanitary landfills and for putting closed landfills to more efficient use.

HAZARDOUS WASTE MANAGEMENT

Generally

RCRA establishes minimum standards for cradle to grave control of hazardous waste. States are provided with the choice to establish and implement a program in place of an EPA-administered program, if the state program is equivalent to the federal program.

The hazardous waste provisions place significant emphasis on identifying what wastes are hazardous. EPA is to promulgate regulations for hazardous waste generators. The regulations include recordkeeping, informing those who transport or dispose of hazardous waste of the characteristics of the waste, and initiating a manifest system so that the hazardous waste can be traced from its generator to a place of legal disposal.

Regulations imposed on the transporters of hazardous waste are developed in cooperation with the Department of Transportation. The manifest system is important for tracking hazardous waste during the transportation stage to the ultimate disposal site.

Those who store, treat, or dispose of hazardous waste are required to receive a permit either from EPA or from an EPA-approved state program. EPA is to make decisions on whether specific wastes well known for their hazardousness can be disposed of safely on land, and, if not, their land disposal is to be prohibited. If EPA cannot make this decision by the deadlines established by RCRA, then land disposal for these wastes is automatically banned.

EPA regulations, regarding the generation, transportation, treatment, storage, or disposal of hazardous waste generally are to take effect six months after they are promulgated. However, EPA may provide a period shorter than six months, or may immediately impose the regulation, when the agency finds that the regulated parties do not need six months to comply, a regulation responds to an emergency situation, or any other good cause determined by EPA.

There are provisions for federal enforcement that include orders from EPA, citizen suits, and criminal and civil penalties.

RCRA defines a waste as hazardous if it exhibits either one of two effects: (1) the waste can cause or significantly causes or contributes to death or serious irreversible or incapacitating illness because of its quantity, concentration, or physical, chemical, or infectious characteristics; or (2) the waste poses a substantial or potential danger to human health or the environment when mismanaged.

Notification of Hazardous Waste Disposal

No later than 90 days after the promulgation of a regulation relating to the identification of a hazardous waste, any person generating the hazardous waste, transporting the hazardous waste, or owning or operating a facility for the treatment or storage of this hazardous waste must file with EPA or an approved state regulatory program a notification stating the location and description of their hazardous waste activities and the hazardous waste that is being handled. The waste may not be transported, stored, or disposed of until notification is properly given.

Hazardous Wastes Subject to Regulation

Identification and Listing of Hazardous Wastes—Generally

In order to be subject to regulation, a waste must be identified as hazardous. The law provides two means or measures by which EPA can establish a waste as hazardous: (1) by being placed on an EPA list of specific wastes EPA determines to be hazardous, or (2) by exhibiting any of the identifying characteristics or criteria that EPA establishes for determining whether a waste is hazardous.

In preparing a list of specified hazardous wastes and a set of identifying characteristics, EPA must take into account such factors as toxicity, persistence, degradability in nature, potential for accumulation in tissue, flammability, corrosiveness, and other hazardous characteristics.

The governor of any state may petition EPA to identify or list a waste as hazardous. EPA must act on the petition within 90 days and notify the governor of his action.

The 1984 amendments to RCRA required EPA to list the following wastes as hazardous by the following dates: chlorinated dioxins and dibenzofurans by May 8, 1985; other halogenated dioxins and dibenzofurans by October 8, 1985; coal slurry pipeline effluent, coke byproducts, chlorinated aliphatics, dioxin, dimethyl hydrazine, toluene diisycanate (TDI), carbamates, bromacil, linuron, organo-bromines, refining wastes, chlorinated aromatics, dyes and pigments, inorganic chemical industry wastes, lithium batteries, and paint production wastes by January 8, 1986.

In addition, EPA, in cooperation with the Agency for Toxic Substances and Disease Registry and the National Toxicology Program, must identify and list wastes that are hazardous solely because they contain recognized hazardous constituents, such as agents causing cancer, genetic damage, or birth defects, at levels that endanger human health. No later than October 8, 1986, EPA must promulgate regulations identifying additional characteristics of hazardous wastes, including measures of toxicity.

EP (Extraction Procedure) Toxicity

A commonly used means of determining whether a waste is capable of leaching toxic substances into a landfill is to conduct what is called an extraction procedure (EP) toxicity test. No later than June 8, 1987, EPA is to improve the EP toxicity procedure to insure that it accurately predicts the leaching potential of wastes that pose a threat to human health and the environment when mismanaged in a landfill.

Hazardous Waste-Derived Fuel Notification

No later than March 8, 1985, anyone who produces or distributes fuel derived hazardous waste was to notify EPA. Hazardous waste-derived fuel may not be transported, treated, stored, or disposed of unless this notification has been given.

Delisting Hazardous Waste

A facility may petition EPA to exclude a waste which it generates from the hazardous waste list. When evaluating a petition, EPA must consider factors in addition to those for which a waste was listed, and must provide notice and comment before making its decision. Any temporary delisting that was granted by EPA prior to November 8, 1984, will automatically lapse if EPA does not make a final decision to grant or deny the delisting petition by November 8, 1986. To the extent practical, EPA must grant or deny a delisting petition within 24 months after EPA has received a delisting application.

Small-Quantity Generator Waste

RCRA makes wastes from small-quantity generators within the ranges specified by the legislation subject to regulation. By March 31, 1986, EPA was to promulgate standards applicable to hazardous waste generators, transporters, and treatment, storage, and disposal facilities covering wastes from generators of 100 to 1,000 kilograms (kg) a month. These are the so-called small generators.

The small generator standards may vary from those for larger generators, but at the very least they must be sufficient to protect human health and the environment. The minimum requirements which EPA must establish in its regulations for small generators are as follows: (1) on-site storage by generators producing less than 1,000 kg per month may occur for up to 180 days without a permit, unless the waste must be shipped over 200 miles, in which case on-site storage is allowed for up to 270 days for up to 6,000 kg of waste; and (2) all other subsequent treatment, storage, or disposal must be at a hazardous waste facility with an RCRA hazardous waste permit for quantities above 100 kg per month. For generators below 100 kg per month, EPA has the discretion to issue regulations requiring permits.

Until March 31, 1986 (or earlier if EPA had issued small-quantity generator rules before), all wastes from generators of 100 to 1,000 kg per month were to go to hazardous waste facilities with an RCRA permit or facilities licensed by the state to manage municipal or industrial wastes. If regulations had not been promulgated by March 31, 1986, then: (1) treatment, storage, disposal by generators of 100 to 1,000 kg per month had to occur at a facility with a hazardous waste permit; (2) exception reports had to be filed twice yearly; and (3) generators had to retain copies of signed manifests for three years.

EPA has the discretion to promulgate standards for generators, transporters, and treatment, storage, and disposal facilities covering wastes of less than 100 kg per month if EPA believes it is necessary to protect human health and the environment.

Oil, Gas, and Geothermal Waste, Mining Waste, Utility Waste, and Cement Kiln Waste

A 1980 amendment to RCRA established separate regulatory requirements for the following types of wastes: (1) drilling fluids, produced waters, and other wastes associated with the exploration, development, or production of crude oil or natural gas or geothermal energy; (2) fly ash wastes, bottom ash wastes, slag waste, and flue gas emission control waste generated primarily from the combustion of coal and other fossil fuels; and (3)) solid waste from the extraction, beneficiation, and processing of ores and minerals, including phosphates and overburden from the mining or uranium ore and minerals; and (4) cement kiln dust waste.

By October 21, 1982, EPA was to submit a study to Congress on the adverse effects, if any, of oil, gas, or geothermal wastes on human health and the environment. Within six months after submitting the study, EPA, after public hearings and opportunity for comment, was to determine whether regulation of these energy wastes was warranted. EPA's decision, along with any regulation, must be submitted to Congress. The regulation will not take effect until authorized by an act of Congress.

Similar studies on adverse human or environmental effects were to be conducted by EPA for utility wastes, mining wastes, uranium mining wastes, and cement kiln dust wastes, and after each study EPA was to determine whether regulations were warranted. EPA was not required, however, to submit regulations for these wastes to Congress for approval.

Used Motor Vehicle Oil

By November 8, 1985, EPA was to propose whether to list used automobile and truck crankcase oil as a hazardous waste, and by November 8, 1986, to make a final decision.

Hazardous Waste Generator Standards

EPA must promulgate standards for generators that are sufficient to protect human health and the environment. EPA's standards are to provide requirements for recordkeeping practices, labeling practices for containers, identifying appropriate containers for hazardous wastes, and furnishing information concerning the chemical composition of hazardous waste to persons transporting, treating, storing, or disposing it, and biennial reports to EPA or a state regulatory program indicating efforts to reduce waste volume and the reduction actually achieved.

EPA is also to impose a manifest system on generators to insure that all hazardous waste generated is designated for treatment, or storage or disposal in, or arrives at a facility (other than the place where the waste was generated) with a hazardous waste permit issued by EPA or an approved state program.

RCRA defines a manifest as a form for identifying the quantity, composition, origin, routing, and destination of a hazardous waste from the point of generation to the point of disposal, treatment, or storage elsewhere. The manifest must contain a generator certification that the waste volume and toxicity of the waste have been reduced to the maximum degree that is economically practicable, and the method of treatment, storage, and disposal is the one currently available to the generator that minimizes the threat to health and the environment. Generators must submit biennial reports to

EPA or a state regulatory program which indicates efforts to reduce waste volume and the reduction actually achieved.

Recycled used motor oil is exempt from EPA hazardous waste generator standards. However, by November 8, 1986, EPA must promulgate special standards for generators of used motor oil that is recycled. Any generator entering into an agreement to deliver used oil to a permitted recycling facility are exempt from manifest requirements, provided the generator does not mix hazardous waste with the oil and keeps records which EPA considers necessary.

Hazardous Waste Transportation

Hazardous Waste Transporter Standards

EPA must issue regulatory standards for the transportation of hazardous waste which at least include requirements for recordkeeping, restricting transportation to properly labeled wastes, compliance with the manifest system, and restricting transportation of hazardous waste only to facilities with an RCRA hazardous waste facility permit.

By November 8, 1986, EPA was to issue regulations establishing standards including the above requirements for the transportation of fuel produced from hazardous wastes, or any other material, which it determined necessary to protect human health or the environment.

Recycled used motor oil is exempt from EPA hazardous waste transporter standards. However, by November 8, 1986, EPA was to promulgate special standards for transporters of used motor oil that was recycled.

RCRA and the Hazardous Materials Transportation Act

RCRA calls for coordination and cooperation between EPA and the Department of Transportation in regulating the shipping of hazardous materials subject to both RCRA and the Hazardous Materials Transportation Act. EPA is authorized to make recommendations to the Department of Transportation for regulating hazardous materials transportation and those wastes which EPA believes should be added to the Department of Transportation list of hazardous materials when transported. EPA is required to delegate to the Department of Transportation the performance of any inspection or enforcement function relating to the transportation of hazardous waste where the delegation would avoid unnecessary duplication of regulatory activity by the two agencies.

The Department of Transportation has primary responsibility for safety regulation relating to the loading, unloading, and handling of hazardous materials in transportation by virtue of the Hazardous Materials Transportation Act. A "hazardous material" means any substance or material in a quantity and form that may pose an unreasonable risk to health and safety or property when transported in commerce. These materials may include, but are not limited to, explosives, radioactive materials, etiologic agents, flammable liquids or solids, poisons, oxidizing or corrosive materials, and compressed gases. The Department of Transportation designates materials which it finds may pose any unreasonable risk to health of safety or property when transported in commerce.

The Department of Transportation is authorized to issue regulations for transporting hazardous materials. The regulations may control the safety aspect which the Department of Transportation deems appropriate and may include, but need not be limited to, packing, repacking, handling, labeling, marking, placarding, and routing of hazardous materials, and the manufacture, fabrication, marking, maintenance, reconditioning, repairing, or testing of a package or container.

The Hazardous Material Transportation Act makes it unlawful to mark or otherwise represent that a container or package for the transportation of hazardous materials is safe, certified, or in compliance with the law, unless it complies with Department of Transportation regulations. The Department of Transportation may establish criteria for handling hazardous materials. The criteria are to include, but need not be limited to, minimum number of personnel; type and frequency or inspection; equipment to be used for detection, warning, and control of risks posed by the hazardous materials; specifications regarding the use of equipment and facilities employed in the handling and transportation of hazardous materials; and a system for monitoring safety assurance procedures for the transporter of the hazardous materials.

The Department of Transportation may require the submission of a registration statement by persons who transport or cause to be transported or shipped hazardous materials or who manufacture, fabricate, mark, maintain, recondition, repair, or test packages or containers that are represented, marked, certified, or sold by the person for use in the transportation of hazardous materials. The registration statement is to include, at the very least, the person's name, principal place of business, the location of each activity handling the hazardous materials, a complete list of hazardous materials handled, and a statement that the person complies with all applicable criteria. The Department of Transportation may issue exemptions from hazardous materials transportation regulations in a manner which insures transportation safety that is at least as good as the level of safety that would be required if there was no exemption, or would be consistent with the public interest and transportation policy for hazardous materials, in the event there was no level of safety established. A person applying for an exemption must provide a safety analysis to justify the granting of the exemption.

The Hazardous Materials Transportation Act applies special provisions to the transportation of radioactive materials on any passenger-carrying aircraft. The transportation of radioactive materials in a passenger airplane is forbidden unless the radioactive materials involved are related to use for research or medical diagnosis or treatment, and as long as these materials when prepared for or in actual transportation do not pose an unreasonable hazard to health and safety.

Treatment, Storage, and Disposal Facility Standards and Requirements

Generally

Central to the hazardous waste management program established by RCRA are the standards which EPA is required to issue for hazardous waste treatment, storage, and disposal facilities which it regards as necessary to protect human health and the environment. At a minimum these standards for treatment, storage, and disposal facilities must include requirements in the seven following areas: (1) recordkeeping; (2) reporting, monitoring, and inspection and compliance with the manifest system; (3) standards for operating methods, techniques, and practices; (4) standards for location, design, and construction of hazardous waste treatment, storage, and disposal facilities; (5) contingency plans for hazardous waste damage occurrences; (6) standards for the continuity of operation, training of facility personnel, and financial responsibility for hazardous waste damage liability; and (7) permit standards for hazardous waste facilities. EPA was also required to establish by May 8, 1987, regulations for monitoring and controlling air emissions at hazardous waste facilities.

The term *treatment* as defined by RCRA means any method, technique, or process designed to change the physical, chemical, or biological character or composition of any hazardous waste so as to neutralize the waste or render it nonhazardous, safer for transportation, or amenable for recovery or storage or reduction in volume.

Storage, for purposes of RCRA, means the containment of hazardous waste, either temporarily or for a period of years, in such a way as not to constitute disposal.

The term *disposal* applies to the discharge, deposit, injection, dumping, spilling, leaking, or placing of hazardous waste into or on land or water so that the hazardous waste or any of its constituents may enter the environment or be emitted into the air or discharged into waters, including groundwaters.

Location Regulations; Air Emissions Regulations

EPA is required to establish regulations for the acceptable location of new and existing hazardous waste facilities. By May 8, 1987, EPA was to establish regulations for air emissions at hazardous waste facilities.

Groundwater Monitoring

By May 1987 EPA was to establish standards for groundwater monitoring. RCRA provides minimal standards for groundwater monitoring at hazardous waste disposal facilities. EPA standards concerning groundwater monitoring at landfills, surface impoundments, waste piles, and land treatment facilities are always to apply whether or not (1) the facility is located above the seasonal high water table; (2) two liners and a leachate system have been installed; or (3) the liners are inspected.

Under certain conditions EPA is authorized to exempt from groundwater monitoring requirements, on a case-by-case basis, engineered land disposal facilities that do not receive or contain liquid hazardous waste. These conditions include that these facilities are designed and operated to prevent liquids from entering the unit, equipped with multiple leak detection systems within the outer layer of containment, provide for continuing operation and maintenance of these leak detection systems during the life of the facility and after it is closed, and for which EPA finds there is a reasonable certainty that releases outside the site will not occur during operation and well after closing. EPA is required to establish guidance criteria identifying areas where groundwater sources are vulnerable.

Prohibition of Land Disposal Methods

The 1984 RCRA amendments directed that the land disposal of hazardous waste be banned unless EPA determined that the prohibition of any of several methods of land disposal was not required in order to protect human health and the environment. In determining whether or not a method of land disposal protects human health or the environment for particular wastes, EPA is to take into account (1) the long-term uncertainties associated with land disposal, (2) the goal of managing hazardous waste in an appropriate manner in the first place, and (3) the persistence, toxicity, and mobility of the hazardous waste and its constituents, as well as their propensity to bioaccumulate. A method of land disposal may not be found by EPA to be protective of human health and the environment, and thus permissible, unless a petitioner for the land disposal method demonstrates that there will be no migration from the disposal area as long as the waste remains hazardous.

EPA is required to promulgate regulations specifying levels or methods of treatment, if any, which substantially diminish the toxicity of waste or substantially reduce the likelihood of migration of hazardous constituents from the wastes to such an extent that threats to human health or the environment are minimized. If a hazardous waste is treated to this beneficial extent, then it is exempt from an EPA ban on a land disposal method which EPA may have otherwise established for the hazardous waste.

Land Disposal Ban for Specified Hazardous Wastes—Schedule for EPA Determinations

Generally. Except for underground injection, by March 8, 1988, the land disposal of hazardous waste containing dioxin and certain solvents identified by the statute is prohibited, except for methods of land disposal which EPA determines will protect human health and the environment. By July 8, 1987, the land disposal of five specific categories of hazardous waste, except for underground injection, was to be prohibited unless EPA determined that a prohibition for any method of land disposal was not necessary to protect human health or the environment. These five categories of wastes specifically listed in RCRA have come to be known as the "California list" because their disposal on land was first prohibited in that state before the enactment of the RCRA amendments. The California list wastes are: (1) liquid wastes containing concentrations of cyanides at 1,000 mg/l or more; (2) liquid hazardous waste containing concentrations in excess of statutory levels for the eight toxic metals of arsenic, cadmium, chromium, lead, mercury, nickel, selenium, and thalium; (3) liquid hazardous waste with a pH up to 2.0; (4) liquid hazardous waste containing polychlorinated biphenyls (PCBs) at concentrations at or above 50 ppm; and (5) hazardous waste containing halogenated organic compounds in total concentrations at or above 1,000 mg/l.

EPA is to determine whether or not the disposal into deep injection wells of the wastes on the California list, and dioxins and solvents, is protective of human health or the environment. By August 8, 1988, EPA must promulgate regulations prohibiting underground injection of any of these wastes if it reasonably determines that this form of disposal endangers human health or the environment as long as the wastes remain hazardous. If EPA fails to make this determination by April 8, 1988, then these hazardous wastes are automatically prohibited from deepwell injection.

By November 8, 1986, EPA was to publish a schedule for determining whether to ban the land disposal of all hazardous waste identified by EPA as hazardous as of November 8, 1984, other than dioxins and solvents and the five categories of California wastes. EPA's schedule is not subject to judicial review, but its failure to develop and publish the schedule can be reviewed by the courts.

The schedule is to set forth a plan by which EPA is to make determinations regarding the imposition of a prohibition on land disposal for one-third of all listed wastes by August 8, 1988, and for all other EPA listed and identified hazardous waste by May 8, 1990. For wastes listed by EPA after November 8, 1984, the agency was to determine by May 8, 1985, whether land disposal should be allowed for them. EPA is to schedule the high-volume wastes that are intrinsically the most hazardous for early review, as the objective of the schedule is to review land disposal for the most hazardous of hazardous waste first. The decision regarding the land disposal of the high volume and highly hazardous listed hazardous waste must be made, to the maximum extent possible, no later than August 8, 1988. For all other listed hazardous wastes, the determination of whether a land disposal ban is needed to protect human health or the environment must be made by May 8, 1990.

Automatic Land Disposal Ban for EPA's Failure to Meet Statutory Deadlines. Land disposal is banned if EPA fails to make a determination as to whether or not to ban land disposal by the statutory deadlines, which for the following wastes are: July 8, 1987, for the five categories of California wastes; November 8, 1986, for dioxins and solvents; and May 8, 1990, for all the listed wastes. EPA is to make determinations regarding the imposition of a prohibition on land disposal for one-third of all listed wastes by August 8, 1988, for two-thirds of all listed wastes by June 8, 1989, and for all the remaining listed and identified hazardous waste by May 8, 1990.

For listed wastes, if EPA fails to make a determination on whether land disposal is to be allowed by the deadlines for either the first third (by August 8, 1988) or the second third (June 8, 1989), disposal in a landfill or surface impoundment may be conducted only if (1) the generator certifies that there is no practical treatment alternative capacity available to the generator, and (2) disposal will take place at a landfill or surface impoundment that complies with RCRA's minimum technology requirements for new facilities of these types. However, after May 8, 1990, if EPA fails to make a determination for any listed waste, land disposal is outright prohibited, regardless of the lack of alternative treatment capacity.

Variances or Extensions for Land Disposal Prohibitions. The statutory prohibitions on land disposal of hazardous waste by EPA are usually to take effect immediately on the date specified in RCRA. However, in certain limited circumstances, EPA may postpone the deadline for a statutory land disposal prohibition.

Another date can be substituted for the statutory deadline banning land disposal of a particular hazardous waste when, on a national scale, adequate alternative treatment, recovery, or disposal capacity for the waste to protect human health and the environment is unavailable. If land disposal is allowed for a particular waste, the surface impoundment or landfill must meet the minimum technical requirements which RCRA imposes on new facilities of this type. The extension of the land disposal ban for lack of adequate alternative capacity is to end at the earliest possible date when adequate alternative capacity is available, but in no event can the extension exceed by more than two years the date specified in EPA regulations or RCRA.

A variance is available to generators of hazardous waste on a case-by-case basis where the applicant for the variance can demonstrate to EPA that it has a binding contractual commitment to construct or provide safe alternative treatment, recovery, or nonland disposal capacity, but due to circumstances beyond the applicant's control such alternative capacity cannot be made available before the land disposal prohibition deadline. This initial individual variance is limited in duration to no more than one year after the deadline, and may be renewed only once for no more than one additional year. For the duration of this variance, the disposal of waste in a landfill or surface impoundment must be conducted at a facility that meets the minimum technology requirements of RCRA for new disposal facilities.

Ban on Liquids in Landfills

After May 8, 1985, the landfilling of bulk or noncontainerized liquid hazardous wastes was to be forbidden. After November 8, 1985, the disposal of nonhazardous waste liquids in landfills was to be prohibited unless the only reasonable alternative was disposal in a nonhazardous landfill or unlined impoundment that contains or may contain hazardous waste, and this disposal would not endanger an underground source of drinking water. By February 8, 1986, EPA was to promulgate regulations that minimize the landfilling of containerized liquid hazardous wastes, minimize the presence of free liquids in containerized hazardous waste, and prohibit the landfilling of liquids that have been absorbed in materials that biodegrade or release liquids when compressed.

Minimum Technology Requirements for Land Disposal Facilities

New Land Disposal Facilities. EPA regulations, at a minimum, require all landfills and surface impoundments submitting permit applications after November 8, 1984, to have two or more liners, a leachate collection system (in the case of a landfill) between the liners, and a groundwater monitoring system. These requirements also apply to replacement or expansion activities that occurred after November 8, 1984, at land disposal sites in existence before this date.

EPA was to promulgate regulations or issue guidance documents by November 8, 1986, for implementing these minimum technology requirements for landfills and surface impoundments. Until these regulations or guidance documents are issued, the minimum technology requirements can be met by installing a top and bottom liner.

The double-liner requirement may be waived for one-liner landfills and surface impoundments containing only foundry furnace emission control wastes or metal castings when these facilities comply with other statutory conditions. Another waiver from the double-liner requirement is available to a landfill or surface impoundment if it can be demonstrated that alternative design and operating practices, together with location characteristics, are as effective in preventing the migration of hazardous waste into groundwater as a double-liner. This waiver from the double-liner requirement is not available for landfills and surface impoundments in Alabama.

Interim Status Land Disposal Facilities. GENERALLY: RCRA establishes a transitional phase in the permit issuance process for hazardous waste treatment, storage, and disposal facilities which is called "interim status" and applies to any qualifying facility in existence prior to the applicability of an RCRA requirement for it. An interim status facility is treated as having an RCRA hazardous waste facility permit until EPA has completed review of the facility's application for a final permit and approved or denied the permit. Interim status applies to any facility that properly applies for a final permit and was in existence prior to November 19, 1980, or the effective date of statutory or regulatory changes under RCRA which would subject the facility to the act's requirements. RCRA established a permit application timetable for interim status facilities. For land disposal facilities, interim status was to terminate on November 8, 1985, unless the facility submitted a so-called Part B application for a final permit which certified that the facility was in compliance with groundwater monitoring and financial responsibility requirements.

EXPANSION OF INTERIM STATUS LAND DISPOSAL FACILITIES: Any expansion of a land disposal facility (landfill, surface impoundment, waste pile, etc.) operating under an interim status permit that receives hazardous waste after May 8, 1985, is subject to the minimum technology requirements of double liners, leachate collection, and groundwater monitoring which are imposed on new land disposal facilities. The owner or operator of an interim status land disposal facility that is expanding must notify EPA (or state, if appropriate) at least 60 days before receiving the waste, and must submit a Part B application for a final permit within six months after providing the notice. EPA is generally prohibited when issuing a permit to an expanding interim status land disposal site from requiring the installation of liners or leak detection systems that differ from those already installed by the owner or operator in good faith compliance with previous EPA regulations or guidance documents. However, EPA may require installation of a new liner when there is reason to believe that any existing liner is leaking.

INTERIM STATUS SURFACE IMPOUNDMENTS—RETROFITTING REQUIREMENTS: The 1984 amendments to RCRA required existing surface impoundments under interim status at the time, with certain allowed exceptions and one allowed modification, either to come into compliance with the minimum technology requirements for new surface impoundments by specified statutory deadlines or to stop receiving wastes. This regulation has the effect of requiring surface impoundments to retrofit to meet the double-liner, leachate collection system, and groundwater monitoring requirements for new surface impoundments. An interim status surface impoundment in existence prior to November 8, 1984, must accomplish the retrofit by November 8, 1988, or it is to be closed. An interim status surface impoundment that receives hazardous waste after November 8, 1984, must accomplish retrofitting within four years of the date it first takes hazardous waste.

An interim status surface impoundment in existence on November 8, 1984, was to file a Part B application to receive a final permit by November 8, 1985, and the impoundment was to certify compliance with applicable groundwater monitoring and financial responsibility requirements, or else the impoundment would lose its interim status.

EXCEPTIONS AND MODIFICATION TO RETROFIT REQUIREMENTS FOR INTERIM STATUS SURFACE IMPOUNDMENTS: RCRA authorizes exceptions and a modification to the general rule that interim status surface impoundments in existence on November 8, 1984, must be retrofitted to meet the minimum technology requirements for new surface impoundments. To obtain an exception or modification from the retrofitting requirements for an interim status surface impoundment, the owner or operator was to apply for an interim status permit and submit the required information by November 8, 1986.

One of the retrofit exceptions is available if the impoundment is not within one-quarter mile of any underground source of drinking water, has at least one liner, has no evidence of leakage, and is in compliance with RCRA groundwater monitoring requirements for facilities receiving permits. This may be characterized as the one-quarter mile exception.

Any surface impoundment that is excluded from the minimum technology requirements because it is not within one-quarter mile of an underground drinking water source and has a natural clay liner must at the time it closes remove or decontaminate all waste residues, all contaminated liner material, and contaminated soil to the extent practicable. If all the contaminated soil is not removed or decontaminated, the owner or operator of the impoundment will be required to comply with the appropriate post-closure requirements, including but not limited to, groundwater monitoring and corrective action.

Another retrofit exception available is meant for interim status surface impoundments at wastewater treatment facilities. In order to qualify, the impoundment must meet the following criteria: (1) use at the time aggressive secondary or tertiary biological treatment facilities that are in compliance with a National Pollutant Discharge Elimination System (NPDES) permit (a water quality permit); (2) meet RCRA's groundwater monitoring requirements for a hazardous waste facility operating with an RCRA permit; and (3) be part of a wastewater treatment facility that complies with the BAT ("best available technology") effluent limitations under the Clean Water Act, or where there is no BAT effluent guideline applicable, the impoundment is part of a wastewater treatment facility with an NPDES permit that is achieving significant degradation of toxic pollutants and hazardous constituents contained in the untreated wastestream.

EPA has the authority to modify retrofitting requirements for interim status surface impoundments if the facility can show that there would be no migration of any hazardous constituent into the groundwater or surface water at any future time. This can be characterized as the no-migration modification. In considering whether to grant the modification, EPA or the state with an authorized regulatory program must take into account the locational criteria that define vulnerable hydrogeology.

An interim status surface impoundment for which EPA has granted an exception or modification from the retrofitting requirements but which, owing to a subsequent change in conditions, including the existence of a leak, no longer qualifies for an exception or modification must then comply with the retrofitting requirements. In other words the exception or modification is lost by such a change in conditions. The compliance need not be immediate; the site has two years to achieve compliance after the disqualifying change in condition has been discovered. Impoundments at wastewater treatment sites that initially qualified for an exception must also comply with the minimum technology requirements, in addition to the retrofit requirements when there is a change in conditions. When an interim status surface impoundment at a wastewater treatment facility is found to be leaking, it must meet the minimum technology requirements unless EPA determines that such compliance is not necessary to protect human health or the environment. The period for achieving compliance after disqualification from the retrofitting exception is three years.

EPA has the discretion to modify or waive the minimum technology requirements for interim status surface impoundments that receive mining wastes, utility wastes, or cement kiln dust as long as the modifications assure protection of human health and the environment. RCRA also authorizes EPA to modify the minimum technology requirements in the case of a surface impoundment whose owner or operator has entered into and is in compliance with a consent decree with EPA or a state-authorized program if the consent decree dictates corrective action intended to protect human health and the environment that is at least equivalent to the minimum technology requirements.

Any exception or modification for interim status surface impoundments can be overridden or removed by EPA. EPA may take such action when necessary to protect human health or the environment, including the application of minimum technology requirements, where EPA determines that hazardous constituents are likely to migrate from the impoundment into groundwater.

When issuing a permit to an interim status surface impoundment, EPA is generally prohibited from requiring the installation of liners or leak detection systems that are different from those installed by the owner or operator in good faith compliance with the minimum technology requirements for surface impoundments. However, EPA may require installation of a new liner when there is reason to believe that any existing liner is leaking.

INTERIM STATUS SURFACE IMPOUNDMENTS USED FOR WASTE TREATMENT OR STORAGE: Impoundments used for storage or treatment of a waste that has been prohibited by EPA from one or more methods of land disposal must meet the minimum technology requirements for new surface impoundments unless the impoundment qualifies as an exception to minimum technology requirements available either because the facility is not within one-quarter mile of an underground source of drinking water or does not experience the migration of hazardous constituents. Surface impoundments operating under an interim status permit which store or treat hazardous waste banned from land disposal must, without exception, meet the double-liner, leachate collection and groundwater requirements imposed on new impoundments. Interim status surface impoundments that treat hazardous waste banned from land disposal can do so only for the purpose of accumulating sufficient quantities to facilitate proper subsequent management, and the hazardous waste residues must be removed within one year of the waste's placement in the impoundment. Interim status surface impoundments used for the treatment or storage of waste that EPA has prohibited from any method of land disposal must remove the treatment residues at least once a year for proper management elsewhere.

Incinerator Standards

Incinerators receiving RCRA permits after November 8, 1984, must achieve the 99.99 percent destruction or removal efficiency that was required by EPA regulations in effect on June 24, 1982.

Interim Control of Underground Injection of Hazardous Waste

By May 8, 1985, or sooner if required by a state, hazardous waste cannot be injected into or above any underground formation that contains an underground source of drinking water within one-quarter mile, unless the injection is part of a federally sponsored hazardous waste cleanup or removal action under RCRA or CERCLA which when completed will be sufficient to protect human health or the environment.

The enforcement of the hazardous waste underground injection ban is to be conducted under the authority of RCRA until EPA or a state has established an underground injection control program under the Safe Drinking Water Act.

Prohibition on Deepwell Injection of Sanitary Wastes, Solvents, and Dioxins

By August 8, 1988, EPA must decide whether to ban the disposal of nonhazardous wastes and solvents and dioxins into deep injection wells. EPA must impose a ban if it determines that the deepwell injection disposal may not be protective of human health and the environment. In determining whether or not deepwell injection of nonhazardous wastes and solvents and dioxins protects human health or the environment, EPA is to take into account the following: (1) the long-term uncertainties associated with deepwell injection; (2) the goal of managing the wastes in an appropriate manner in the first place; and (3) the persistence, toxicity, mobility, and bioaccumulation propensity of the wastes and their constituents.

Disposal Prohibition for Underground Formations

The disposal of noncontainerized or bulk liquid hazardous wastes in the four types of geological formations of salt domes, salt beds, underground mines, or caves is prohibited until EPA determines that any form of these kinds of disposal protects human health or the environment. Should EPA find that the disposal of noncontainerized or bulk liquid hazardous waste is safe in any of these geological formations, it must promulgate performance and permitting standards for such disposal. The disposal of containerized hazardous waste is prohibited in these places until such a facility receives an RCRA hazardous waste permit.

The Waste Isolation Pilot Project in New Mexico is not subject to the restrictions on disposal in salt domes, salt beds, underground mines, and caves.

Facility Standards for Hazardous Waste Used as Fuel

By November 8, 1986, EPA was required to promulgate technical standards for facilities that produce, burn and distribute, or make fuel derived from hazardous waste, as might be needed to protect human health and the environment. Until EPA promulgates these regulations, it is unlawful to distribute or market fuel derived from hazardous waste unless a label appears on the invoice or bill of sale accompanying the fuel which warns that the fuel contains hazardous waste. EPA may exempt from the preregulation warning label requirement fuels that are produced from petroleum refining production where the oil containing hazardous waste from the refining process is returned for use for that refining process.

Until EPA promulgates fuel facility standards for hazardous waste, cement kilns in cities with a population of 500,000 or more are prohibited from burning fuel derived from hazardous waste unless they comply with EPA's incinerator standards.

Anyone who produces, uses, distributes, or markets waste burned or blended for fuel must notify EPA. If the notification is not given, the fuel derived from hazardous waste cannot be transported, treated, stored, or disposed. EPA is required to issue recordkeeping requirements for operations that handle such fuels.

Petroleum-refining wastes converted into petroleum coke are exempt from the hazardous waste fuel facility standards, labeling, and recordkeeping requirements. EPA may exempt from these same requirements facilities that burn *de minimis* quantities of hazardous waste as fuel, provided the waste is generated at the facility, the waste is burned for energy recovery, and the burning device is designed and operated at a destruction and removal efficiency sufficient to assure protection of human health and the environment.

Recycled Used Oil

As of November 8, 1986, EPA must subject recycled used motor oil to it's conventional standards for treatment, storage, and disposal facilities. The standards for used oil regulation are established by EPA to whatever extent it finds to be necessary to protect human health and the environment, as well as to promote recycling.

Waste Oil Dust Suppressants

Waste oil or other materials contaminated with hazardous wastes (except ignitable wastes) cannot be used as a dust suppressant.

Financial Responsibility for Cleanups

RCRA authorizes EPA to establish financial responsibility standards for owners and operators of hazardous waste treatment, storage, and disposal facilities. Financial responsibility generally refers to the capability and liability of the facility owner or operator to pay for the proper maintenance and operation of the site, for the site's proper closing, for the long-term care of the closed site, and for remedial action and damages resulting from the release of hazardous waste into the environment. EPA may require that the owner or operator of the facility establish financial responsibility through the use of insurance, guarantees, surety bond, letter of credit, or self-insurance.

A guarantor is any person who provides evidence of financial responsibility for a facility owner or operator. The total liability of the guarantor is the amount it has guaranteed for evidence of financial responsibility. However, RCRA does not limit the liability of the guarantor under state or federal statutory, contractual, or common law, including the liability for bad faith in negotiating a settlement of a claim.

Direct action is authorized against a guarantor who provides financial responsibility where no solvent owner or operator can be found or the owner or operator is bankrupt. The guarantor is permitted in a direct action lawsuit brought against it to invoke the rights and defenses of the owner or operator of the facility.

RCRA also expressly is not intended to diminish the liability of any person in respect to the federal Superfund law.

Corrective Action Beyond the Boundaries of a Hazardous Waste Facility

EPA regulations require that cleanup and remedial action for hazardous waste releases take place beyond the boundary of a treatment, storage, and disposal facility where necessary to protect human health and the environment. The owner or operator of the facility is not responsible for undertaking corrective action beyond the facility's boundaries if he or she can demonstrate to EPA's satisfaction that despite the owner or operator's best efforts he or she cannot obtain necessary permission.

Modification of Facility Standards for Mining Waste, Utility Waste, and Cement Kiln Dust

If mining waste, utility waste primarily from the combustion of coal or other fossil fuels, or cement kiln dust is made subject by EPA to hazardous waste facility regulations, the agency is allowed to modify the minimum requirements relating to liquids in landfills, prohibitions on land disposal, minimum technology requirements, deepwell injection, corrective action, and retrofitting interim status surface impoundments to take into account the special characteristics of any of these wastes. The EPA modifications can be employed only if they assure protection of human health and the environment.

RCRA Permits for Hazardous Waste Treatment, Storage, and Disposal

Generally

RCRA establishes a permit program for hazardous waste treatment, storage, and disposal activities. These facilities must obtain an operating permit issued by EPA or by an authorized state program. The purpose of the permit is to ensure that hazardous waste facilities fully comply with EPA standards.

Treatment, storage, or disposal of any hazardous waste is prohibited except in accordance with a permit. A permit is required before construction of a hazardous waste facility can begin, except for polychlorinated biphenyl (PCB) incinerators approved by EPA under the Toxic Substances Control Act.

An application for a permit must contain such information as EPA may require concerning the composition, quantities, and concentration of hazardous waste as well as the site at which the hazardous waste or products of treatment of the hazardous waste will be disposed of, treated, transported to, or stored. Permits can be issued only to facilities that comply with EPA standards for treatment, storage, and disposal of hazardous waste.

Permits are to be for a fixed term not exceeding ten years for land disposal, incineration, storage, or treatment. Land disposal permits must be reviewed within five years after issuance to assure compliance with currently applicable requirements. A permit may be reviewed and modified at any time. Permit renewals are to consider improvements in the state of control and measurement technology, as well as changes in applicable regulations. Permit applications for landfills and surface impoundments must be accompanied by an assessment of the potential of public exposure to hazardous substances released from these units.

All permits issued after November 8, 1984, for a hazardous waste treatment, storage, or disposal facility must require corrective action for releases of hazardous waste at any unit at the facility, regardless of whether the releases began prior to the permit or before any unit was closed. Where the corrective action cannot be completed prior to the issuance of the permit, the permit must contain schedules for corrective action and assurances of financial responsibility.

As a condition for an on-site permit (a permit for a facility where the waste is generated, as opposed to an off-site facility where waste is transported for management), the generator must certify at least once yearly that the volume or quantity and toxicity of the waste have been reduced to the maximum degree that is economically practicable. Another condition to the on-site permit is that the generator must show that the proposed method of treatment, storage, or disposal is one currently available to the generator which minimizes threats to human health and the environment.

Permit Decision Timetable

EPA or the state with permit issuance authority must approve or deny permits for facilities that apply for a permit before November 8, 1984, in accordance with a statutory timetable. For land disposal facilities, permits must be processed by November 8, 1988; for incinerators, by November 8, 1989; and for all other facilities, by November 8, 1992.

Interim Status Permit

RCRA establishes a transitional phase in the permit issuance process for hazardous waste treatment, storage, and disposal facilities which is called "interim status" and applies to any qualifying facility in existence prior to the applicability of an RCRA requirement to it. An interim status facility is treated as having a permit until EPA has completed review of the facility's application for a final permit and has approved or denied the application for the final permit. Interim status applies to any facility that properly applies for a final permit and was in existence prior to November 19, 1980, or the effective date of statutory or regulatory changes under RCRA which would subject the facility to the act's requirements.

Interim status is to be denied to any facility that has been previously denied an interim status permit or had an interim status permit terminated.

RCRA established a permit application timetable for interim status facilities. For land disposal facilities interim status was to terminate on November 8, 1985, unless the facility submitted a so-called Part B application for a final permit certifying that the facility was in compliance with groundwater monitoring and financial responsibility requirements. For incinerators, interim status is to terminate on November 8, 1989, unless a Part B application for a final permit was submitted by November 8, 1986. For all other facilities, interim status terminates on October 8, 1992, unless a Part B application for a final permit is submitted by November 8, 1988.

Research, Development, and Demonstration Permits

EPA is authorized to issue temporary permits for experimental facilities without first issuing permit standards. These experimental permits are limited to one year but are renewable each year for up to four years. EPA may immediately terminate a research, development or demonstration permit when it determines that it is necessary to protect human health and the environment.

Used Oil Recycling Facilities

Owners and operators of used oil recycling facilities are deemed to have a permit if they comply with the standards which EPA promulgates for the management of used oil, unless EPA determines that an individual RCRA permit is necessary to protect human health and the environment.

State Permit Programs

Any state can choose to administer and enforce a hazardous waste control program in lieu of EPA if EPA authorization is obtained.

There are two types of authorization for state programs—interim and final. Interim authorization is available to those states with existing hazardous waste control programs that did not qualify for final authorization at the time RCRA regulations first went into effect but wish time to build a control program capable of obtaining final authorization. To obtain interim authorization, a state control program must be substantially equivalent to EPA's own comprehensive program and EPA requirements for a fully authorized state program. Interim authorizations in effect as of November 8, 1984, may not last beyond January 31, 1986.

To qualify for final authorization, the state program must be equivalent to the federal program, be consistent with federal and state programs nationwide, and provide adequate enforcement for compliance with EPA regulations. To obtain or maintain final authorization, states must make available to the public any information they have obtained on treatment, storage, and disposal facilities to the extent that such information would be available if EPA were conducting the program.

Any requirement or prohibition that was imposed by the 1984 amendments to RCRA is to be enforced immediately by EPA in the state with an interim or finally authorized program until the state can revise its program to incorporate the new requirement or prohibition. States with provisions substantially equivalent to the new requirements could apply for interim authorization to administer the requirements in place of EPA.

EPA is authorized to enter into cooperative agreements with states to assist in the administration of the requirements and prohibitions of the 1984 RCRA amendments pending interim or final authorization of any of the state programs by EPA. EPA is also authorized to jointly issue permits with a state for those requirements or prohibitions of the 1984 amendments that have not yet been incorporated into the state program.

No state or political subdivision may impose requirements less stringent than those authorized by EPA regulations. However, a state or political subdivision may impose more stringent requirements than those imposed under RCRA. States are authorized to require that copies of manifests for intrastate shipments of hazardous waste be sent to them. Any action taken by a state under an approved hazardous waste program has the same force and effect as the action taken by EPA. EPA may withdraw state authorization to administer the hazardous waste program if the state is not properly administering and enforcing the program. EPA must first notify the state of the deficiency and hold a public hearing, and if corrective action is not taken within 90 days, EPA is to withdraw authorization.

Burning of Municipal Solid Waste Containing Hazardous Waste

Dioxin Emission Study

The 1984 amendments direct EPA, as soon as practicable, to submit a report to Congress on the risk of dioxin emissions from resource recovery facilities that burn municipal solid wastes, and on operating practices appropriate for controlling these emissions.

Household Waste Exclusion from RCRA Hazardous Waste Provisions for Municipal Energy Recovery Facilities

The burning of municipal solid waste at an energy recovery facility is exempt from the hazardous waste requirements of RCRA provided it burns residential and nonhazardous wastes only and establishes procedures to ensure that hazardous wastes will not be burned at the facility.

Domestic Sewage

Since February 8, 1986, EPA has been required to report to Congress on hazardous wastes that are exempt from RCRA because they are mixed with domestic sewage or other wastes that pass through a sewer system to a publicly owned wastewater treatment works. Within 18 months after submitting the report, but not later than August 8, 1987, EPA must revise or promulgate regulations to adequately control these wastes. By November 8, 1987, EPA must submit a report to Congress on wastewater lagoons at publicly owned wastewater treatment works and their effects on groundwater. The inspection and notification requirements of the hazardous waste provisions of RCRA apply to solid and dissolved materials in domestic sewage in the same way that they apply to other hazardous wastes.

Inventory of Federal Hazardous Waste Facilities

Each federal agency must biennially submit to EPA an inventory of each treatment, storage, and disposal facility which it owns or operates or has owned or operated. Federal agencies need not resubmit information which they submitted under the federal Superfund, or for hazardous waste facility permits under RCRA, or in notification to EPA that hazardous waste is being handled as required by RCRA. EPA must conduct the inventory when federal agencies fail to do so.

EPA Dissemination of Health and Safety Information Related to Hazardous Waste Activities

EPA is to provide to the Department of Labor (DOL) and director of the National Institute for Occupational Safety and Health (NIOSH), information on hazardous waste cleanup activities, identify the hazards to persons whose work involves exposure to or handling hazardous waste, incidents of worker injury, and harm related to hazardous waste activities. EPA is also to provide DOL and NIOSH with notifications and reports which the agency receives from hazardous waste generators, transporters, and treatment, storage, and disposal facilities.

Exposure Assessments for Hazardous Waste Landfills and Surface Impoundments

Permit applications for landfills and surface impoundments must be accompanied by an assessment of the potential of public exposure to hazardous substances released from these units. The Agency for Toxic Substances and Disease Registry is to conduct health assessments of communities surrounding these facilities where the exposure assessment indicates the presence of substantial risk. Members of the public may submit evidence of releases of or exposures to hazardous wastes from landfills or surface impoundments, or evidence on the risks or health effects associated with the releases or exposure to EPA, the Agency for Toxic Substances and Disease Registry, or a state with an authorized program.

Hazardous Waste Exports

After November 8, 1986, no person was to export hazardous waste unless: (1) they had filed a notification of intention to export with EPA; (2) the receiving country agreed in writing to accept the hazardous waste; (3) a copy of the receiving country's written consent was attached to the manifest; and (4) the shipment conformed to the terms of the consent. These requirements do not apply if the United States and the receiving country have an agreement establishing a hazardous waste export procedure. No later than November 8, 1985, EPA was required to promulgate regulations necessary to control hazardous waste exports.

Inspections

EPA and state officials may enter at reasonable times any establishment or other place where hazardous wastes are or have been generated, stored, treated, or disposed of, or transported from. Upon their request, an EPA or state official is to have access to, and the right to copy, all records relating to hazardous waste, at a reasonable time and under reasonable conditions. EPA or the state can inspect and obtain samples of any hazardous waste and samples of any containers or labeling from such wastes. Prior to leaving the premises, the inspecting authority must give the owner, operator, or their agent a receipt describing the samples obtained, and if requested a portion obtained by EPA or the state. If any analysis of the samples is made, a copy of the results is to be furnished to the owner, operator, or agent in charge of the facility. Any records or information obtained by EPA are to be made available to the public, except upon a showing satisfactory to EPA that such records, if made public, would disclose confidential trade secrets protected from disclosure by federal law.

EPA must inspect yearly each hazardous waste facility operated by a state or municipality. At least every two years, EPA, or the authorized state, must inspect privately operated treatment, storage, and disposal facilities. EPA must, and authorized states may, inspect each federally owned or operated treatment, storage, and disposal facility once a year.

Enforcement

On the basis of information regarding a violation of RCRA's hazardous waste provisions, EPA may issue an administrative compliance order or commence a civil action in federal district court for appropriate relief, including a temporary or permanent injunction. The federal district court may assess a civil penalty of up to $25,000 for each violation per day.

If the violation of an RCRA hazardous waste requirement or prohibition occurs within a state with an EPA-authorized program, EPA is to give the state notice of a violation 30 days before issuing a compliance order or commencing a civil action. The EPA compliance order must specify with reasonable certainty the nature of the violation and the time for compliance. EPA may order compliance immediately. An EPA order may include suspension or revocation of any hazardous waste permit issued by EPA or a state. As part of the order EPA may issue administrative monetary penalties, and these penalties may be imposed on past as well as present violations of RCRA. An administrative penalty may be assessed for up to $25,000 for each day of noncompliance per violation. In assessing the penalty, EPA is to take into account the seriousness of the violation and any good faith effort to comply with the law.

If the violator fails to take corrective action within the time specified in an EPA compliance order, the agency may assess an administrative penalty of up to $25,000 for each day of continued noncompliance with the order and may suspend or revoke any permit issued to the violator, whether issued by EPA or a state.

An order, suspension, or revocation of a permit becomes final unless within 30 days the person subject to the EPA action requests a public hearing. If a public hearing is requested, EPA must promptly grant it. In connection with any administrative violation proceeding, EPA may issue subpoenas for the attendance and testimony of witnesses and the production of relevant documents, and may promulgate rules for discovery procedures.

EPA is authorized to issue an administrative abatement order requiring corrective action for releases of hazardous waste from interim status facilities, and EPA may commence a civil action for appropriate relief. An EPA order for a interim status facility may include suspension or revocation of authorization to operate. EPA may assess a civil penalty of up to $25,000 for failure to comply with an order for an interim status facility for each day of non-compliance.

Criminal fines or imprisonment can be imposed on any person convicted of doing any of the following: (1) knowingly transporting hazardous waste to a facility that does not have a federal or state permit; (2) knowingly treating, storing, or disposing of hazardous waste without having obtained a permit; (3) knowingly violating a material condition or requirement of such a permit; (4) knowingly violating a material condition or requirement of interim status standards; (5) knowingly omitting material information or making a false material statement or representation in any record or document used by EPA or a state under RCRA; (6) knowingly hauling hazardous waste and knowingly destroying, altering, or concealing any document required by EPA or a state under RCRA; (7) knowingly transporting or causing to be transported hazardous waste without a manifest; and (8) knowingly exporting hazardous waste without the consent of the receiving country or in violation of any international agreement between the United States and the receiving country regarding hazardous waste procedures.

The first conviction of a violation can result in a fine of up to $50,000 for each day of the violation, or a jail term of up to two years (five years for a violation of 1 to 4 referred to in the previous paragraph), or both. For subsequent convictions, the maximum fine and prison term are doubled.

A substantially heavier criminal penalty is applied to the knowing violations referred to above when the violator also knowingly places another person in imminent danger of death or serious bodily injury. Conviction of such a situation of knowing endangerment can result in a maximum fine of $250,000 and a prison term of fifteen years, or both, for an individual, and a maximum fine of $1 million when the convicted party is an organization.

If EPA determines that the presence of any hazardous wastes at facility or site poses a substantial hazard to humans or the environment, it may issue an order requiring monitoring, testing, analysis, and reporting. EPA may impose monitoring, testing, and reporting requirements on an immediate previous owner or operator of a site or facility if this party can reasonably be expected to possess actual knowledge about the presence of hazardous waste, but the current owner or operator does not. EPA can commence a civil action in federal district court against anyone who failed or refused to comply with an EPA order to conduct monitoring, analysis, testing, and reporting. The court can assess a civil penalty of up to $5,000 for each day during which the failure or refusal to comply with an EPA order occurs.

Imminent Hazards

EPA may bring suit in federal district court to immediately restrain the handling, storage, treatment, transportation, or disposal of solid or hazardous waste that presents an imminent and substantial danger to health or the environment. EPA itself may also issue an order to restrain an imminent hazard. A person willfully violating, or failing or refusing to comply with, an EPA imminent hazard order is subject to a judicial fine of up to $5,000 for each day the violation or noncompliance occurs.

EPA must provide the affected state with notice of an imminent hazard suit or order the agency may undertake. Local government agencies must be provided with immediate notice when EPA receives information that waste at the site presents an imminent hazard. EPA must require that notice of the imminent danger be posted at the site where the waste was located. EPA must provide for public notice and comment prior to entering into a settlement or covenant not to sue in any imminent hazard action.

CITIZEN SUITS

Citizens are allowed to bring civil action in federal district court against any person or government entity alleged to be in violation of RCRA, or against EPA to perform any mandatory act or duty under RCRA. Citizen suits may also be brought where past, as well as present, management or disposal of hazardous or solid waste has contributed to an imminent and substantial hazard. A plaintiff bringing a citizen suit for an imminent hazard is required to serve a copy of the complaint on EPA and the Justice Department.

Before a citizen suit may be commenced, the plaintiff must provide 60 days' notice of the RCRA violation (other than for an imminent hazard) to EPA, to the state where the alleged violation occurred, and to the violator. In the case of a citizen suit for an imminent hazard, 90-day notice must be given to EPA, the state, and the alleged perpetrating party, except that the action may be brought immediately after this notice is given if there is a violation of RCRA's hazardous waste provisions as well.

If EPA or the state is diligently prosecuting a civil or criminal action, the citizen suit is precluded.

A citizen suit on an imminent hazard is prohibited in the following cases: (1) with respect to the siting and permitting of hazardous waste facilities (except the prohibition does not apply to a state or local government bringing suit in this case); (2) where EPA has begun and is diligently prosecuting actions under the imminent hazard provisions of RCRA or of CERCLA; (3) while EPA or a state is actually engaging in a cleanup under CERCLA or has incurred costs to initiate a Remedial Investigation/Feasibility Study (RI/FS) under CERCLA and is diligently proceeding with a remedial action; and (4) where EPA has obtained a court order (including a consent decree) or issued an administrative order under the imminent hazard provision of CERCLA, or where under the imminent hazard provisions of CERCLA a party is diligently conducting cleanup-related measures.

A railroad common carrier is not considered to have contributed to a situation that poses an imminent hazard, for which a citizen suit has been brought, if the railroad has merely transported the waste under a sole contractual agreement and has exercised due care.

EPA, if not already a party to a citizen action, may intervene as a matter of right. In a citizen suit for an imminent hazard, intervention as a matter of right is allowed to any person whose interest relating to the action may be impaired or impeded by the disposition of the suit. However, such intervention is not allowed as a matter of right if EPA or the state shows that the prospective intervener's interest is adequately represented by existing parties to the suit.

The federal district court in its final order in a citizen suit can award the costs of litigation, including reasonable attorneys' and expert witness fees, but these fees are limited to the prevailing or substantially prevailing party. The court may require a bond or equivalent security if a temporary restraining order or preliminary injunction is sought in a citizen suit. Bringing a citizen suit does not nullify or preclude exercise of any rights that a party to the litigation would have under other statutes or common law to seek enforcement of any standard or requirements relating to the management of hazardous waste or to seek other relief, including relief against EPA or a state agency.

CITIZEN PETITIONS FOR RULEMAKING

Any person may petition EPA to issue, amend, or repeal an RCRA regulation. Within a reasonable amount of time, EPA must take action on the petition and publish notice of the action together with its reasons in the Federal Register.

JUDICIAL REVIEW

Judicial review of final RCRA regulations and of EPA action on a citizen petition for issuing, amending, or repealing a regulation is restricted to the District of Columbia Court of Appeals. EPA's actions on these final regulations, for which judicial review is exclusively restricted to the District of Columbia Court of Appeals, cannot be challenged by a defendant in civil or criminal proceedings.

A petition for judicial review must be filed within 90 days from the date of EPA's final action, but may be allowed after this time if the question for review is based solely on grounds arising after the ninetieth day.

Judicial review of an EPA action regarding a permit for the treatment, storage, or disposal of hazardous waste or regarding authorization or interim authorization of a state hazardous waste program may be instituted by any interested person in a federal court of appeals having jurisdiction where the person lives or transacts business. EPA's actions regarding a treatment, storage, or disposal facility permit or authorization of a state program for which judicial review is allowed cannot be challenged by a defendant in civil or criminal proceedings.

FEDERAL RESPONSIBILITIES

Application of Federal, State, and Local Law to Federal Facilities

Subject to a presidential exemption for the paramount interest of the United States, any federal agency with jurisdiction over a solid waste or hazardous waste facility, or engaged in an activity resulting in disposal, is subject to all federal, state, interstate, and local requirements for permits, judicial enforcement, and reasonable service charges. Executive branch agencies and any unit of Congress are specifically required to comply with EPA guidelines for solid waste management.

Federal Procurement to Maximize Resource Recovery

The RCRA provisions regarding federal procurement apply only where the purchase price of the procured item or fair market value of the quantity purchased during the previous fiscal year exceeds $10,000.

Each federal procuring agency is directed to procure items composed of the highest percentage of recovered materials that is practicable, and in the case of paper products, consistent with maintaining a satisfactory level of competition. The requirement to use recovered materials and waste paper does not apply where the items are not reasonably available within a reasonable amount of time, the items do not meet performance standards, or the items are available only at an unreasonable price. Federal contracting officers must require vendors to certify the percentage of recovered material to be utilized in the performance of a contract.

Federal agencies that generate heat, mechanical, or electrical energy from fossil fuels and that have the capability of using discarded materials as a primary or supplementary fuel must do so to the extent practicable.

The procurement specifications of federal agencies cannot contain any exclusion of recovered materials from federal contracts, cannot require the items to be manufactured mainly from virgin materials, and must require that reclaimed materials be used to the maximum extent possible without jeopardizing the intended end use of the item. EPA, after consultation with the General Services Administration and Department of Commerce, must issue, and revise from time to time, procurement guidelines for federal agencies that maximize the use of discarded materials and waste paper. Each procuring agency is required to develop a program to promote the preferential purchase of items containing recovered materials and waste paper.

EMPLOYEE SAFEGUARDS

Employee Protection

RCRA prohibits an employer from discharging an employee or otherwise discriminating against an employee with respect to compensation, terms, conditions, and privileges or employment because the employee commenced or caused to be commenced a legal proceeding under RCRA, or testified, or is about to testify in a proceeding, or assisted or is about to assist in a proceeding to carry out the purposes of RCRA.

A remedy is provided to employees who are improperly discharged or discriminated against. This employee can file a complaint with the Department of Labor within 30 days after the alleged violation occurs, and the Department of Labor is to notify the person named in the complaint that it has been filed. The Department of Labor must investigate, provide an opportunity for a public hearing at the request of any party, and make fundings of fact based on the investigation. If the Department of Labor finds that a violation did occur, it will issue a decision, which is to include any order necessary, requiring the party committing the violation to take necessary affirmative action to abate the violation, including but not limited to, reinstating the employee to his or her former position with compensation.

Employment Effects

Any employee who is discharged, or laid off, threatened with discharge or layoff, or otherwise discriminated against by a person because of administration or enforcement of RCRA, may request EPA to conduct a full investigation. As part of the investigation, EPA must hold public hearings at the request of any party. EPA is to make findings of fact on the effect of the administration and enforcement of RCRA on employment and on the alleged discharge, layoff, or discrimination and must issue recommendations it deems appropriate. Any report, findings, and recommendation by EPA are to be made available to the public.

UNDERGROUND STORAGE TANKS

Generally

The 1984 amendments to RCRA established a program to control underground storage tanks containing petroleum products and certain hazardous substances. These amendments created a regulatory program for imposing standards on underground tanks. The Superfund Amendments and Reauthorization Act of 1986 further amended RCRA to confer authority on EPA and EPA-approved state programs to undertake corrective actions for responding to and cleaning up releases from underground petroleum tanks. A $500 million fund, called the Leaking Underground Storage Tank Trust Fund, was established to pay for the corrective actions. The fund was financed by a 1-cent tax per gallon gasoline, diesel fuels, and other petroleum-based fuels, with the tax to expire at the end of 1991.

By March 1, 1985, EPA was to issue final permitting standards for underground tanks containing hazardous wastes that cannot be entered for inspection. By November 1988, EPA was to modify its underground storage tank regulations, if necessary, to cover the minimum requirements dictated by the statute concerning leak detection, prevention, and correction measures for underground storage tanks containing petroleum products and hazardous substances. EPA was directed to promulgate standards for new underground petroleum tanks by May 8, 1987, standards for new nonpetroleum tanks by November 8, 1987, and standards for existing nonpetroleum tanks by November 8, 1988.

Tank owners and operators were required to notify state and local authorities of the existence and characteristics of their underground storage tanks containing hazardous substances and petroleum products. Tank owners and operators were required to comply with financial responsibility requirements established by EPA which could adequately pay for the cost of taking corrective action in the event of damaging or polluting releases from the tanks. States were given the authority to administer the underground tank regulatory program when approved by EPA. Underground storage tanks were also to be subject to regulatory information requests, inspections, monitoring, and testing. EPA was given the authority to undertake administrative and judicial enforcement actions against violators of the underground tank regulatory program.

An underground storage tank is defined as a tank with 10 percent or more of its volume underground, including the volume of pipes. Excluded are farm and residential tanks storing less than 1,100 gallons of motor fuels, heating oil tanks on the premises, septic tanks, and pipelines regulated under the Natural Gas Pipeline Safety Act or the Hazardous Liquid Pipeline Act, surface impoundments, stormwater and wastewater collection systems, flow-through process tanks, oil and natural gas production liquid traps, and storage tanks situated in an underground area if the tank is on or above the surface of the floor.

The RCRA program for underground tanks applies only to "regulated substances." These regulated substances include petroleum products (which are liquid at standard temperature and pressure) and substances designated hazardous substances by the Comprehensive Environmental Response, Compensation, and Liability Act (CERCLA), commonly known as the Superfund Act, but not including hazardous wastes regulated under RCRA. The CERCLA hazardous substances that are subject to regulation when in underground storage tanks are hazardous substances and toxic pollutants designated as being substantially dangerous pursuant to CERCLA, hazardous air pollutants designated under the Clean Air Act, and any imminently dangerous chemical designated under the Toxic Substances Control Act.

Underground Tank Regulations

EPA is to promulgate final underground storage tank regulations for various types of tanks by statutorily prescribed dates, and these standards must be sufficient to protect human health and the environment. EPA regulations for the underground tank control program must include, at a minimum, a monitoring system to identify releases, recordkeeping on the monitoring system, requirements for corrective action in response to releases, requirements for closing out tanks after their use to prevent future releases from the inactive tank, requirements for maintaining financial responsibility to cover the costs of taking corrective action and compensating third parties for damages due to releases, and performance standards for new underground tanks.

EPA is authorized to establish three types of regulations to control underground storage tanks: (1) new tank performance standards; (2) minimum requirements for an underground tank control program; and (3) requirements for financial responsibility for tank owners and operators. The new tank performance standards apply to underground storage tanks that are brought into use after the effective date of final standards for existing underground storage tanks. The new tank performance standards must include, but are not limited to, design, construction, installation, release detection, and compatibility standards.

RCRA establishes a timetable for the promulgation of regulations by EPA for three categories of underground tanks. EPA was directed to promulgate new tank standards and regulations for all petroleum tanks by May 8, 1987, standards and program regulations for new nonpetroleum tanks by November 8, 1987, and standards and program regulations for existing nonpetroleum tanks by November 8, 1988.

Until the effective date of the final performance standards for new underground storage tanks, RCRA forbids the installation of any new underground storage tank unless the following conditions are satisfied: (1) the tank prevents releases due to corrosion or structural failure during its operational life; (2) the tank is cathodically protected, constructed of noncorrosive material, or designed in a manner to prevent the release of stored substances; and (3) the material used in constructing or lining the tank is compatible with the substance to be stored; or (4) in place of the previous requirements, the tank is located in soil with a resistivity greater than 12,000 ohm/cm (unless EPA has established a stricter standard). The last soil condition requirement is meant to allow a bare steel tank to be placed underground until EPA issues final tank standards. The above requirements in effect constitute interim standards for the installation of underground tanks until final performance standards for new underground tanks are promulgated.

Financial Responsibility Regulations

EPA is required to promulgate regulations requiring tank owners or operators to maintain financial responsibility sufficient to pay the cost of corrective action and compensating third parties for bodily injury and property damages due to releases from an underground storage tank. EPA must promulgate the financial responsibility requirements no later than November 8, 1988. The EPA regulations may require financial responsibility to be established through insurance, guarantees, surety bond, self-insurance, a combination of any of these measures, or any other method chosen by EPA.

In promulgating financial responsibility standards, EPA is given the authority to differentiate various classes and categories of tanks and to vary the amount of financial responsibility that is required according to these classes and categories. A minimum amount of $1 million per occurrence of financial responsibility must be maintained, unless EPA sets a lower amount by regulation for a class or category of underground tank. EPA can only lower the amount of financial responsibility by regulation and on the basis of categories or classes of tanks, not as an ad hoc decision granted for individual tanks. EPA cannot lower the financial responsibility coverage below the $1 million minimum for underground tanks that are engaged in petroleum production, refining, or marketing activities, nor can EPA lower the $1 million minimum coverage for underground tanks that contain very large volumes. EPA also has the authority to establish financial responsibility above the $1 million minimum coverage, but must do so on the basis of classes and categories of underground tanks. The EPA financial responsibility regulations can require aggregate coverage.

EPA can temporarily suspend financial responsibility requirements for a particular class or category of underground tanks or in a particular state. The suspension may only last 180 days. The suspension is not available for the purpose of giving relief to a particular tank owner or operator who cannot get insurance. EPA may suspend financial responsibility requirements only after making a determination that no method of demonstrating financial responsibility is generally available to a category of underground tank owners or operators or in the state. Before granting a suspension, EPA must find that the underground tank owners or operators in the affected class or category are taking steps to form a risk retention group or that the state is taking steps to form a fund for such owners or operators. At the end of the 180-day suspension period, EPA must make a new set of determinations that a suspension is warranted if another suspension is requested.

Direct action is authorized against a guarantor providing financial responsibility when the owner or operator is in bankruptcy or insolvent. A guarantor is any person who provides evidence of financial responsibility for the tank owner or operator. The guarantor is permitted in a direct action lawsuit to invoke the rights and defenses of the owner or operator of the tanks had the lawsuit been brought against the operator and which would have been available to the guarantor had the owner or operator sued him. The liability of the guarantor is generally limited to the total amount guaranteed for financial responsibility to the tank owner or operator.

State Programs

No later than May 8, 1987, states may apply to EPA to establish their own underground storage tank control programs in place of EPA conducting the program. States have the choice to submit programs covering only tanks containing petroleum products, or only tanks containing hazardous substances, or for both. In order to be approved by EPA, the state program must include and be no less stringent than the federal program in respect to major elements and must provide for adequate enforcement. Within six months of the state submission, EPA must decide whether the state program conforms with the requirements for the federal program. If it does, EPA is to approve the state program and permit the state to have primary enforcement responsibility for regulating underground storage tanks. States or local governments can adopt underground storage tank requirements that are more stringent than federal regulations.

If EPA determines that a state with an approved underground tank program is not administering it properly, it is to notify the state of this determination. If the state does not take action to correct the program's inadequacies within 180 days, EPA must withdraw approval for the state program and administer the underground tank program itself.

Underground Tank Notification

The states are to designate what state or local agency will receive notification of the existence and characteristics of the underground storage tanks from their owners and operators. EPA is directed to design the notification form used by tank owners or operators. Owners or operators were to provide notification of the existence of the underground tank to the designated state or local agency by May 8, 1986, specifying the age, size, location, and uses. Owners of tanks taken out of the operation after January 1, 1974, were to provide notification by May 8, 1986. Any owner who has brought an underground storage tank into use since May 8, 1985, is to provide notification within 30 days of the existence of the tanks. Distributors of regulated substances and tank sellers must inform owners and operators of the tanks that they have an obligation to provide notification to the proper state or local agency, once EPA has established new tank performance standards.

There are exemptions to the notification requirement. The exemptions are available to those tank owners who have already provided notification under the provisions of CERCLA to tanks taken out of the ground, and to tanks taken out of operation before January 1, 1974.

Corrective Action (Cleanup) Response Program and Leaking Underground Storage Tank Trust Fund for Petroleum Releases

The Superfund Amendments and Reauthorization Act of 1986 further amended RCRA to confer authority on EPA and EPA approved-state programs to undertake corrective actions for responding to and cleaning up releases from underground petroleum tanks. A $500 million fund, called the Leaking Underground Storage Tank Trust Fund, was established to pay for the corrective actions. The Fund is financed by a 1-cent per gallon tax on gasoline; diesel fuel; special motor fuels; liquid fuels used in motor vehicles, boats, and trains; liquid aviation fuels; and fuels used in commercial transportation on inland waterways. The tax expires on December 31, 1991, or when the net revenue exceeds $500 million.

It should be emphasized that only releases of petroleum products, not any other substances, are covered by the response program whose corrective actions are financed by the Leaking Underground Storage Tank Trust Fund. The kinds of response actions that can be taken for petroleum releases include issuing orders to tank owners and operators to perform corrective action, enforcing orders, governmental corrective action at sites where the owners or operators will not respond, and recovery of the costs of corrective actions paid by the Fund.

Upon approval by EPA, a state is allowed to conduct a response program for releases from underground petroleum tank releases. In order for a state to engage in response measures that are financed by the Fund, EPA must determine that the state has the capability to carry out effective corrective actions and enforcement measures. The state must enter into a cooperative agreement with EPA, setting out the response activities for which the state will be responsible. The state is required to pay 10 percent of the cost of any corrective action undertaken by it or EPA under a cooperative agreement using money from the Fund, after the underground petroleum tank regulations are promulgated. Until that time, the full costs of the state actions under a cooperative agreement are paid by the Fund. The Fund may also pay the full cost of a corrective action after the date of the regulations but only where the corrective action is necessary to respond to an imminent and substantial danger to human health and the state refuses to pay its 10 percent share of the costs.

Neither EPA nor a state can use the Fund to undertake a corrective action at a facility that has failed to maintain required financial responsibility. The failure of an underground petroleum tank owner or operator to maintain financial responsibility does not preclude EPA or the state from using money from the Fund to take corrective action outside the boundaries of the facility or where necessary to respond to a release or threatened release that poses an imminent and substantial danger to human health or the environment.

In all cases, the underground tank owner or operator is to undertake a corrective action for a petroleum release in accordance with an EPA or state order, if the owner or operator has the financial capability to respond and will comply with the order. Where these conditions are not met, EPA or the state can use the Fund to undertake corrective action and sue the tank owner or operator to recover the costs.

The underground petroleum tank response program is divided into two parts, one providing authority to respond before regulations for petroleum tanks are issued, and one providing authority to respond consistent with these regulatory provisions when they are promulgated. EPA was required to establish regulations for petroleum tanks by May 8, 1987.

EPA is given the authority to conduct corrective measures in response to petroleum releases before EPA has promulgated underground tank regulations. Prior to the regulations, EPA or an approved state program can take enforcement action to require the underground tank owner or operator to promptly and properly respond to a petroleum release. EPA or the state may unilaterally undertake a corrective action for an underground petroleum tank release when it is found necessary to protect human health and the environment. EPA must use money from the Leaking Underground Storage Tank Trust Fund to pay for an enforcement action to require corrective measures by tank owners and operators and to pay for the costs of corrective action undertaken by EPA or an approved state program prior to the promulgation of regulations. Priority must be given to corrective actions by EPA or a state to insolvent tank owners or operators who cannot afford to properly undertake correction actions themselves.

After the regulations for underground tanks containing petroleum are promulgated, which by law is supposed to be May 8, 1987, EPA or an authorized state can also use the Leaking Underground Storage Tank Trust Fund to undertake corrective action for petroleum releases. However, the post-regulation response actions financed by the Fund are limited to the general condition that the actions be necessary to protect human health and the environment and only be used in one or more of four specific circumstances: (1) where no person can be found who is subject to the regulations and has the capacity to undertake a corrective action; (2) where EPA or an authorized state needs to respond promptly to protect human health and the environment; (3) where the tank owner or operator has refused to cooperate with an order from EPA or a state; or (4) where the total cost of the corrective action exceeds the required financial responsibility coverage for a tank owner or operator and their paying the costs of corrective action above the required coverage amount would significantly impair the ability of the tank owner or operator to stay in business.

EPA and authorized state programs can issue orders to compel an underground tank owner or operator to conduct a corrective action or comply with regulations. In issuing orders, priority must be given to releases of petroleum which pose the greatest risk to human health and the environment.

Petroleum tank owners and operators are liable to EPA or a state for the costs of any corrective action they make take. EPA or the state has the discretion to forego full-cost recovery where the tank owner or operator has maintained the required amount of financial responsibility coverage, but it is not adequate to pay the cost of a corrective action without significantly impairing its ability to continue in business. No indemnification, hold harmless, or similar agreement or conveyance would be effective to transfer liability from the tank owner or operator who may be liable for a release to any other person.

Information, Inspections, Monitoring, and Testing

At the request of the appropriate state or federal agency, any owner or operator of an underground storage tank must furnish information relating to its tanks, allow access to records related to the tanks, and conduct monitoring and testing when required. The information obtained from a tank owner or operator must be made available to the public, except if the information is a trade secret and therefore entitled to be protected as confidential.

For the purpose of developing or assisting in the development of any regulation, conducting any study, taking corrective action, or enforcing the underground tank requirements, EPA may inspect establishments or other places where an underground tank is located, inspect and obtain samples from tanks, and conduct monitoring and testing of tanks, associated equipment, contents, surrounding soils, air, surface water, or groundwater.

Enforcement

If EPA determines that any person is in violation of the underground tank requirements, it may issue an administrative compliance order or commence a civil action in federal district court for appropriate relief, including a temporary or permanent injunction. If a violation occurs in a state with an approved underground storage tank program, EPA must give notice to the state prior to taking an enforcement action. If a violator fails to comply with enforcement directives within the time period specified in an order, he or she is liable for a civil penalty up to $25,000 for each day of continued noncompliance. Orders become final within 30 days unless the person charged requests a hearing.

EPA has subpoena power for the attendance of witnesses and production of documents, and may issue discovery rules, in connection with an administrative proceeding regarding a violation.

Any tank owner or operator who knowingly fails to notify state or federal authorities, or submits false information about its tanks, is subject to a civil penalty of up to $10,000 a tank for each day the violation occurs. Any owner or operator who installs or begins using an underground tank for storing hazardous substances without complying with EPA regulations is subject to a civil penalty of up to $10,000 a tank for each day the violation occurs.

Federal Facilities

Each federal agency with underground storage tanks containing hazardous substances is subject to and must comply with all federal, state, interstate, and local requirements for its tanks. The president may exempt underground storage tanks owned by a federal agency from compliance with federal requirements if it is determined to be in the paramount interest of the United States. No exemption can be granted due to the lack of appropriated federal funds unless the president had specifically requested the appropriation from Congress but they were denied. A presidential exemption is limited to a year, unless the president issues a new exemption.

7 Comprehensive Environmental Response, Compensation, and Liability Act (Superfund) (42 U.S.C. §§ 9601 et. seq.)

OVERVIEW

The Comprehensive Environmental Response, Compensation, and Liability Act of 1980 (CERCLA), then commonly and unofficially known as the Superfund Act, was landmark legislation that established a federally directed program to clean up the nation's most dangerous hazardous waste and chemical contamination sites. This legislation enabled the federal government to respond to actual or threatened releases of dangerous substances at sites and facilities by undertaking cleanup actions, to administratively or judicially abate releases posing an imminent or substantial danger to public health or welfare or the environment, and to recover damages for the destruction or harm of natural resources. CERCLA also allowed private parties to conduct a cleanup or remedial action at a site and then recover the costs from responsible parties or from what the 1980 legislation designated as the Hazardous Substances Response Trust Fund, or informally but widely known as the Superfund. This first Superfund consisted of $1.6 billion, 86 percent of which was financed by taxes on oil and certain chemical substances and the remainder by federal appropriations. The purpose of the Superfund was to finance government and private cleanup actions and to pay claims for damages to natural resources.

The original Superfund legislation proved to be a disappointment, if not a failure, because the EPA, which was responsible for administering the act, had by 1986 been able to begin cleanup of only eight dangerous sites, out of the hundreds, if not thousands, around the country. In addition, the entire $1.6 billion was spent to achieve this dismal performance. In response to the failures of the 1980 legislation and the fact that its funding and taxing authorization had expired, Congress enacted the Superfund Amendments and Reauthorization Act of 1986, which amended CERCLA.

The Superfund reauthorization bill of 1986 substantially expanded and toughened the cleanup authority of the federal government and provided a fivefold increase, to $8.5 billion, for the Superfund. The Hazardous Substance Response Trust Fund, informally called the Superfund, was replaced by a newly named fund, the Hazardous Substances Superfund, which made the name "Superfund" official in the legislation. The new $8.5 billion Superfund would be established for five years, and funding would include $2.75 billion from a tax on petroleum, $1.4 billion from a tax on raw chemicals, $2.5 billion from corporate income tax, $1.25 billion from federal appropriations, $0.3 billion from interest, and $0.3 billion from government recoveries of cleanup costs from companies responsible for damages. The new taxes to fund the Superfund would generally take effect after December 31, 1986, and would end before January 1, 1992.

The 1986 Superfund Amendments set strict new standards for cleaning up contaminated and polluted sites and mandated the federal government to begin work at 375 sites within five years. The 1986 amendments stressed the use of permanent cleanup methods, including detoxifying hazardous wastes whenever possible, rather than burying them in landfills, or transferring wastes from one site to another. The 1986 amendments retained and strengthened the key reason for the Superfund, and that is to authorize direct action by the federal government to undertake itself and direct others to undertake the abatement and cleanup of hazardous substance threats and releases. The federal government may order a polluter to remove or control any hazardous substance endangering public health, welfare, or the environment. Also retained and strengthened by the 1986 amendments was the authority of the federal government and members of the public to enforce the act's provisions and compel responsible parties to pay the costs of response actions undertaken under the law and to reimburse the Superfund for initially financing these response actions.

DEFINITIONS

The definitions in CERCLA are important because they determine the parties, substances, and activities covered by the act.

The scope of CERCLA coverage for hazardous substances is broad. CERCLA defines hazardous substances to include hazardous and toxic substances identified under other federal environmental statutes and additional substances designated by EPA. These include substances designated as hazardous or toxic pollutants under the Clean Water Act, hazardous under the Resource Conservation and Recovery Act, any hazardous air pollutant listed under the Clean Air Act, and imminently hazardous substances as defined by the Toxic Substances Control Act. Hazardous substances encompassed by CERCLA also include substances designated by EPA under the act itself. Substances designated as hazardous by EPA pursuant to CERCLA are to include those which, when released into the environment, may present substantial danger to the public health or welfare or the environment. Petroleum and natural gas are specifically excluded from the definition of hazardous substances. CERCLA also excludes from its coverage the release of nuclear materials or byproducts, normal field application of fertilizers, engine exhausts, and releases in the workplace if the injured party may assert a claim against the employer.

The release of hazardous substances and pollutants is the very threat for which CERCLA was enacted to respond and abate and is broadly defined to include any spilling, pumping, pouring, emitting, discharging, injecting, escape, leaking, dumping, or disposal into the environment. The release of pollutants includes the abandonment of barrels of other contaminants, regardless of whether they have broken open or leaked. Releases not covered by CERCLA are those that are allowed by permits under other federal pollution control statutes.

CERCLA authorizes responses not only to hazardous substances, but also to any other "pollutant or contaminant" not listed as hazardous if the release may present an imminent or substantial danger to the environment. Pollutant or contaminant is defined to encompass, but not be limited to, any substance, including disease-causing agents that after release into the environment and upon exposure, inhalation, or assimilation into any organism, either directly from the environment or indirectly by ingestion through food chains, will or may be reasonably anticipated to cause death, disease, behavioral abnormalities, cancer, genetic mutation, physiological malfunctions (including reproductive malfunctions), or physical deformities in these organisms or their offspring.

One of the most important powers established by CERCLA is authorizing the federal government to order removal and other remedial action for hazardous substances.

The distinction between removal and remedial action as responses is important in the legislation because some provisions refer to only one or the other. Removal generally is an immediate action taken primarily to bring a release of a hazardous substance under control. Removal is not intended for the mitigation or elimination of long-term problems. Remedial actions, on the other hand, are meant to be permanent and thorough responses. A remedial action is synonomous with permanent cleanup. The essential difference between removal and remedial actions is that removal is directed at immediate and necessary cleanup operations, while remedial actions are concerned with more extensive and permanent efforts to rehabilitate the environment and repair the damage caused by the release of hazardous substances.

Removal is defined to include containment, disposal, or other action to minimize danger to public health or the environment. Removal may also include limiting access to sites, providing alternative drinking and household water supplies, temporary evacuation and housing for threatened persons, and any emergency assistance that may be provided under federal disaster relief.

Remedial actions are activities that involve permanent remedies, that is, long-term cleanup, taken in addition to or in place of removal actions, in order to prevent or minimize the release of hazardous substances so that they do not migrate to cause substantial danger to present or future public health or welfare or the environment. Remedial action includes, but is not limited to, cleanup, confinement, diversion, destruction, or treatment of the hazardous substances at the site of the release, providing alternative water supplies, and monitoring. Remedial action also encompasses the permanent relocation of residents and business and community facilities, where it is more cost effective and environmentally preferable than removing the hazardous substances from the place of release to some other place, or where necessary to protect public health or the environment. Remedial action specifically includes off-site transportation or other off-site removal measures to secure disposition of the hazardous substances.

Under CERCLA the owners and operators of facilities from which releases occur are liable for reimbursing the federal government for the costs of response actions and natural resource damages. CERCLA specifies that the definition of an owner or operator does not include state and local governments if they acquire a facility involuntarily (due to bankruptcy, foreclosure, tax delinquency, abandonment, or similar means) and have not contributed to the pollution problem. This is important because under current law, the state or local share of cleanup costs increases from 10 to 50 percent when a state or local government is considered the owner or operator of a facility.

FEDERAL RESPONSE AUTHORITY

Generally

CERCLA confers extensive authority on the federal government to respond to the release of hazardous substances. This authority is given in most instances to the president, who may delegate his or her responsibilities to other federal officials and agencies. Most of the responsibilities have been conferred on EPA.

Federal remedial or removal actions must be consistent with the National Contingency Plan (NCP), which is mandated by CERCLA. The NCP is the chief body of regulations that govern how CERCLA is to be carried out. The federal government must promulgate regulations for the establishment of an administrative record that is to form the basis for selecting a response action. The administrative record is to be made available to the public at or near the site. For the purpose of engaging in response actions by the federal government, high priority must be given to sites where releases of hazardous pollutants have closed drinking water supplies or contaminated a principal drinking water supply. The federal government must make reasonable efforts to identify and notify potentially responsible parties before selecting a response action.

CERCLA confers on the federal government the authority to order an owner or operator of a site releasing or threatening to release hazardous substances to take emergency corrective action, without the need of court approval, in order to protect against imminent and substantial dangers to public health or welfare of the environment.

One of the most important powers conferred on the federal government is the authority to take direct action. The federal government may order the removal or other remedial action for any release or threatened release of hazardous substances. Primary attention is to be given to releases of hazardous substances that threaten public health. When a substance defined by CERCLA as hazardous has been released or threatens release, the federal government may unilaterally undertake remedial or removal action and do so without determining that the release presents a danger to public health or the environment.

The federal government's response action is financed by the withdrawal of money from the Superfund. This money may be subsequently recovered from any party responsible for the release in an action brought by the federal government in federal district court.

The federal government may allow a cleanup action to be carried out by a facility owner or operator or any other responsible party (such as a dumper), if it is determined that the party is qualified and will do the work properly and promptly.

The federal government is still principally responsible for properly overseeing the cleanup activities undertaken by others.

The federal government is greatly restricted from undertaking a Superfund-financed cleanup action for releases of naturally occurring substances in unaltered form, releases from products that are part of the structure of buildings, or releases into a drinking water system which are due to the ordinary deterioration of the system. The federal government may undertake cleanup in these otherwise restricted situations if the release constitutes a public health or environmental emergency and no other person with the authority or capability to respond will do so quickly enough.

Any short-term cleanup action undertaken under CERCLA should, to the maximum extent that is practicable, contribute to effective long-term cleanup. With certain exceptions, federal short-term remedial actions cannot continue after $2 million has been obligated for the activity or after 12 months have elapsed from the date of the initial response to the release or the threatened release of the hazardous substance. The federal short-term remedial action can continue beyond the $2 million/12-month cutoff in cases where EPA determines that a continued response is needed to deal with the emergency and there is a risk to public health or welfare, assistance will not be otherwise provided on a timely basis, or continued response is considered otherwise appropriate or consistent with the remedial action to be taken.

Public Participation in Response Actions

CERCLA requires that the federal government allow and facilitate public participation in the selection of response actions. The federal government is to issue regulations for establishing participation by the public in the development of the administrative record that forms the basis for the selection of a response action. The regulations are also to include participation by potentially responsible parties in the development of this record.

Before undertaking a remedial action at a site, the federal or state government must prepare a remedial action plan. For remedial actions, the procedures established by the federal government must, at a minimum, include (1) notice to the public and potentially affected persons regarding its remedial response plan; (2) a reasonable opportunity for the public to comment and provide to the public information regarding the plan; (3) an opportunity for a public meeting near the site; (4) a response to significant comments, criticism, and information from the public; and (5) a statement of the basis and purpose of the remedial action strategy selected by the federal government.

The federal, or state government, whichever is engaging in the remedial action, must take certain steps before finally adopting a remedial action plan and embarking on the implementation of that plan. The first step is publishing a notice and brief analysis of the plan and making the plan available to the public. The notice and analysis must include sufficient information to provide a reasonable explanation of the proposed plan. The second step is to provide reasonable opportunity for the submission of written and oral comments, and an opportunity for a public meeting near the site, regarding the proposed plan and any waivers being considered for requirements relating to cleanup standards. The federal government or state must keep a transcript of the meeting and make the transcript available to the public. Finally, the federal government or state must publish the significant differences, if any, between the final remedial action plan that has been prepared and any actual remedial action, settlement, or enforcement action that may instead be adopted. The federal government or state must include in this published material the reasons why the changes were made. These differences and changes must be published, at a minimum, in a major local newspaper of general circulation.

Federal Cleanup Schedules

CERCLA establishes timetables governing the progress of cleanup and other response actions under CERCLA.

The act establishes as a "goal" the federal government's completion by January 1, 1988, as is maximally practicable, of preliminary assessments of all facilities which EPA's Comprehensive Environmental Response, Compensation, and Liability Information System (CERCLIS) contained as of October 17, 1986. By January 1, 1989, a date also set as a goal, the federal government must have assured actual inspection of the sites for which there has been a positive decision to inspect. The date of October 17, 1990, is stated as a goal by which each facility in CERCLIS should be evaluated, if the federal government determines that an evaluation is needed on the basis of the site inspection or preliminary assessment. For any facility listed in CERCLIS after October 17, 1986, the facility is to be evaluated.

If the federal government fails to achieve any of the goals for completing preliminary assessments, deciding which sites should be inspected, or evaluating facilities on the CERCLIS list, it must publish an explanation of why not by the date set as the goal for the particular activity.

The original CERCLA directed the federal government to establish a National Priorities List (NPL), which consisted of the nation's worst sites that were to receive priority in federal response actions. The 1986 amendments established deadlines for the federal government to begin studies, called Remedial Investigation Feasibility Studies (RI/FS), on how to clean up a site on the National Priorities List. In addition to studies that already had been begun by October 17, 1986, the federal government must start at least another 275 RI/FSs before October 17, 1989. If the federal government fails to meet the 275 RI/FS target of October 17, 1989, then it must begin no fewer than an additional 175 RI/FSs by October 17, 1990, and an additional 200 RI/FSs by October 17, 1991—for a total of at least 375 RI/FSs to be undertaken by October 17, 1991.

The federal government is directed to assure that substantial and continuous on-site remedial action (long-term cleanup) is started at facilities on the National Priorities List, in addition to those facilities for which remedial action was begun prior to October 17, 1986, the date of enactment for the CERCLA amendments. The CERCLA amendments established a schedule for these cleanups: 175 sites during the period before October 17, 1989; and 200 more sites during the period between October 17, 1989, and October 17, 1991—for a minimum total of 375 sites for which cleanup must be scheduled by October 17, 1991.

Cleanup Standards

Generally

The Superfund Amendments of 1986 imposed general standards to govern federal cleanup actions for hazardous substances—regardless of whether the cleanup was for pollutants on-site or for pollutants that had to be transported elsewhere off-site.

Whatever long-term or permanent cleanup action is chosen by the federal government, it must adopt a method that is cost effective for both the short term and long term and that is in accordance with the National Contingency Plan. Moreover, the remedial action that is selected must assure protection of human health and the environment. The Conference report for the Superfund Amendments of 1986 addresses the issue of what takes precedence in the choice of a remedial action—environmental and health protection or cost considerations. The Conference report indicates that the federal government is to determine an adequate level of protection of human health and the environment, and then, afterwards and secondarily, it selects a cost-effective means to achieve the adequate level of protection chosen. The protection of human health and the environment, in all cases, is the minimum standard that must be employed as the degree of cleanup required. Moreover, the cleanup method chosen by the federal government must be relevant and appropriate to the circumstances.

In choosing a remedial action, the federal government should prefer methods of treatment that permanently and significantly reduce the volume, toxicity, or mobility of hazardous substances over other treatment methods that do not achieve these reductions. Furthermore, off-site movement and disposal without reduction treatment, where it is available, is the least favored alternative. If the federal government does not follow the act's preference for reduction methods, it must publish an explanation as to why. In choosing a remedial action for a site, the federal government must prepare an assessment of the long-term effectiveness of permanent solutions and alternative treatment technologies or alternative resource recovery technologies that will permanently reduce the volume, toxicity, or mobility of the hazardous substances. In assessing these alternatives for remedial action, the federal government must, at a minimum, consider: the long-term uncertainties posed by land disposal; the goals and requirements of the Solid Waste Disposal Act (also known as the Resource Conservation and Recovery Act); the substances' persistence, toxicity, mobility, and tendency to bioaccumulate; the short-term and long-term threats to human health; the long-term maintenance costs; the potential for future cleanup costs if the remedial action were to fail; and the potential threat to health and the environment associated with the excavation, transportation, redisposal, or containment of the hazardous substances.

The federal government may select a cleanup method even though it may not have been successfully tried at a similar site. In making this selection, the federal government may consider the degree of support for this untried method by parties with an interest in seeing the site cleaned up.

If the federal government chooses a cleanup method that leaves any hazardous substances at the site, it is required to review the site at least once every five years to assure that human health and the environment are protected. The federal government must take further action or require a responsible party to take such action if this required review of the site determines that any is necessary. The federal government is required to report to Congress the sites that are subject to reviews, the result of the reviews, and any action taken because of the reviews.

On-site Standards

The CERCLA amendments of 1986 provided standards for response actions directed against pollutants left on-site, in addition to the general standards that as a minimum human health and the environment must be protected. For any pollutant left on-site and where other more stringent federal or state standards apply, the cleanup method must meet the other more stringent standards rather than those established under CERCLA. These other more stringent federal or state requirements must be met where they are legally applicable to the hazardous substances or pollutant or they are relevant and appropriate under the circumstances. The federal environmental laws with which on-site response actions must comply include, but are not limited to, the Toxic Substances Control Act, the Safe Drinking Water Act, the Clean Air Act, the Clean Water Act, the Marine Protection, Research and Sanctuaries Act, and the Solid Waste Disposal Act. On-site cleanups must also meet the Maximum Contaminant Level Goals under the Safe Drinking Water Act and the water quality criteria under the Clean Water Act, where these requirements are relevant and appropriate under the circumstances.

Where the federal government chooses on-site land disposal, a state standard that could effectively result in a statewide ban on land disposal of hazardous substances generally will not apply. However, the act allows such statewide bans to stay in effect for on-site disposal if all the following existing conditions are present: the state standard applies generally and was formally adopted; the standard was adopted for hydrogeological purposes and not to prevent on-site cleanups and other land disposal strategies for reasons unrelated to the protection of health and the environment; and the state guarantees payment of extra costs for methods of disposal other than the land disposal method prohibited by the state standard. This provision in CERCLA restricting a state's ability to establish a standard with the effect of creating a statewide ban on land disposal is not meant to establish a system of federal preemption. The provision also is not meant to restrict the right of a state to undertake cleanup or to recover the costs of cleanup under state law or CERCLA.

CERCLA allows flexibility in the choice of technology to conduct on-site cleanups that may initially violate a particular federal or state standard or requirement of environmental law. The federal government may select an alternative on-site cleanup method that does not meet a particular technology requirement or standard imposed by another state or federal law in only six circumstances: (1) when it finds that the cleanup action is part of a larger one that will meet the requirements or standards; (2) compliance with the prevailing requirement or standard will threaten human health and the environment more than the alternative; (3) compliance is technically impractical from an engineering perspective; (4) the cleanup method selected will attain a level of performance equal to that demanded by the avoided standard or requirement; (5) a state has not applied its requirement or standard consistently; or (6) the legally required remedy would be so costly as to drain the Superfund of money needed to protect public health at other sites.

No federal, state, or local permit can be required for a cleanup action conducted entirely on-site, where the cleanup complies with the act's requirements for on-site response action.

Off-site Transfer Standards

Material transferred off-site as part of a cleanup action can be taken only to a facility in compliance with the Resource Conservation and Recovery Act (also known as the Solid Waste Disposal Act) and other applicable state and federal laws and requirements, including permit requirements. CERCLA allows the off-site disposal of hazardous materials, but only under two conditions. First, the unit at the off-site facility to where the materials are transferred must be a place which the federal government determines is not releasing any hazardous materials into the groundwater, surface water, or soil. Second, any releases at other units at the facility are being controlled under a corrective action measure approved by the EPA under the Resource Conservation and Recovery Act.

NATIONAL CONTINGENCY PLAN (NCP); NATIONAL PRIORITY LIST (NPL); HAZARD RANKING SYSTEM

Federal response actions for hazardous substance releases must be consistent with the National Contingency Plan (NCP), which is the chief body of regulations under which CERCLA is administered. The NCP is to include methods for discovering and investigating facilities containing hazardous substances; methods for evaluating and remedying substantially dangerous releases; methods and criteria for determining the level of remedial or removal action under CERCLA; assignment of appropriate roles in cleanup efforts for federal, state, and local governments and for interstate and nongovernmental agencies; and the means for undertaking remedial actions that are cost effective over the period of potential exposure to the hazardous substances or contaminated materials.

Among the most important provisions of the National Contingency Plan are those for establishing criteria for cleanup priorities and establishing an annual list of sites designated as receiving top priority for Superfund response actions based on these criteria. The list in the National Contingency Plan is called the National Priorities List (NPL). The purpose of the NPL is to identify for the states and public those sites that appear most to warrant cleanup. The sites on the National Priority List are to be the first targets for federal cleanup actions. Among the top 100 priority sites, at least one must be designated by each state. A state is allowed to designate its highest priority facility only once. For the purpose of placing facilities on the list and engaging in response actions or imminent danger abatement actions, the federal government must give high priority to facilities where releases of hazardous substances or contaminants have caused the closing of drinking water wells or have contaminated a principal drinking water supply.

The criteria for choosing sites that make up the National Priority List come together in the Hazard Ranking System. This system must accurately reflect the degree of risk to human health and the environment posed by site. The federal government's establishment of the priority criteria in the Hazard Ranking System for determining the placing and ranking of sites on the NPL must be based on the following factors: relative hazard to public health or the environment, taking into account the population at risk; hazardous potential of the substances at the site; potential for contamination of drinking water supplies; direct contact or destruction to sensitive ecosystems; damage to natural resources which may affect the human food chain; ambient air pollution; and state preparedness to assume the costs and responsibilities of cleanups.

STATE AND FEDERAL CLEANUP INTERACTION

The federal government is required to issue regulations that provide for substantial and meaningful state participation in the initiation, development, and selection of cleanup actions to be undertaken in any state. This state involvement includes, among other things, notice to the state of federal negotiations potentially with responsible parties and the opportunity to participate in these negotiations and be a party to any settlement.

If the federal government's selection of a cleanup action to abate an imminent and substantial danger (pursuant to Section 106 of CERCLA) is not one that meets other federal or state laws or requirements, before the federal government enters into any consent decree with the offending party the state must be given at least 30 days' notice. The state may remain silent, and the imminent hazard cleanup will proceed, or the state may concur and join in the consent decree. If the state does not concur in the federal choice of an imminent hazard cleanup that does not meet other state or federal requirements and the state desires a cleanup that does, it has the right to intervene in federal district court before the entry of the consent decree to challenge the decree. If the state establishes on the record during federal administrative proceedings that the federal government's selection of an imminent hazard cleanup method that does not meet other federal and state requirements is not properly justified, the federal court must order a cleanup action that does conform with these requirements. If the state fails to show in federal court that the federal government decision was not supported by substantial evidence, it can pay the extra costs of the stricter requirements and have them carried out.

Before a Superfund-financed remedial or removal action can be initiated by the federal government, it must first consult with any affected state. Before a remedial action can be undertaken, the federal government must first enter into a contract or cooperative agreement with the state obligating the state to assume future maintenance of removal and remedial actions during the expected life of these actions as determined by the federal government. In this cooperative agreement, the state is obligated to assure the availability of hazardous waste facilities in the state which comply with the Resource Conservation and Recovery Act that will receive any hazardous substances that need to be handled off-site. The cooperative agreement must also obligate the state to pay or assure payment of 10 percent of the remedial action costs if the facility was not owned or operated by the state or local government, and to pay or assure payment of at least 50 percent if the facility was owned or operated by the state or a local government.

While the federal government shares the cost with state government for the construction and installation of cleanup measures at a hazardous waste site, the state government is responsible for 100 percent of the costs of operating and maintaining measures to restore ground and surface water quality after the cleanup action has been finished. This post-cleanup operation and maintenance of the site at state expense must be set and sustained at a level that protects human health and the environment. However, the operation of these water quality restoration methods for a period of up to ten years after a cleanup method has been constructed and installed is considered part of the cleanup period for which the state and federal government share costs. This is in contrast to activities required to maintain the effectiveness of the cleanup measures following the ten-year period after they have been installed and operated to complete the cleanup. Carrying out these post-cleanup activities to maintain thereafter an adequate level of health and environmental protection for the site is a cost to be fully borne by the state.

The federal government has the discretion to enter into a contract or agreement with any state to let the state conduct any or all of the response activities and related enforcement measures. The federal government has 90 days to make a decision on a state application to take on these responsibilities through a cooperative agreement or contract between the two. The kinds of cleanup activities which the state is eligible to fully take on in place of the federal government include any of those the federal government could conduct under CERCLA for the site. In other words, the state can, with the federal government's permission, carry out any cleanup action under CERCLA which the federal government can.

The federal government can enter into an agreement to reimburse a state or local government for part or all of the response activity conducted by the state or local government. The federal government is authorized to reimburse local governments for the expense of carrying out temporary emergency response measures for hazardous substance releases. Reimbursement cannot include payment for normal expenditures by the local government that are incurred in the course of providing what are traditionally local services and responsibilities for hazardous substance responses, such as routine emergency firefighting. The federal reimbursement to a local government for an emergency response is limited to $25,000 for each response.

CERCLA provides for granting credits to the states against their share of cleanup costs for money which the state has spent on a cleanup action under a cooperative agreement with the federal government which is in excess of the state share.

After October 17, 1989, the federal government is forbidden from providing any cleanup action in a state unless the state provides assurances that there will be adequate capacity and access for facilities to treat and dispose of all that state's hazardous waste for the next 20 years and these facilities are in compliance with the federal hazardous waste regulatory program. The reference to hazardous waste in CERCLA in this regard is intended to cover all hazardous waste generated within the state, and not just hazardous wastes taken from Superfund sites in a response action. This provision is a prod to states to select and develop hazardous waste treatment and disposal sites by threatening loss of Superfund assistance.

USES OF THE SUPERFUND

The Superfund Amendments of 1986 authorized taxing measures and appropriations authority to provide $8.5 billion for Superfund-financed activities. The Superfund, formally known as the Hazardous Substances Superfund, may in general be used for all the federal costs of response and cleanup. The Superfund can be used to compensate private parties for their necessary costs of carrying out response activities for the federal government, in accordance with the National Contingency Plan. The Superfund also covers the cleanup costs if a solvent party responsible for the hazardous substance damage cannot be found or if cleanup costs exceed the liability limits of responsible parties. The federal government can use the Superfund only for the administrative costs of carrying out CERCLA to the extent that they are reasonably necessary and incidental to the implementation of the act.

The Superfund can be used to pay for claims by the federal government or states for injury to and the destruction or loss of natural resources. The primary obligation of the Superfund, up to 85 percent, is to be devoted to the costs of removal and remedial actions, and the remainder, 15 percent but no more, can be directed to natural resource damage. Claims for natural resource damage can only be claimed or recovered by the federal government or a state government acting on behalf of the public. Except in a situation requiring action to avoid an irreversible loss of natural resources or to prevent or reduce any continuing danger to natural resources or similar need for emergency action, the Superfund cannot be used for natural resource damage until a plan for the use of the Superfund is adopted by affected federal agencies and any state sustaining damage to its natural resources. Before adoption, the plan is subject to public notice, opportunity for a hearing, and is open to public comment. CERCLA prohibits use of the Superfund for payment of natural resources damage claims until the claimant has exhausted all administrative and judicial remedies to recover the amount of the claim from a liable party. Use of the Superfund to pay natural resource damage claims is prohibited in any year the federal government determines that the fund is altogether needed for responses to threats to public health.

In addition to financing removal and remedial actions, the permissible uses of the Superfund for governmental response activities and related costs include: (1) costs of assessing the damage to or destruction of natural resources; (2) costs of federal and state efforts in the restoration, rehabilitation, or replacement of damaged or lost natural resources; (3) costs of investigations and enforcement action against hazardous substance releases; (4) costs of epidemiological studies, maintaining a national registry of persons exposed to hazardous substances, and diagnostic services otherwise not available to determine whether people exposed to hazardous substances as a result of a release are suffering from diseases with a long latency; (5) costs of equipment and similar overhead needed to supplement equipment and services for contractors and other nonfederal entities and costs of establishing and maintaining damage assessment capability for response activities; and (6) costs to protect the health and safety of response workers.

The Superfund can be used to pay up to $15 million for the cost of a pilot program authorized by the 1986 amendments for the removal or permanent treatment of lead-contaminated soil in one to three urban areas of the federal government's choosing.

CERCLA allows public groups to participate in decisions regarding sites on the National Priority List which affect the groups. The Superfund may be used to provide grants to help these public groups obtain technical assistance in interpreting information and decisions related to the site. Generally, the grant cannot exceed $50,000, and the local groups are required to pay 20 percent of the costs, although these requirements can be waived.

CLAIMS FOR RECOVERY OF CLEANUP COSTS AND DAMAGES

Recovery for Response Costs Against Responsible Parties

Response costs incurred by the federal government, or by a private party appointed to carry out a response action pursuant to the National Contingency Plan, may be recovered from a party held liable under CERCLA, or as reimbursement by making a claim to be paid directly from the Superfund.

Claims for response costs must first be presented to the party responsible for the release, if known by the claimant, before a claim may be made on the Superfund. No claim to the Superfund may be approved by the federal government during a pending court action brought by the claimant to recover the costs which are the subject of that party's claim. A party has three years to present a claim; otherwise it is not collectible under the act. If a claim is not satisfied within 60 days of presentation to the responsible party, the claimant can then present the claim to the Fund for payment.

Claims Against the Superfund

Generally

When a person has incurred costs as a result of carrying out a response action pursuant to the National Contingency Plan, and the responsible party fails to satisfy the claim within 60 days after it is presented to that party or the responsible party is unknown, the claimant may present the claim to the Superfund for payment. In other words, before a claim may be made on the Superfund, claims for response costs must first be presented to the party responsible for the release, if known by the claimant. A claim against the Superfund is an alternative to court action against the responsible party.

Knowingly giving false information as part of a claim can subject the violator to criminal penalties that include a fine of up to $25,000 or imprisonment of up to a year, or both. CERCLA limits the liability of the United States to the amount in the Superfund. That is, any claim against the Superfund may be paid only out of the Superfund, and CERCLA is not to be construed to authorize payment by the federal government for any additional amount from any source other than the Superfund. In the event the Superfund is not adequate to meet claims, they must be paid in the order in which they were finally determined by the federal government.

CERCLA imposes statutes of limitations on claims seeking payment directly from the Superfund. For a claim submitted against the Superfund for recovery of costs for a response action, a time limit of six years is set, the period beginning at the time the response action is completed. For natural resource damages, the limit is three years from the discovery of the loss or the issuance of EPA regulations governing natural resource damages, whichever is later.

Claim Payment Procedure

A party seeking payment of a claim submits it first to the federal government. The federal government may, if satisfied that the information developed during the processing of the claim warrants it, pay all or part of the claim. The federal government must reduce any claim payment to the extent that a judicial award has been made for the costs for which payment is requested. If the federal government declines to pay all or part of the claim, the claimant may request an administrative hearing. The claimant has 30 days to request a hearing after receiving notice of the federal government's decision. The claimant has the burden of proving his or her claim at the hearing. A claimant or the federal government has 30 days to appeal after receiving notice of the award or decision by the administrative hearing. The venue for appeal is the federal district court for the district where the release occurred. The administrative hearing's decision is binding and conclusive and cannot be overturned by the district court unless there has been an arbitrary or capricious abuse of discretion.

RECOVERY FOR DAMAGES TO NATURAL RESOURCES— CLAIMS BY FEDERAL AND STATE GOVERNMENTS

The parties on which CERCLA imposes liability for hazardous substance releases are subject to recovery actions by either the federal government or a state for damages due to injury to or loss or destruction of natural resources, including the reasonable costs of assessing the injury, destruction, or loss. The claim for damages against a responsible party may be made by the federal government or state government acting on behalf of the public as trustee of the natural resources. No more than 15 percent of the Superfund can be used to respond to or provide compensation for natural resource damages. Claims for natural resource damage can only be claimed or recovered by the federal government or a state government acting on behalf of the general interest of the public, and cannot be claimed or recovered by another person.

EPA was required to issue, no later than April 17, 1987, regulations for assessing damages to natural resources from releases of hazardous substances. The federal government designates who is to act as trustee for natural resources under CERCLA. The trustee assesses the damages to natural resources and gets any funds recovered from responsible parties to pay damages to natural resources.

Damages to federally owned natural resources are assessed by those federal officials whom the president has designated under the National Contingency Plan. The assessment by federal officials has the force and effect of a rebuttable presumption on behalf of any claimant, including the federal government, in any judicial proceeding under CERCLA.

Where a claim made to a responsible party for damage to natural resources is not satisfied within 60 days of its presentation, the federal government or the state may commence a court action against the responsible party or may present a claim to the Superfund for payment. A court action to recover damages for the loss, injury, or destruction of natural resources must be brought in a federal district court.

LIABILITY FOR RELEASES OF HAZARDOUS
SUBSTANCES

CERCLA establishes broad liability for those responsible for hazardous substance problems, and they are obligated to reimburse the Superfund and the states for cleanup costs, natural resource damages, response costs borne by other parties consistent with the National Contingency Plan, and the costs of health studies authorized under the act. The responsible parties are also liable for interest, calculated from either the date payment is demanded in writing or the date the expenditures are made. CERCLA imposes liability on any person who owns or operates a vessel or facility releasing hazardous substances, or who owns or operates a facility where hazardous substances are disposed, or who arranges with a transporter for the disposal or treatment of its own hazardous substances at a facility owned or operated by another party, or any person who accepts or has previously accepted hazardous substances for transport to a disposal or treatment facility.

CERCLA overrides state statutes of limitations governing when a person can sue for an injury caused by hazardous substances. Under CERCLA, for a person bringing a lawsuit, a state statute of limitation begins at the time the person knew, or reasonably should have known, that the injury was caused by the hazardous substance, not when the damage occurred, albeit unseen. This provision allows people to sue who are suffering from latent illnesses caused by exposure to hazardous substances since the damage caused by the exposure to the body often occurs long before the illness becomes apparent. In the case of minor persons, the statute begins to run on the later date of when adult age is reached or when the persons knew or had reason to know that their injury was caused by the hazardous substance. For incompetent persons, the statute of limitations begins to run when the person becomes competent.

CERCLA provides several exceptions and exclusions from liability. CERCLA does not impose liability for response costs or damages for releases permitted under any other provisions of federal law. Service station owners who collect used oil are exempt from CERCLA liability after they have relinquished control of the oil. In order to qualify for the exemption, the service station dealers cannot mix the used oil with other hazardous substances and the recycled oil must be managed in compliance with federal standards under the Safe Drinking Water Act and state and local standards for management of recycled oil. Transporters who are independent contractors, which many are, are liable only while they are hauling hazardous substances, unless they select the storage or disposal. The use of pesticides registered under the Federal Insecticide, Fungicide, and Rodenticide Act is excepted from the response costs and liability provisions of CERCLA. State and local governments are not liable for nonnegligent emergency actions taken to deal with a release of hazardous substances by another person. A person is not liable for nonnegligent actions taken or omitted in accordance with the National Contingency Plan or at the discretion of the federally approved coordinator of the response action at the site.

As defenses, no liability is imposed for damages caused solely by an act of God, an act of war, or an act or omission of a third party. The third party defense is available to a government entity that acquired the property by escheat, involuntary acquisition, or eminent domain. The third party defense is also available to a landowner who acquired the site by inheritance. The defenses of act of God, act of war, or third party responsibility are not available to a person who fails to provide the federal or state government with notice of the existence of hazardous substance releases of which the person is aware.

The third party defense is not available unless the defendant exhibits by a preponderance of evidence that due care was exercised to prevent damaging consequences of foreseeable acts or omissions by another third party. Parties responsible for hazardous substance releases cannot use the third party defense when the release resulted from the acts or omission of contractors hired by the federal government to undertake response actions at the site. The third party defense also does not apply if the defendant has entered into a contractual relationship, direct or indirect, with the third party (except with common carriers by rail). This means that a person cannot use contractual arrangements that appear to make a third party responsible as a shield from liability. However, a contractual relationship does not deprive the third party defense to a person who acquires property under a land contract, deed, or other instrument without knowing there is a pollution problem at the site. In order to qualify for protection from liability under the third party defense, the landowner must exercise reasonable due care upon learning of a release or threat of a release.

CERCLA invalidates indemnification, hold harmless, or similar agreements that seek to shift the liability of the responsible party to another person. However, a person is not prohibited from entering into an agreement to insure, hold harmless, or indemnify the party to the agreement for liability for hazardous waste damage.

CERCLA imposes unlimited liability for the costs of remedial or removal actions, except in the case of vessel or vehicle owners or operators. A limit is set on a per gross ton basis for vessels that carry hazardous substances, and another limit is set for other means of transporting hazardous substances. For vessels that carry any hazardous substances as cargo residue, Superfund liability is limited to $300 per gross ton, or $5 million, whichever is greater. For other vessels, liability is $300 per gross ton, or $500,000, whichever is greater. For motor vehicles, aircraft, pipelines, or rolling stock, the limit is set at $50 million or such lesser amount as the president establishes by regulation, but no less than $5 million, or for releases into navigable waters, no less than $8 million. There is no liability limit for the costs of response actions for facilities. However, there is a $50 million liability limit for damages to natural resources.

The limitations on liability for response costs as to vessels, motor vehicles, aircraft, pipelines, and rolling stocks do not apply, and there is unlimited liability where the release or threatened release was the result of willful misconduct or willful negligence or where the responsible party fails to or refuses to provide reasonable cooperation and assistance in connection with response activities. The limitations on liability are also not applicable for any person who fails to give the government notice of the existence of a hazardous waste facility.

CERCLA provides some protection from liability for parties performing cleanup or response actions for federal or state governments under the Superfund provisions. CERCLA protects these response action contractors from liability under federal law for injuries, costs, damages, and expenses or other liability that results from releases or threatened releases at cleanup jobs undertaken by the contractors for federal or state governments. Response action contractors are not liable under federal law for their nonnegligent actions while conducting jobs for the federal or state government, but they are liable for releases and their damages which are the result of the contractor's negligence, gross negligence, or intentional misconduct. The liability exemption under CERCLA for response action contractors does not preempt state law with respect to contractor liability, and the states are free to establish their own liability standards for these contractors. The limitation on liability also applies to claims against the response action contractor for indemnification, contribution, or by a third party. The same CERCLA exemption from liability for nonnegligent acts also applies to state or local government employees who provide services similar to those of response action contractors and are acting within the scope of their authority. The limitation on liability for response action contractors, whether private or governmental, does not affect the liability of any other person. The liability exemption expressly does not affect the liability of any person under any warranty under federal, state, or common law. It does not apply to the liability of an employer who is a response action contractor in regard to its employees under any other law, including worker's compensation laws of the state.

The federal government may enter into indemnification agreements with response action contractors for liability due to the contractor's negligence on the job. Indemnification cannot be provided for contractor conduct that is grossly negligent or for intentional misconduct. Indemnification is allowed only when or to the extent that fair and reasonable insurance is not available to the contractor for the response job.

The federal government has an automatic lien on all real property and related rights subject to or affected by a response action of a person who is liable for costs and damages under CERCLA. A maritime lien is created in favor of the federal government on a vessel causing damages and costs under CERCLA.

SUPERFUND LITIGATION

Contribution

Contribution is the sharing of a loss or payment among two or more parties. A person sued by the federal or state government for recovery of response or cleanup costs can seek contribution from any other person who is actually or potentially liable. A contribution claim may be brought during or after the original suit. The court may allocate costs among the parties which it deems equitable.

CERCLA allows parties settling with the government for response costs to obtain contribution from nonsettling parties. A person whose liability to the federal government for response costs has been settled is protected from contribution claims regarding matters covered in the settlement. Such a settlement does not discharge other responsible parties from liability from suit or contribution, but it does reduce the amount of their potential liability for such a suit or contribution by the amount of the settlement. If the federal or state government recovers less than its full cost in a settlement, it can sue the nonsettling party for the remainder.

Statutes of Limitations for Federal Recovery Suits

Statutes of limitations are established for suits to recover damages for natural resource destruction, to recover remedial and cleanup costs, to obtain contribution for any response costs or damages, and to recover idemnification payments which the government makes to a response action contractor.

For a civil action brought to recover damages to natural resources, the suit must be brought within three years after the later of (1) the date of discovery of the loss and its connection with the release in question or (2) the date on which final federal natural resource damage regulations pursuant to CERCLA are promulgated. A substitute deadline on natural resource damage litigation is provided in place of the above dates for any facility on the National Priorities List, any federal facility, or a site where a remedial action is already scheduled. This deadline is no later than three years after the completion of the remedial action occurring at the facility. Civil action for damages to natural resources generally must be delayed until completion of the remedial investigation and feasibility study (RI/FS) at the National Priority site and other sites where the federal government, or a responsible party under its direction, is proceeding with the RI/FS.

There are different statutes of limitations for government suits to recover the costs for remedial actions (short-term or temporary measures) and removal actions (permanent cleanup), For a removal action the government must sue for recovery of its response costs within three years after completion of the removal action. For a remedial action the government must bring suit to recover its costs within six years after the start of on-site construction of the remedial action.

The statute of limitations for a party bringing a contribution suit is three years from the date of the judgment or settlement or the date of an administrative order in small settlements.

The statute of limitations for a federal government suit seeking recovery from a responsible party of idemnification it has paid a response action contractor is anytime before three years from the date the indemnification payments were made.

Covenants Not to Sue

Under certain conditions, the federal government may choose as part of a settlement to provide a covenant not to sue in the consent decree which releases a party from further liability to the government resulting from a remedial action at the site which is ordered by the decree. Among the conditions for the government entering into such a discretionary covenant not to sue are that the covenant be in the public interest, expedite a response action, and be consistent with the National Contingency Plan and the settlement agreement. In addition to the discretionary covenant not to sue, CERCLA provides for two special mandatory covenants not to sue. The first is to be included in a settlement agreement where the federal government, in its discretion, has rejected an on-site remedial action and has ordered the hazardous substances to be taken off-site. The second special mandatory covenant not to sue is to be used for a remedial action when the hazardous substance is to be permanently destroyed. Before either special mandatory covenant not to sue can be employed, it must also meet the conditions of the discretionary covenant not to sue mentioned above, including the condition that such a covenant be determined to be in the public interest. Where settlement negotiations involve a release that has resulted in damages to natural resources, the federal government must notify the trustee of the negotiations, encourage the trustee's participation, and obtain the trustee's written approval for any covenant not to sue.

Subrogation Claims

When the Superfund pays any claim, the claimant must subrogate to the federal government any claim against the parties responsible for the release. Subrogation means that the federal government is substituted in place of the original claimant in respect to the claim and thus may bring the suit against the responsible parties to recover the payment made from the Superfund. The attorney general is responsible for bringing an action on behalf of the Superfund to recover any compensation paid by the fund to a claimant, and without regard to any limitation of liability, including all interest, administrative and adjudicative costs, and attorneys' fees incurred by the Superfund. The action may be brought against any owner, operator, or guarantor, or against any other person who is liable to the compensated claimant or to the Superfund, for the damages or costs for which compensation was paid out of the fund. Moreover, any person, including the Superfund, who pays compensation under CERCLA to any claimant for damages or costs resulting from hazardous substance releases will be subrogated to all rights, claims, and causes of action that the claimant has under CERCLA or any other law.

IMMINENT AND SUBSTANTIAL DANGER ABATEMENT

In addition to any action taken by a state or local government, when the federal government determines that there may be an imminent and substantial danger to public health or welfare or the environment because of an actual or threatened hazardous substance release, the attorney general can bring an action in federal district court to obtain necessary orders to abate the danger.

The federal government may also attempt to compel the offending party to abate a hazardous substance release that poses an imminent and substantial danger, without need for court approval, by issuing an administrative order directing necessary action to protect public health and welfare and the environment. Anyone who willfully, without sufficient cause, violates an imminent hazard abatement order may be fined up to $25,000 per day in federal district court. Any person who fails without sufficient cause to conduct a corrective action in compliance with an imminent hazard abatement order is subject to a federal civil action brought in federal district court for punitive damages at least equal to, and not more than three times, the amount taken from the Superfund to finance a proper corrective action.

A person who paid cleanup costs under a federal imminent hazard abatement order for which the person was not liable may be reimbursed from the Superfund by submitting a claim petition. If the petition is refused, the person may institute a reimbursement suit in federal district court. In order to obtain reimbursement, the person must show that the federal imminent hazard abatement order requiring that person to take corrective action was arbitrary, capricious, or unlawful.

SETTLEMENTS

The federal government can negotiate settlement agreements with parties actually or potentially responsible for hazardous substance releases requiring these parties to pay for or conduct a cleanup. The purposes of the settlement procedures are to facilitate settlements, expedite remedial actions, and minimize litigation. A settlement by the federal government must be in the public interest and consistent with the National Contingency Plan.

Choosing to negotiate a settlement is an option available to the federal government in place of suing the responsible parties. The federal government is not required to engage in settlements; its authority to settle is discretionary. A decision of the federal government as to whether to engage in settlement negotiations is not subject to judicial review. However, the courts are not precluded from reviewing a consent decree for the settlement, which is submitted for court approval in order make the settlement judicially enforceable. This court approval of the consent decree for a settlement determines whether the relevant requirements of CERCLA have been met and whether entry of the consent decree is in the public interest.

Any federal agency with authority to engage in a response action under the National Contingency Plan can settle a claim for response costs. However, if the total response cost exceeds $500,000, the settlement must receive prior written approval by the attorney general. A party who has resolved its liability in a settlement agreement with the federal government is not liable for claims for contributions regarding matters addressed in the settlement.

CERCLA authorizes expedited settlement procedures for parties contributing only minor (*de minimis*) amounts of pollution at a site. The use of these procedures is entirely at the federal government's discretion. A covenant not to sue may be included in a *de minimis* settlement agreement. In order to be eligible for a *de minimis* settlement, a potentially responsible party must not have contributed to the release or threatened release of the hazardous substance. A *de minimis* settlement protects a party from contribution suits from others. If the *de minimis* settlement embodied in an administrative order relates to a facility where the total response costs exceed $500,000, the administrative order for the settlement must be approved by the attorney general.

Arbitration can be used to settle federal claims under CERCLA where total response costs for the facility do not exceed $500,000, excluding interest.

Mixed funding is authorized for settlements. Mixed funding means that the settling parties agree to pay their share of the response costs and the federal government pays the rest from the Superfund on behalf of the responsible persons who are unknown, unavailable, or refuse to settle. The federal government is still able to pursue collection of the remaining costs from the other nonsettling parties who have not paid. Parties who settle may do the cleanup work and be reimbursed from the Superfund for amounts in excess of their share of the response costs.

Any settlement agreement voluntarily reached by the federal government must be approved by the U.S. attorney general and be entered in an appropriate federal district court as a consent decree. The proposed judgment must be filed 30 days before a final judgment is entered. During this time, the attorney general must provide an opportunity for the public to comment on the proposed judgment, and must file with the court any written comments. The attorney general may withdraw or withhold its consent to the proposed judgment as a result of the comments. The attorney general may withdraw or withhold its consent to the proposed judgment as a result of the comments.

If the federal government decides that a period of negotiation could facilitate a settlement with potentially responsible parties for their taking cleanup actions and speed up a remedial action, it may notify these parties and provide them with the names and addresses of all others involved, the amount of each pollutant contributed by each, and the ranking by volume of pollutant at the site. These parties may not use participation in settlement negotiations as an admission of liability in a court. A 120 moratorium is imposed on any federal response action or imminent hazardous abatement action after such notice in order to provide a period for the settlement negotiations. Moreover, the federal government must abide by a 90-day moratorium on commencing a remedial investigation and feasibility study (RI/FS) for the affected site after notice to other parties of negotiations regarding a settlement with the responsible parties. Negotiations during these moratoria or any other period used by the parties do not prevent the federal government from acting against any significant threat to health or the environment. Persons receiving notice of settlement negotiations have 60 days to offer a proposal for undertaking or financing a response action. If the federal government decides that a party has not made a good faith offer within this 60-day period for a settlement to undertake or finance a response action, it can bring a lawsuit to compel cleanup or payment. If an additional potentially responsible party is identified during the negotiation period or after an agreement has been made following the negotiation, the federal government may bring the additional party into the negotiation or enter into a separate agreement with that party.

The federal government must develop guidelines for engaging in nonbinding preliminary allocations of responsibility (NPAR) as a tool for expediting settlement negotiations. The NPAR is meant to allocate percentages of the total cost of the response action among the potentially responsible parties. The federal government's decision to engage in an NPAR in any instance is discretionary and thus not subject to citizen suits to enforce CERCLA or to judicial review. The factors which the federal government may consider in developing guidelines for NPARs include volume, toxicity, mobility of the hazardous substances, strength of evidence, ability to pay, litigation risks, public interest considerations, precedental value, inequities, and aggravating factors. In preparing an NPAR for a site, the federal government may subpeona information from anyone. The allocation cannot be used as a basis for establishing liability, is not admissible in any court, and is not subject to judicial review.

The federal government must provide its reasons in writing when it rejects, in its discretion, a substantial offer from a party following a preliminary allocation of responsibility. The rejection is not subject to court review.

Under certain conditions, the federal government may choose as part of a settlement to provide a covenant not to sue in the consent decree that releases a party from further liability to the government resulting from a remedial action at the site ordered by the decree. Among the conditions for the government entering into such a discretionary covenant not to sue are that the covenant be in the public interest, that it expedite a response action, and that it be consistent with the National Contingency Plan and the settlement agreement. In addition to the discretionary covenant not to sue, CERCLA provides for two special mandatory covenants not to sue. The first can be included in a settlement agreement where the federal government, in its discretion, has rejected an on-site remedial action and has ordered the hazardous substances to be taken off-site. The second special mandatory covenant not to sue is to be used for a remedial action when the hazardous substance is to be permanently destroyed. Before either special mandatory convenant not to sue can be employed, it must also meet the conditions of the discretionary covenant not to sue mentioned above, including the condition that such a covenant be determined to be in the public interest. Where settlement negotiations involves a release that has resulted in damages to natural resources, the federal government must notify the trustee of the negotiations, encourage the trustee's participation, and obtain the trustee's written approval for any covenant not to sue.

If a party fails to pay a claim that has been settled, the attorney general can bring a civil action to enforce the claim, plus costs, attorney's fees, and interest. Under CERCLA a party failing or refusing to comply with a settlement agreement is also subject to civil penalties.

FINANCIAL RESPONSIBILITY AND POLLUTION INSURANCE

Financial responsibility requirements are imposed on offshore facilities, certain vessels, and ocean incineration vessels to meet potential liabilities under CERCLA. An operator or owner of an offshore facility or vessel (except a nonself-propelled barge that does not carry a hazardous substance as cargo) over 300 gross tons must maintain financial responsibility of $300 per gross ton. Vessels carrying hazardous substances, regardless of their weight, must maintain financial responsibility of at least $5 million. The federal government may require additional evidence and amounts for financial responsibility for vessels engaged in the ocean incineration of hazardous substances.

Where an owner or operator has more than one vessel, evidence of financial responsibility need be established only to meet the maximum liability applicable to the largest vessels. Financial responsibility may be established by insurance, guarantee, surety bond, or self-insurance, or any combination of these. A bond that is filed must be issued by a bonding company authorized to do business in the United States.

Failure to comply with the financial responsibility requirements will make a vessel subject to denial of entry into a U.S. port or to detention.

The federal government is directed to promulgate financial responsibility requirements for land-based facilities that produce, transport, and treat, store, or dispose of hazardous substances. Methods of financial responsibility for these facilities can include insurance, guarantees, surety bond, letter of credit, or self-insurance.

Evidence of financial responsibility for motor carriers is to be determined under another piece of legislation, the Motor Carrier Act of 1980.

A lawsuit for recovery for liability or claims may be brought directly against the guarantor, insurer, and so on, providing the financial responsibility for a facility or vessel. Direct action lawsuits against a guarantor of a hazardous substance site are restricted to cases where the owner or operator or others responsible for the release are insolvent or bankrupt. In direct action suits the guarantor, such as an insurance company, is liable for no more than the amount of the guarantee, insurance policy, surety bond, letter of credit, or similar instrument.

The direct action suit must be brought in federal district court. In defending such a suit, the guarantor may invoke all the rights and interests that would be available to the owner or operator of the vessel or site in defending a lawsuit. The defense that the incident was caused by the willful misconduct of the owner or operator can be used by a guarantor of a vessel but not for a facility on land. The guarantor of a vessel is unable to invoke any claim or defense that might have been available in a suit brought against him by the owner or operator of the vessel, but the guarantor of a facility on land can assert these claims and defenses.

Federal financial responsibility requirements preempt similar state requirements.

CERCLA authorizes companies to form risk retention groups and purchasing groups as a means of providing pollution insurance to parties who otherwise may have difficulty in obtaining commercial liability insurance. A risk retention group is an insurance company that consists of several member insurers and whose purpose is to assume and spread the risks of liability for insurance underwritten by the group among the group's members. A purchasing group consists of several parties who purchase insurance on a group basis. CERCLA exempts risk retention groups and purchasing groups created for CERCLA pollution insurance purposes from state laws that might otherwise prohibit or hinder them.

FEDERAL FACILITIES

All the provisions of CERCLA apply to facilities owned or operated by the federal government, except with respect to financial responsibility. Moreover, for federally owned or operated sites not on the National Priorities List, state laws also generally apply.

EPA is required to establish a Federal Agency Hazardous Compliance Docket to serve as a central repository for information from federal agencies on hazardous substance releases and sites submitted under CERCLA and the Solid Waste Disposal Act. The docket is to be updated by EPA at least every six months. By April 17, 1988, EPA is to ensure that a preliminary assessment is conducted for each facility on the docket. Where appropriate, following the preliminary assessment, EPA must conduct further evaluations for determining priorities among releases and place facilities on the National Priorities List. A deadline of April 17, 1989, has been imposed on EPA to complete the evaluation and listing of federal sites for the NPL.

A federal agency operating a federal site placed on the NPL must begin a cleanup study (remedial investigation and feasibility study) within six months after the site is listed. The cleanup study must be conducted in consultation with EPA and the state where the site is located. EPA is required to review the results of cleanup studies by other federal agencies. The federal agency operating the site must enter into an interagency agreement with EPA for expeditious remedial action within six months after the review. The interagency agreement must include a review of alternate remedial actions that were considered and selection of a remedial action plan by EPA, a schedule of completion, and arrangements for long-term operation and maintenance.

The remedial action at the site must begin within 15 months after the study's completion. The cleanup action must be finished as expeditiously as practicable. Federal agencies are required to include in their annual budget requests a statement of the costs of cleaning up their sites, along with a statement of the hazards which the sites pose to human health, welfare, and the environment.

Responsibility for selecting a remedial action at a federal site is shared by the federal agency that owns or operates the site and EPA. If they fail to agree, EPA is required to exercise ultimate authority to select the remedial action. Each agency must submit an annual report to Congress and the affected states on the progress of remedial actions. EPA and the federal agencies are required to comply with the public participation requirements of CERCLA. State and local governments must be allowed to participate in the planning, formulation, and selection of remedial actions by EPA at federal sites.

Whenever the federal government sells or transfers property, it must provide information on any hazardous substances handled or released there.

A deed transferring federal property where released hazardous substances were handled or where hazardous substances were released must contain a covenant warranting that all necessary cleanup measures had been completed prior to the transfer or, if discovered afterwards, that cleanup will be undertaken by the federal government.

The president may grant national security waivers for federal facilities from CERCLA's requirements. These waivers are available for up to a year and may be renewed several times, but each renewal can be for no more than a year. A national security waiver should be applied only on a site-specific and instance-specific basis. Requirements of the Atomic Energy Act and all executive orders concerning the handling of classified information apply to requests for information under CERCLA.

REPORTING AND RECORDKEEPING REQUIREMENTS

Generally

CERCLA requires two separate types of notification to the federal government. One type of reporting is applied to facilities that handle or have the potential to release hazardous substances. The other reporting requirement is for giving notification of actual releases of hazardous substances. CERCLA also authorizes the promulgation of regulations for the facilities' notification of releases to parties who are possibly exposed as a result of the releases.

Facility Reporting

With certain exceptions provided by CERCLA, any person who owns or operates or who at the time of disposal owned or operated a facility at which hazardous substances have been stored, treated, or disposed, or who transported hazardous substances, must notify EPA of the existence of the facility. This report must specify the amount or type of any hazardous substance at the facility and any known, suspected, or likely releases. EPA has the authority to determine minimum reportable quantities of hazardous substances from facilities below which no report will be required. EPA has the discretion to require details in the manner and form of the reports provided by the facilities. EPA is to notify other government agencies and the governors of affected states of the hazardous substance facility notifications.

CERCLA provides criminal penalties for not complying with the facility notification requirements. Failure to comply with the notification requirements is punishable by a fine in accordance with the Federal Uniform Criminal Code, or maximum imprisonment of up to three years for the first offense and five years for subsequent offenses, or both a fine and imprisonment.

Hazardous substance facility notification and information obtained as a result of the notification cannot be used in a criminal prosecution, except for perjury or giving a false statement.

There are three exceptions to the hazardous substance facility reporting requirement. First, facility notification is not required of a hazardous waste treatment, storage, or disposal facility operating with a permit obtained under the Resource Conservation and Recovery Act—in other words, a valid hazardous waste facility permit. Second, notification is not required for any facility at which hazardous substances have been temporarily stopped in transit, incidental to transportation, and part of the transportation process and not for the purpose of storage. Finally, notification is not required for a pesticide registered under the Federal Insecticide, Fungicide, and Rodenticide Act (FIFRA) when used by a farmer.

EPA is authorized to issue rules and regulations for recordkeeping by facilities that are required to provide notification to EPA of hazardous substances. These records must be retained for at least 50 years. EPA may require that the records be kept more than 50 years if necessary to protect public health or welfare. The destruction of the records is punishable by the monetary fines in the Federal Uniform Criminal Code or by imprisonment of up to three years for the first offense and five years for subsequent offenses, or both a fine and imprisonment.

Reporting of Releases

Persons in charge of a vessel or of an offshore facility must immediately report the release of any hazardous substance to the National Response Center, established under the Clean Water Act. The center, in turn, must expeditiously notify other government agencies and the governors of affected states. The requirement that the National Response Center receive immediate notification of hazardous substance releases does not apply to releases permitted or authorized under other federal laws.

An exception to the hazardous substance notification requirement is provided to the use by a farmer of a pesticide registered under the Federal Insecticide, Fungicide, and Rodenticide Act. A release report is not required of a continuous release, stable in quantity or rate, of a hazardous substance either from a facility for which facility notification has been provided or for which release notification has been given for a period sufficient to establish the continuity, quantity, and regularity of the release. This exemption is conditioned on furnishing the National Response Center with annual reports of the continuous releases or with reports any time there is an increase in releases above that previously reported or occurring.

Notification to Potentially Injured Parties

CERCLA requires federal rules and regulations for furnishing notice to potentially injured parties by an owner or operator of any vessel or facility from which a hazardous substance has been released.

INFORMATION-GATHERING AND INVESTIGATION POWERS

The federal government may engage in investigations, monitoring, surveying, or other information-gathering activities in connection with responding to hazardous substance releases or threatened releases, or health complaints and harm associated with releases, or to enforce CERCLA. To assist in determining the need for responding to a release of hazardous substances or for enforcement of CERCLA, the federal government or the state may require any person who handles or has handled hazardous substances to provide information and allow access to and the copying of records. The federal government or the state is allowed to enter places where hazardous substances are handled and to inspect and obtain samples of substances and any containers or labeling for these substances. The records, reports, or information obtained from a person are to be made available to the public, unless the person from whom the information is obtained satisfactorily demonstrates to the federal government or the state that it is entitled to the confidential treatment. Confidential information can be disclosed to the federal government for the purpose of carrying out CERCLA's provisions.

JUDICIAL REVIEW, JURISDICTION, VENUE

Judicial Review of Federal Response Actions

CERCLA prohibits persons from suing the federal government to challenge its selection of a response action or imminent hazard abatement order, except in a limited set of circumstances. Judicial review of federal response decisions or activities is allowed in the following instances: (1) cost recovery actions against responsible parties; (2) suits for imminent hazardous abatement orders to recover a penalty for violation of such an order; (3) an action for reimbursement of potentially responsible parties for response costs made pursuant to an abatement order; (4) an action under the citizen suit provision of CERCLA alleging that the response action violated the requirements of CERCLA, except that the action may not be brought in regard to a removal that involves an off-site remedial measure; and (5) an imminent and substantial danger action which the federal government is using to compel a remedial action.

Judicial review of the selection of a response action is limited to the administrative record on which the selection was based. Whenever a suit is brought under CERCLA for judicial review, notice of the suit must be given to the attorney general and EPA. The party seeking judicial review and objecting to a federal response action or order has the burden of proving it is arbitrary, capricious, or unlawful. If the burden is not satisfied by the challenger, the court must sustain the federal government's decision in selecting a response action.

Pre-enforcement Judicial Review of Regulation

Judicial review of CERCLA regulations may occur only in the Circuit Court of Appeals for the District of Columbia, and a party must institute suit for this review within 90 days of promulgation. Otherwise the opportunity for review of the regulation is lost. Any matter with respect to which this judicial review could have been obtained at the time cannot be subject later to judicial review in any civil or criminal proceeding for enforcement or obtain damages or recovery of response costs.

Federal District Court Jurisdiction; Venue

Federal district courts have exclusive jurisdiction over all controversies arising under CERCLA, including suits to recover response costs or natural resource damages or appeals of arbitration decisions or EPA awards. Venue is in any district court in which the hazardous substance release or damage occurred, or in which the defendant resides, may be found, or has his or her principal office. The jurisdiction of the federal district courts is without regard to the citizenship of the parties or the amount in controversy.

CITIZEN SUITS

Citizens may bring suits in federal district court against others, including the federal government, who violate CERCLA. CERCLA authorizes citizen suits against two categories of persons or organizations: (1) any party, including the federal government, alleged to be in violation of any requirement, agreement, or order that has become effective pursuant to CERCLA; and (2) federal officials and agencies, including EPA, for failing to perform any mandatory duty or act under CERCLA. As to the first kind of suit, it may not be instituted where the federal government has commenced and is diligently pursuing a suit to obtain compliance with a requirement, agreement, or order under CERCLA or the Solid Waste Disposal Act.

Venue for citizen suits is confined to the federal court district in which the violation occurred, or for failures to perform mandatory acts, either in the district where the violation occurred or in the District of Columbia District Court.

The plaintiff in a citizen suit is required to give notice to parties it intends to sue for violation of CERCLA and must wait 60 days after giving notice before bringing the suit. The 60-day notice requirement does not apply to suits against the federal government for failure to carry out mandatory duties.

CIVIL AND ADMINISTRATIVE PENALTIES

CERCLA provides for civil penalties for violations and gives EPA authority to assess civil penalties administratively.

The act provides for two kinds of administrative penalties: Class I and Class II. The Class I penalty involves an informal administrative process and a single monetary penalty imposed on a per violation basis, whereas the Class II penalty involves a formal administrative process and a monetary penalty assessed on a per violation per day basis and escalates with subsequent violations. CERCLA also provides for a judicial process for imposing civil penalties. Consequently, for any given violation the federal government can choose between two types of administrative penalties and a judicial action.

For Class I administrative penalties, the monetary penalty is a maximum $25,000 per violation. The Class I civil penalty cannot be assessed without notice and an opportunity for a hearing, but the hearing is not a formal Administrative Procedures Act hearing. Judicial review of a Class I civil penalty is to occur in federal district court.

For Class II administrative penalties, the monetary penalty is set at a maximum $25,000 per day per violation (as opposed to per violation only for Class I penalties), increasing for second and subsequent violations to a maximum $75,000 per day per violation. For a Class II penalty a formal Administrative Procedures Act hearing is required before the penalty may be assessed. Judicial review of a Class II penalty is with the District of Columbia Court of Appeals.

The federal government can bring an action in federal district court to assess and collect a penalty up to a maximum of $25,000 per day for each day of the violation, and a maximum $75,000 for each day of the second and subsequent violations.

Class I and Class II administrative penalties and the judicial penalty apply to each of the following kinds of violations of CERCLA: failure to provide notice of releases or submission of false or misleading information under the notice provisions: failure to comply with the financial responsibility requirements; failure to comply with an order or request under the information-gathering and access provisions; and failure to comply with an order, decree, or agreement under the settlement provisions and federal facilities provisions of the act.

RELATIONSHIP WITH OTHER LAWS

CERCLA does not generally preempt a state from imposing additional liability or requirements for controlling hazardous substances. However, there are several exceptions to the authority conferred upon states to engage in hazardous substance regulation under CERCLA. CERCLA's financial responsibility requirements for vessels and facilities preempt any similar state or local requirements. A state is to accept evidence of compliance with CERCLA financial responsibility requirements in lieu of other requirements of financial responsibility for hazardous substance releases. CERCLA bars double recoveries under the Superfund and other state or federal laws for removal costs, damages, or claims concerning hazardous substances.

LEGISLATIVE VETO

CERCLA establishes a legislative veto, requiring all CERCLA regulations to be submitted to Congress for possible disapproval before they can become effective.

FEDERAL HEALTH ASSISTANCE AND STUDIES

When originally enacted, CERCLA created the Agency for Toxic Substances and Disease Registry (ATSDR), which is administered by the surgeon general. In the original CERCLA, the ATSDR was given responsibility to provide medical care and testing to people in cases of public health emergencies caused by exposure to toxic substances. In these public health emergencies, exposed persons are eligible for admission to Public Health Service hospitals and facilities.

CERCLA requires that the ATSDR and EPA conduct a series of health-related studies and programs.

ATSDR and EPA are required to prepare a list of substances commonly found at Superfund sites. By April 17, 1987, ATSDR and EPA was to prepare a list, in order of priority, of at least 100 hazardous substances commonly found at Superfund sites which these agencies believe pose the most significant threat to human health because of their toxicity and potential for human exposure. By October 17, 1988, at least 100 more substances must be added to the list, and during each of the following three years, no fewer than 25 substances must be added.

ATSDR, then, is required to prepare toxicological profiles on all the listed substances, in accordance with guidelines developed jointly with EPA. If information on the health effects of the toxic substances is inadequate, ATSDR must assure initiation of a research program to determine the health effects of these substances. EPA and ATSDR are to coordinate the health research program with the National Toxicology Program and with testing under the Toxic Substances Control Act and the Federal Insecticide, Fungicide, and Rodenticide Act. Congress expressed its sense that the costs of research programs on health effects should be borne by manufacturers and processors of the hazardous substances for which the research is conducted. By October 17, 1987, EPA was to issue regulations for the payment of these health research program costs under CERCLA, the Toxic Substance Control Act, and the Federal Insecticide, Fungicide, and Rodenticide Act.

ATSDR is required to perform a health assessment for each site on the National Priorities List. The assessment must be completed within one year after a site is included on the National Priorities List.

Citizens and physicians may request ATSDR to conduct health assessments for sites that are probable sources of exposure. ATSDR must provide a written explanation if it does not conduct a health assessment.

Where a health assessment is done at a site on the National Priorities List, ATSDR is to complete it promptly, and to the maximum extent practicable, before completion of a remedial investigation and feasibility (RI/FS) at the site.

A health assessment is defined to include a preliminary assessment of the potential risk to human health posed by a site, based on number of factors, such as the nature and extent of contamination, potential pathways of human exposure, and size and susceptibility of the affected community. The purpose of the health assessment is to aid in deciding what future necessary actions ATSDR or EPA must take to reduce human exposure to hazardous substances and whether further health studies should be conducted.

ATSDR must give its results and recommendations to EPA and the appropriate states. If the health assessment indicates a serious threat to human health or the environment from a release, ATSDR must notify EPA, which must promptly evaluate the release to determine whether the site should be placed on the NPL. If the site is already on the NPL, ATSDR may recommend to EPA that the site be given a higher priority.

The costs of a health assessment for a site can be recovered from parties liable for the hazardous substance releases that necessitated the health study. If the results of the assessment warrant, ATSDR is authorized to conduct a pilot or full-scale epidemiological study of the affected human population. Where a health assessment indicates a significant risk to human health, ATSDR is to consider establishing a registry of exposed persons. Where ATSDR has determined that there is a significant increased risk of adverse human health effects from exposure to hazardous substances based on the results of a health assessment, exposure registry, or epidemiological study, ATSDR must initiate a health surveillance program for the affected population to screen various groups for disease and refer them for treatment.

If any ATSDR health study shows a significant risk to human health, the federal government must take the steps necessary to reduce human exposure and eliminate or substantially mitigate the risk. The steps can include providing alternative water supplies, permanent or temporary relocation, or any other necessary steps. It is not necessary for the federal government to await the results of any health study before acting to abate an imminent hazard.

WORKER PROTECTION STANDARDS AND EMPLOYEE DISCRIMINATION STANDARDS

The Department of Labor is required to establish regulations for the health and safety protection of workers engaged in hazardous waste operations. The regulations must cover site-specific plans for worker protection, training, remedial surveillance, protective equipment, engineering controls, maximum exposure limits, information programs, handling, decontamination, and emergency protection of workers. Moreover, the training standards must require that general site workers receive at least 40 hours of initial instruction off the site and three days of actual field experience. Supervisors directly responsible for the hazardous waste operations must receive the same training as general site workers and eight additional hours of special training. The training standards must also establish a program for certifying hazardous waste workers and prohibit untrained and uncertified workers from engaging in hazardous waste operations.

No employer may fine, or in any way discriminate against, or cause to be fired or discriminate against, any employee or any authorized representative of employees because the employee or representative has provided information to the state or federal government or has commenced or caused to be commenced a proceeding under CERCLA. No employer may fire or discriminate or cause the firing or discrimination against an employee or employee representative because he or she either has testified or is about to testify in any proceeding resulting from the administration or enforcement of CERCLA.

Any employee or employee representative who has been fired or discriminated against may apply to the Department of Labor for a review of the firing or alleged discrimination. The Department of Labor is to conduct an investigation, providing an opportunity for a public hearing, at the request of any party to the review, and is to make findings of fact based on the investigation. If the Department of Labor finds that a violation did occur, it is to require the employer to take such affirmative action to abate the violation, including but not limited to, the rehiring or reinstatement of the employee or employee representative to his or her former position with compensation. The violator may be assessed the costs and expenses of the Department of Labor proceeding, including attorneys' fees.

An employee who deliberately violates CERCLA requirements is not covered by the employee discrimination provisions of the act.

8 Emergency Planning and Community Right-to-Know Act of 1986 (42 U.S.C. §§ 11001 et. seq.)

OVERVIEW

The Superfund Amendments and Reauthorization Act of 1986 contained a new free-standing piece of legislation entitled the Emergency Planning and Community Right-to-Know Act of 1986. The Right-to-Know Act established emergency planning, reporting, and notification requirements that were meant to protect the public in the event of a release of hazardous substances. It gave the public the fundamental "right-to-know" about the existence of hazardous substances handled by private companies in their community.

STATE COMMISSIONS, PLANNING DISTRICTS, AND LOCAL COMMUNITIES

The governor of each state is required to appoint a state emergency response commission, which may be one or more existing emergency response organization. If no state commission is appointed, the governor serves as the commission and is responsible for performing the duties assigned by the act to the commission.

The emergency response commission is responsible for designating emergency planning districts and must appoint local emergency planning committees for the districts. The commission is responsible for supervising and coordinating the activities of the local emergency planning committees. Each committee must include representatives from each of the following groups or organizations: elected and local officials; law enforcement, civil defense, firefighting, health, local environmental, hospital, and transportation personnel; broadcast and print media; community groups; and owners and operators of hazardous waste or substance sites. The local emergency response committee and state emergency response commission must designate an official to serve as a coordinator for information. The state commissions and local committees must formulate procedures for handling public information requests under the Right-to-Know Act.

SUBSTANCES AND FACILITIES COVERED FOR EMERGENCY PLANNING AND FACILITY NOTIFICATION

Facilities covered by the act's emergency planning requirements are those that have a substance on the list published by EPA in November 1985 in Appendix A of the "Chemical Emergency Preparedness Program Interim Guidelines" in excess of a threshold planning quantity for the substance. The substances on the EPA list are designated as extremely hazardous. EPA sets the threshold quantity for these substances, but if it fails to do so for any substance the threshold planning quantity is set at 2 pounds by the law. EPA can revise the list and thresholds from time to time. The governor or state emergency response commission may designate additional facilities to be subject to the emergency planning requirements.

The owners of facilities where extremely hazardous substances exist in excess of the threshold planning quantity must notify the state commission. The state commission must notify EPA of the facilities where substances covered by the act are found.

COMPREHENSIVE EMERGENCY RESPONSE PLANS

By October 17, 1988, the local emergency planning committee must develop comprehensive emergency plans. The plans must be reviewed at least once a year. At the minimum, each local emergency plan must include the following: identity of the facilities covered; methods to be followed by the facilities and local emergency and medical personnel in response to a release; identify of facility and community emergency coordinators; procedures for notification of emergency personnel and the public of a release; methods for release detection and the population to be affected by a release; identification of emergency equipment and facilities in the community; evacuation plans; training programs; and methods and schedules for carrying out the plan.

Facility owners are required to notify the local emergency planning committee of the facility representative who will participate in the emergency planning process as a facility emergency coordinator. The facility must promptly inform the local committee of any relevant changes at the site as the changes occur or are expected to occur. The facilities are required to provide the local committees with information needed to develop and carry out the plan.

The emergency plan completed by the local committees for a district are reviewed by the state commission and Superfund regional response teams.

EMERGENCY NOTIFICATION OF HAZARDOUS
SUBSTANCE RELEASES

Facilities are required to give immediate notice of a release of a listed extremely hazardous substance in three specific instances. The emergency release notice requirements of the act do not apply to on-site releases; only those that extend beyond the boundaries where the facility is located are applicable. First, notice must be given for an extremely hazardous substance if the release also requires notice to EPA's National Response Center under CERCLA. Second, notice is required for the release of an extremely hazardous substance that is not specifically listed under CERCLA as requiring notice but that is not federally permitted in excess of the amount set by EPA (or 1 pound, if no amount has been set), and the release occurs in a manner that would require notice under CERCLA. Third, notice is required where the substance is not a listed extremely hazardous substance but the release must be reported to EPA under CERCLA. For the third kind of release, notification must be given to local and state emergency response organizations if the release exceeds a reportable quantity established by EPA under CERCLA, or if the release occurs after April 30, 1988, it exceeds the fallback threshold under CERCLA of 1 pound.

Facilities must immediately give notice of releases to the community emergency coordinator for the local emergency planning committee and to the state emergency planning commission. This notice can be transmitted by telephone, radio, or in person. Where the release is related to transportation of the substance or storage incident to transportation, the notice must be accomplished by calling the 911 emergency telephone operator and reporting the release.

The notice of an off-site release given by a facility to the local committee and state commission must include eight items of information: (1) chemical identity of the released substance; (2) indication of whether the substance is a listed extremely hazardous substance; (3) quantity of the release; (4) time and duration of the release; (5) medium into which release occurred (air, land, or water); (6) known or active chronic health effects; (7) proper precautions to take as a result of the release, including evacuation; (8) name and telephone number of person(s) to contact for further information.

As soon as practical after the immediate notice of the release, the facility is required to provide a written followup emergency notice to the local committee and state commission. The followup written notice must update the information provided in the initial notification and must include three additional items of information: (1) actions taken to respond to the release; (2) known or anticipated acute or chronic health risks; and (3) medical attention necessary for exposed individuals.

REPORTING REQUIREMENTS

Material Safety Data Sheets

Facilities are required to report the presence of hazardous chemical substances in addition to those listed as extremely hazardous. These are the hazardous substances that must currently be reported on "material safety data sheets" (MSDS) under the Occupational Safety and Health Act of 1970. Facilities are required to submit the MSDS form, or a list of such chemicals for which an MSDS form is required, to the local committee, state commission, and the local fire department.

The Right-to-Know Act exempts from the definition of hazardous chemical, and thus from the MSDS reporting requirement, certain substances, including (1) food, food additives, drugs, or cosmetics regulated by the Food and Drug Administration; (2) solids contained in maufactured products; (3)

personal, family, or household products; (4) substances used in research and medical facilities; and (5) substances used in routine farming operations.

EPA has the authority to establish threshold quantities below which no facility would be required to report a hazardous substance release.

Local communities are required to make the MSDS form available upon request by any person.

Any state or local law enacted after August 1, 1985, which requires the submission of an MSDS form from a facility must require that the data sheet be identical to the one required by EPA. State or local governments may require supplemental sheets to the federally formatted MSDS form to acquire additional information.

Emergency and Hazardous Chemical Inventory Reporting Forms

The Right-to-Know Act establishes a reporting program under which facilities are to provide chemical inventory information on forms required by the act. A two-tier process for reporting is established. The first tier is essentially a summary of the information on all covered hazardous chemicals at a facility which is submitted to authorities under the act, with this summary in the form of an annual report. The second tier is information on specific hazardous chemicals which is to be made available by the facility on request rather than in an annual report. Another distinction is that Tier I information relates to categories of hazardous chemicals and Tier II information concerns individual chemicals.

The first tier consists of an annual report to the local committee, state commission, and fire department on chemicals for which an MSDS form would be required. The information on the Tier I annual report includes an estimate (in ranges) of the amount and general locations of the categories of hazardous chemical. The first annual report is due no later than March 1, 1988.

The Tier II report, which must be available on request, includes the same information on the amount and location of a specific hazardous chemical that is provided for aggregate chemicals on the Tier I annual report, as well as a description of the manner of storage of the particular hazardous chemical and the location of the facility. In addition, the form for a Tier II report should indicate whether the facility elects to keep the location information confidential from disclosure to the public.

For acquiring the Tier II specific chemical information, different procedures apply to different parties. These parties are separated into three groups: (1) state emergency response commissions, local emergency planning committees, and local fire departments; (2) other state and local officials; and (3) the public. As to the first category, state commissions, local committees, and local fire departments can directly request the Tier II information on a specific chemical identity from the facility. Other state and local officials have access to the Tier II information only through a request to the state commission or local committee. The request to the local committee or state commission, when made by the other local or state official acting in an official capacity, cannot be denied. Public access to the Tier II specific chemical information is acquired from the state commission or local committee. A member of the public must make the information request in writing and must indicate the specific facility for which the information is requested. If the Tier II specific chemical identity information has already been provided to the state commission or local committee, the person will be given access to it. If the state commission or local committee does not have the Tier II information in its possession, whether it will obtain the information from the facility and provide it to a member of the public is affected by the amount of the chemical at the facility. If the facility has stored 10,000 or more pounds of the hazardous chemical at the facility during the preceding calendar year, then the state commission or local committee must acquire the information on the chemical at the request of a member of the public and make that information available to that person. When the amount stored is less, the member of the public making the Tier II request must state a reason for needing the information, and the state commission or local committee has the discretion whether to grant it. The local committee or state commission must respond within 45 days of receiving the request from the member of the public.

Fire departments are given access to conduct on-site inspection of any facility required to file the annual Tier I chemical inventory form. At such an inspection the facility must provide specific location and volume information on chemicals kept at the site.

Toxic Chemical Release Forms

The Right-to-Know Act established requirements for annual reporting on routine releases of certain toxic or dangerous chemicals into the environment. This reporting covers releases that occur as a result of normal business operations, as distinct from abnormal, emergency releases for which there is the different and distinct emergency notification requirement. The toxic chemical release forms are to be submitted to EPA and the state on an annual basis, by July 1 of every year. These forms must report data reflecting releases that occurred during the preceding calendar year.

Not all industries are required to prepare toxic chemical release forms for routine releases. Only facilities that are part of industries included in the SIC (Standard Industrial Classification) Codes 20–39 are covered by the requirement to prepare these forms. EPA may add or delete SIC codes, which represent categories of industries. EPA's deletion and addition authority is limited, however, to SIC codes for facilities that manufacture, process, or use toxic chemicals. EPA may also apply the requirements to specific facilities, and not just to SIC codes. This discretionary authority to add a particular facility to the requirement for preparing a toxic chemical release form is limited to a facility that manufactures, processes, or uses toxic chemicals and on the condition that EPA determines that including the facility is warranted on the basis of the toxicity of the chemical, proximity to other sites that release the toxic chemical or to population centers, the history of releases of the chemical at the facility, and other factors which EPA deems appropriate.

The Right-to-Know Act specifies a list of chemicals for which the annual toxic chemical release forms are required. The list is found in Committee Print Number 99–169 of the Senate Committee on Environment and Public Works and is entitled "Toxic Chemicals Subject to Section 313 of the Emergency Planning and Community Right-to-Know Act of 1986." EPA can add or delete substances to the list on its own initiative or on petition, if they meet certain criteria.

EPA may add a chemical to the list for which annual routine toxic chemical release forms are required if it determines that the chemical causes, or can reasonably be anticipated to cause, any of three problems: (1) significant adverse human health effects beyond the boundaries of the plant; (2) cancer, birth defects, serous or irreversible reproductive dysfunctions, nuerological disorders, heritable genetic mutations, or other chronic effects, whether these health effects occur inside or outside the boundaries of the plant; or (3) significant adverse effects on the environment. Chemicals capable of causing significant adverse environmental effects can make up no more than 25 percent of the chemicals on the list. EPA may delete a chemical from the list if it determines that none of the three effects mentioned above are caused by it. Any person may petition EPA to add or delete a toxic chemical to the list on the grounds that it is (for inclusion) or is not (for deletion) capable of significantly harming human health. A chemical connot be added or deleted on the grounds that it causes significant adverse environmental effects. EPA must publish an explanation of why a petition to add or delete a toxic chemical is denied. A state governor may make a petition to add or delete a chemical to the list on the same criteria of health and environmental harms applying to EPA's decision to add or delete chemicals.

The Right-to-Know Act requires that toxic chemicals be included in the annual report for routine releases only if the chemicals are present above certain thresholds. For chemicals simply used at the facility for purposes other than manufacturing or processing of the chemical, the threshold for reporting is 10,000 pounds per year. For listed chemicals manufactured or processed at a facility, the threshold is 75,000 pounds until July 1, 1988; 50,000 pounds until July 1, 1989; and 25,000 pounds per year for annual reports submitted as of July 1, 1990, and thereafter.

EPA was to provide by June 1, 1987, a uniform toxic chemical release form for the annual reports submitted by facilities. If the required form is not published by EPA, the reports submitted by a facility must be made by letter which contains the required information. The form prepared by EPA, or the letter if there is no form, must report the following information: (1) name, location and principal business activities of the facility; (2) appropriate certification regarding the accuracy and completeness of the report, signed by a senior official with management responsibility for the person(s) preparing the report; (3) use of the chemicals; (4) estimate of the maximum amount of each toxic chemical present at the facility at any time during the year; (5) methods of waste treament or disposal used for each wastestream and an estimate of the amounts of the substance remaining in the wastestream after treatment; and (6) amount of each listed toxic chemical released into the environment during the year.

Facilities are allowed to base their toxic chemical release report on readily available data required to be collected by other laws, or reasonable estimates when such data are not available. A facility is not required to undertake new monitoring in addition to that required by other laws just to satisfy the annual toxic chemical release reporting requirement.

The toxic chemical release reports are required on an annual basis. Begining with the report due in 1994, EPA has the authority to alter the reporting frequency but cannot require more than one per year. Beginning with the 1994 report, EPA can modify the reporting frequency either nationally or in specific geographic areas for all toxic chemicals covered, for a class of these toxic chemicals or a category of facilities, or for a specific toxic chemical or a specific facility. To make any changes in the reporting frequency, EPA must make several determinations: the extent to which the information has been used by EPA, other federal agencies, states, and local governments, health professionals, and the public; the extent to which this information is readily available to potential users from other sources and is provided to EPA under other programs; and (when shortening reporting frequency) the extent to which this change imposes additional and unreasonable burdens on the facility's submitting reports.

WITHHOLDING TRADE SECRETS

A facility subject to the reporting and information requirements of the Right-to-Know Act may withhold information on the specific chemical identity of a substance if they establish that the information is a trade secret. When the specific chemical identity is claimed as a trade secret, the generic class or category of the hazardous or toxic chemical must be submitted.

The trade secret protection cannot be used to prevent disclosure of chemical information from health professionals and public health officials. The trade secret provisions of the act are expressly prevented from being used to withhold as a trade secret information which other provisions of the act give health professionals access to. Trade secret protection does not apply to emergency notification for the release of hazardous chemicals. When a specific chemical identity is withheld from the public because of a claim of trade secrecy, the governor or state emergency response commission must identify the appropriate adverse health effects associated with the chemical if it is hazardous or extremely hazardous and must provide this information to any person requesting the information about the chemical.

In order to withhold the specific chemical identity of a substance as a trade secret, it must be shown that the information has not been disclosed to any other person, that it is not required to be disclosed under any other law, that disclosure is likely to cause substantial harm to the company's competitive position, and that the chemical identity is not readily discoverable through reverse engineering.

Procedures have been established to enable review of a claim that a specific chemical identity be protected from disclosure as a trade secret. A review may be initiated by EPA, or it may be in response to a petition seeking disclosure of the chemical, which any person may make. If a petition for a review to dispute a trade secret claim is filed, EPA is required within 30 days to review the explanation for the claim provided by the claimant who acquired the trade secret protection and EPA must determine whether the explanation presents sufficient assertions, which if true, justify the claim for the trade secret protection. A petitioner does not have the burden of proving the inadequacy of an explanation submitted to justify a trade secret claim.

EPA follows two procedures in reviewing a claim made by a facility for trade secret protection of a specific chemical identity. The first procedure is followed if the original assertions made for the trade secret protection claim are sufficient to justify the claim. The second is followed if the original assertions are not, upon review by EPA, found to be sufficient to justify the claim for trade secret protection.

If EPA finds that the claimant's explanation presents sufficient assertions to support a finding that the specific chemical identity is a protectable trade secret, EPA must notify the claimant for the trade secret that he or she has 30 days to supplement the explanation with detailed information to support the assertions. If, after review of the supplemental information, EPA determines that the assertions in the explanation are true and that the specific chemical identity deserves continued trade secret protection, EPA must notify the petitioner against the trade secret protection. The petitioner may seek judicial review of EPA's determination. If after review of the supplemental information, EPA determines, that the assertions in the explanation are incorrect and that the specific chemical identity does not deserve trade secret protection, then EPA must notify the claimant that it intends to release the specific chemical identity. The claimant has 30 days to appeal the adverse determination to EPA and may seek judicial review if the appeal is unsuccessful.

Another procedure is followed if EPA, in response to a petition or on its own initiative, determines that the explanation accompanying the claim of continued trade secrecy protection presents insufficient assertions to support a finding that the chemical identity deserves to be a trade secret. In this case EPA must notify the claimant for trade secret protection of this determination, and the claimant has 30 days to appeal EPA's decision, or, upon a showing of good cause, to amend the original explanation by providing supplementary assertions to support the trade secret claim. If EPA does not reverse its determination on the insufficiency of assertions to support a trade secret claim after an appeal or review of the supplementary material, then EPA is required to notify the claimant, who may seek judicial review. If EPA does reverse its determination, then the petitioner against trade secret protection must be notified and may seek judicial review of EPA's decision.

Upon a request by the state's governor, EPA is required to provide trade secret information to a state.

INFORMATION TO HEALTH PROFESSIONALS, DOCTORS, AND NURSES

The Right-to-Know Act requires facilities claiming trade secret protection for a chemical to provide access to the trade secret information for various health professionals who need it. In order to get this trade secret information, the health professional must make a written request for it. Except in the case of a medical emergency, the written request must be accompanied by a written statement of need, and the health professional must enter into a confidentiality agreement limiting the use and disclosure of the information. In the case of a medical emergency where the specific chemical identity is necessary for or will assist in emergency or first-aid diagnosis or treatment, the physician is entitled to the information without a written statement of need.

AVAILABILITY OF INFORMATION TO THE PUBLIC

Except for trade secrets, each emergency response plan, material data safety sheet, inventory form, toxic chemical release report, and written followup to emergency notification must be made available to the general public at government offices designated by EPA, the state, or the local emergency planning committee. Each local committee must annually publish notices in local newspapers that such information is public.

ENFORCEMENT AND CIVIL SUITS

Federal Enforcement

The Right-to-Know Act provides a system of administrative, civil, and criminal penalties for enforcing the emergency planning and right-to-know provisions.

EPA may order a facility to provide the information required by the act for emergency planning by a local committee or to provide notification of extremely hazardous substances in excess of the threshold planning quantity. A facility that fails to obey the order is subject to a civil penalty of up to $25,000 for each day of the violation.

The Right-to-Know Act provides for two kinds of administrative penalties—Class I and Class II—to be imposed against parties violating the emergency notification requirements of the law. EPA may chosse one or the other administrative penalty to pursue against a violator of the emergency notification requirements, but not both. The difference between the two penalties is that the Class I invovles an informal administrative process and a single monetary penalty per violation, whereas the Class II involves a formal administrative process and monetary penalties that are assessed on a per day basis and escalate with subsequent violations.

EPA may assess a Class I administrative penalty of up to $25,000 for a violation of the emergency notification requirements. This administrative penalty cannot be assessed unless the person accused of the violation is given notice and opportunity for a hearing. The Class II administrative penalty that EPA may seek for violation of the emergency notification requirements includes a monetary penalty of up to $25,000 per violation per day for the first violation, and up to $75,000 per day per violation for the second and subsequent violations. Before EPA may assess a Class II penalty, it must conduct and conclude a formal hearing process.

EPA can bring a civil action in federal district court to assess and collect a penalty for violation of the emergency notification requirements of the act. The federal district court can impose a maximum penalty of $25,000 per day for the first violation and a maximum of $75,000 for each day of a violation for the second and subsequent violations.

Criminal penalties may be imposed for the knowing and willful violation of the emergency notification requirements. For the first conviction, the criminal penalties include a fine of up to $25,000 or a prison term of up to two years, or both. In the case of a second and subsequent criminal convictions, the maximum fine increases to $50,000, and the maximum prison term increases to up to five years.

EPA may initiate a civil action or an administrative action for violation of the requirements relating to the annual emergency hazardous chemical inventory reports and to the annual reporting of routine toxic chemical releases. An administrative or judicial fine of up to $25,000 per violation may be imposed for violating these requirements. Likewise, EPA may seek judicial civil and administrative penalties of up to $10,000 per violation for violations of the requirements regarding the Material Safety Data Sheets, requirements for providing needed information to health professionals in cases of medical emergencies, and requirements for providing information in support of an application for trade secret protection claims. Judicial civil and EPA administrative penalties of up to $25,000 per violation can be imposed for assertion of a frivolous trade secret claim. A criminal penalty of up to $20,000 or imprisonment of not more than one year, or both, is provided for unlawful disclosure of trade secret information.

Health professionals may bring an action in federal district court to obtain information from a facility which they have requested in accordance with the act but which has not been complied with.

Civil Actions by Citizens, State Governments, and Local Governments

The Right-to-Know Act allows any person to bring civil enforcement suits against facilities, EPA, state and local agencies, and officials for violations of the act.

Any person may bring a civil enforcement suit against a facility for failure to do any of the following: submit a followup emergency notice; submit a material safety data sheet or list; complete and submit an annual Tier I chemical inventory report; or complete and submit a toxic chemical report release form.

Any person may bring a civil enforcement suit against EPA for its failure to do any of the following: publish chemical inventory forms; respond within 180 days to a petition to add or delete a chemical from the list of those for which a toxic chemical release form is required; establish a computer data base of the nation's toxic chemical inventory; promulgate trade secret regulations; and render a decision within nine months on a petition for review of the granting of chemical trade secret protection.

Any person may bring a civil enforcement suit against EPA, a state governor, or a state emergency response commission for failure to provide a mechanism for public availability of emergency response plans, material safety data sheets and lists, annual chemical inventory forms, toxic chemical release forms, and other information that must be made available to the public. Any person may bring a civil enforcement suit against a state governor or state emergency response commission for failure to respond to a request for Tier II specific chemical identity information within 120 days after receiving the request.

State or local governments may bring a civil enforcement suit against a facility for failure to do any of the following: provide notification to the emergency response commission that extremely hazardous substances exist at the site in excess of the threshold planning levels; submit a material safety data sheet or list; make available material safety data sheet information to the state emergency response commission; or complete and submit a Tier I annual chemical inventory form.

Any state emergency response commission, local emergency planning committee, or local fire department may bring a civil enforcement suit against a facility for failure to provide the information which they are required to provide to these groups, including a Tier II specific chemical identity report.

A state may sue EPA for failure to provide the state with trade secret information otherwise unavailable to the public and others.

Prior to bringing suit, a person must give 60 days' notice to EPA, appropriate state and local officials, and the alleged violator. A civil enforcement suit cannot be brought if EPA is diligently prosecuting an enforcement action for the same violation. The court may award the costs of litigation, including attorneys' fees, to any substantially prevailing party.

Citizens are given a limited right to intervene in government enforcement actions instituted in federal court. EPA may intervene as a matter of right in any civil enforcement suit described in this section.

RELATIONSHIP WITH OTHER LAWS; EXEMPTION OF TRANSPORTATION FROM THE ACT'S REQUIREMENTS

The Right-to-Know Act expressly does not preempt any local or state law or modify the obligations or liabilities of any person under other federal laws. Among other things, a state or locality may impose stricter requirements for emergency planning, reporting, and notification regarding the releases of toxic chemicals.

The Right-to-Know Act exempts from its requirements the transportation of chemicals (including the transportation and distribution of natural gas), as well as storage incident to transportation.

Index

About the Author

SIDNEY M. WOLF is a Professor in the Social Science Division at Northeastern State University in Tahlequah, Oklahoma. His previous positions have included being an environmental planner for the State of Alaska, pollution law attorney for the City of Detroit, and a lobbyist on environmental and energy issues for Environmental Action and the Environmental Policy Center in Washington, D.C. Mr. Wolf has testified on numerous occasions on environmental and energy issues before congressional committees. He has appeared as a guest on *Good Morning America* and the *McNeil/Lehrer Report*. His articles on environmental issues have appeared in prestigious journals such as *Environmental Law, Boston College Environmental Affairs Law Review*, and the *Bulletin of the Atomic Scientists*.